THE NEW CLARENDON BIBLE
(NEW TESTAMENT)

General Editor: THE REVD H. F. D. SPARKS, D.D., F.B.A.

———

THE GOSPEL ACCORDING TO
JOHN

St. John the Evangelist: St. Mark's Basilica, Venice; twelfth century

THE GOSPEL ACCORDING TO
JOHN

IN THE
REVISED STANDARD VERSION

With introduction and commentary

by

J. C. FENTON

PRINCIPAL, ST. CHAD'S COLLEGE
DURHAM

OXFORD
AT THE CLARENDON PRESS
1970

Oxford University Press, Ely House, London W.1

GLASGOW NEW YORK TORONTO MELBOURNE WELLINGTON
CAPE TOWN SALISBURY IBADAN NAIROBI DAR ES SALAAM LUSAKA ADDIS ABABA
BOMBAY CALCUTTA MADRAS KARACHI LAHORE DACCA
KUALA LUMPUR SINGAPORE HONG KONG TOKYO

GENERAL EDITOR'S PREFACE

LIKE its predecessor, the New Clarendon Bible (New Testament) sets out to provide concise but scholarly commentaries on individual books of the New Testament in English suitable for candidates taking G.C.E. 'A' level, students in universities and colleges of education, and others who need something less ambitious than the full-scale 'academic' commentary.

In the old series the English text used as the basis of the commentaries was the Revised Version. At the time the old series was projected the choice could hardly have been otherwise. But now, when there are so many newer English versions available, the problem is more difficult. After taking what seemed the best advice the publishers have chosen the American Revised Standard Version for the new series, believing that this is the version which in the foreseeable future is most likely to be found suitable for examination purposes in schools and colleges; they hope also that the publication of a Catholic edition of RSV, which differs only slightly from the original, will enable commentaries based on the RSV to be more generally useful. And they wish to express their gratitude to the National Council of Churches of Christ in the United States of America for the permission, so readily given, to make use of the RSV in this way.

The design of the new series follows that of the old, except that it has been thought more practical to print both text and notes on the same page. Subjects requiring more comprehensive treatment than the scope of the notes allows will be found as before in the Introductions and in appendices at the end of the volumes.

CONTENTS

LIST OF ILLUSTRATIONS

ABBREVIATIONS

Barrett	C. K. Barrett, *The Gospel according to St John* (London, 1955)
Bernard	J. H. Bernard, *A Critical and Exegetical Commentary on the Gospel according to St. John* (edited by A. H. McNeile) (Edinburgh, 1928)
Dodd, *HTFG*	C. H. Dodd, *Historical Tradition in the Fourth Gospel* (Cambridge, 1963)
Dodd, *IFG*	C. H. Dodd, *The Interpretation of the Fourth Gospel* (Cambridge, 1953)
ET	English Translation
Gk.	Greek
Guilding	A. Guilding, *The Fourth Gospel and Jewish Worship* (Oxford, 1960)
Hoskyns	E. C. Hoskyns, *The Fourth Gospel* (edited by F. N. Davey) (London, 1940)
JTS, NS	*The Journal of Theological Studies*, New Series
Lightfoot	R. H. Lightfoot, *St. John's Gospel* (edited by C. F. Evans) (Oxford, 1956)
mg.	margin
MS, MSS	manuscript, manuscripts
NEB	New English Bible: O.T. 1970; N.T. 1961 (Second Edition 1970)
N.T.	New Testament
O.T.	Old Testament
RSV	Revised Standard Version: O.T. 1952; N.T. 1946
RSVCE	Revised Standard Version Catholic Edition: N.T. 1965
RV	Revised Version: O.T. 1884; N.T. 1881
Strachan	R. H. Strachan, *The Fourth Gospel, its Significance and Environment* (London, 1946)
Westcott	B. F. Westcott, *The Gospel according to St. John* (London, 1908)

LITERATURE ON JOHN

A. COMMENTARIES

For the Commentaries of Barrett, Bernard, Hoskyns, Lightfoot, Strachan, Westcott, see Abbreviations.

Two commentaries in English have been published since this book was written:

J. MARSH, *The Gospel of St John* (Harmondsworth, 1968).

J. N. SAUNDERS, *A Commentary on the Gospel according to St John* (edited by B. A. Mastin) (London, 1968).

B. OTHER BOOKS ON JOHN

See Abbreviations for the books of Dodd and Guilding.

P. GARDNER-SMITH, *Saint John and the Synoptic Gospels* (Cambridge, 1938)

W. GROSSOUW, *Revelation and Redemption* (London, 1958)

W. F. HOWARD, *The Fourth Gospel in Recent Criticism and Interpretation* (revised by C. K. Barrett) (London, 1961)

E. KÄSEMANN, *The Testament of Jesus* (London, 1968)

F. MUSSNER, *The Historical Jesus in the Gospel of St John* (Freiburg, 1967)

E. M. SIDEBOTTOM, *The Christ of the Fourth Gospel* (London, 1961)

D. M. SMITH, *The Composition and Order of the Fourth Gospel* (New Haven and London, 1965)

INTRODUCTION

1. *The Johannine Problem*

From as early as the second century, the Gospel according to John, for all its usefulness and attractiveness, has been a problem; it has raised questions which have not been easy to answer. The best way to approach it will be to set out these questions as clearly as possible, though it must be said at once that at the present time there are no agreed answers to them.

First, every careful reader of the New Testament will have noticed that there is something about John's Gospel which marks it off from the other three; for example, it may be difficult to remember whether a given passage is from Matthew, or from Mark, or from Luke; but it is comparatively easy to determine whether it is from one of these three (i.e. the Synoptic Gospels) on the one hand, or from John on the other.

The distinguishing mark by which one decides in this matter, is John's language. For example, the expression 'the kingdom of God' (or 'the kingdom of heaven') occurs frequently in the Synoptic Gospels, but only twice in John; and, conversely, sayings in the form 'I am the . . .' identify a passage as Johannine, because there are no such sayings in the Synoptics.

Another difference between John and the Synoptics is the order of events in the Gospel: in Mark, for example, Jesus goes from Galilee to Jerusalem only once (Mark 10¹); in John he makes the journey three times (John 2¹³, 5¹, 7¹⁰). In Mark the cleansing of the temple comes towards the end of the Gospel (Mark 11¹⁵) whereas in John it is placed near the beginning (John 2¹³ ff.).

In addition to these differences of language and order, there is another which is of much greater importance—the picture of Christianity which the reader forms. In the Synoptic Gospels the picture is that of following Jesus during the few remaining days of this age into the kingdom of God which is coming soon; in John, this idea of the imminence of the end of the world is no longer prominent, and seldom mentioned; according to John, the believer enters eternal life in the present.

So far, we have been looking only at some of the differences between the Synoptic Gospels and John; but the problem which these differences create is made more complicated by the fact that there are also certain similarities between all four Gospels: some of the events in the life of Jesus are described in both the Synoptic Gospels and John in ways which are so similar that it is possible that there is a literary dependence on one side or the other. (A good example of this is the account of the anointing of Jesus: Matt. 26[6 ff.], Mark 14[3 ff.], Luke 7[36 ff.], John 12 [1 ff.]; see also below pp. 3 ff.).

The questions then which arise from a comparison of John with the Synoptic Gospels are:

(a) Why does John differ from them (in language, order, and content) more than any one of them differs from the other two?

(b) Is there some literary dependence? Did John use one or more of the Synoptic Gospels, or did they use John?

(c) If there is no dependence in either direction, how are we to account for these similarities and agreements?

These questions only arise because we have other Gospels with which to compare John; but even if they had not survived we should still have had a Johannine problem; John's Gospel taken by itself, and apart from any comparison with the Synoptics, presents us with a series of questions.

(a) Who wrote it? Three passages (John 1[14], 19[35], 21[24]) have been taken to indicate that it was written by one who was an eye-witness of the life of Jesus, and indeed this was the view which was held from the second century until modern times. Scholars today are not so certain that this is so; the three passages may not mean what they have been taken to mean, and the book itself may show that its author was not so closely or personally connected with the events which he describes.

(b) Was there one author, or were there more than one? Some scholars maintain that the book bears the marks of having been written by a number of hands, while others deny this.

(c) Has the book suffered dislocation and rearrangement? Again, opinion is divided.

(d) What was the background of the author, or authors? Was it Judaism, or the Greek world? And for whom was the book written: Christians or non-Christians, Jews or Gentiles?

All of these questions arise when we begin to look at this Gospel on its own, and it is not possible to be certain about the answer to any of them.

But there is still a further aspect of the Johannine problem. In the New Testament there is one book which claims to have been written by a man called John (which this Gospel itself does not claim), namely the Revelation; and there are three Letters attributed by tradition to John. Are all or any of these by the author of the Gospel? Scholars are not unanimous in their answers; many of them maintain that the three Letters were by the Evangelist, few that the Revelation was by him, though it contains some things which are similar to the Gospel.

2. *An Illustration of the Problem*

It may help to clarify some of these problems, and to intro-duce the questions we must put to the text, if we take as a sample one chapter in John where most of the difficulties we have mentioned are present, namely, Chapter 6.

The events in the previous chapter had all taken place in Jerusalem ($5^{1 \, f.}$), but Chapter 6 begins:

After this Jesus went to the other side of the Sea of Galilee, which is the Sea of Tiberias.

It is a strange connection: the Sea of Galilee is about 60 miles from Jerusalem, so one would not normally say that one went from Jerusalem to the other side of it. The chapter begins as if the previous narrative had been describing events in Galilee, beside the lake. For this reason a number of scholars have sug-gested that the chapters of the Gospel were rearranged at an early date; that originally Chapter 6 followed on immediately after Chapter 4 (in which Jesus was in Cana in Galilee, 4^{46}) and that Chapter 5 followed Chapter 6.

6^{1-14} describes the Feeding of the Five Thousand, a miracle which is also recorded by Matthew, Mark, and Luke; but while the Synoptic accounts agree fairly closely, John contains elements which set him apart from them and these can best be seen if the texts of Mark and John are placed side by side, with the words which are identical (or nearly so) in italics:

Mark 6³²⁻⁴⁴

And they went away in the boat to a lonely place by themselves. Now many saw them going, and knew them, and they ran there on foot from all of the towns, and got there ahead of them. As he landed he *saw a great throng*, and he had compassion on them, because they were like sheep without a shepherd; and he began to teach them many things. And when it grew late, his disciples came to him and said, 'This is a lonely place, and the hour is now late; send them away, to go into the country and villages around and *buy* something *to eat*.' But he answered them, 'You give them something to eat.' And they said to him, 'Shall we go and buy *two hundred denarii* worth of *bread*, and give it to them to eat?' And he said to them, 'How many *loaves have* you? Go and see.' And when they had found out, they said, '*Five, and two fish*.' Then he commanded them all to sit down by companies upon the green *grass*. So they *sat down* in groups, by hundreds and by fifties. And *taking the* five *loaves* and the two fish he looked up to heaven, and *blessed*, and broke the loaves, and gave them to the disciples to set before the people; and he divided the two fish among them all. And they all ate and were satisfied. And they took up *twelve baskets full* of *broken pieces* and of the fish. And those who ate the loaves were *five thousand men*.

John 6¹⁻¹⁴

After this Jesus went to the other side of the Sea of Galilee, which is the Sea of Tiberias. And a multitude followed him, because they saw the signs which he did on those who were diseased. Jesus went up into the hills, and there sat down with his disciples. Now the Passover, the feast of the Jews, was at hand. Lifting up his eyes, then, and *seeing* that a *multitude* was coming to him, Jesus said to Philip, 'How are we to *buy* bread, so that these people *may eat*?' This he said to test him, for he himself knew what he would do. Philip answered him, '*Two hundred denarii* would not buy enough *bread* for each of them to get a little.' One of his disciples, Andrew, Simon Peter's brother, said to him, 'There is a lad here who *has five* barley *loaves and two fish*; but what are they among so many?' Jesus said, 'Make the people *sit down*.' Now there was much *grass* in the place; so the *men* sat down, in number about *five thousand*. Jesus then *took the loaves*, and when he had *given thanks*, he distributed them to those who were seated; so also the fish, as much as they wanted. And when they had eaten their fill, he told his disciples, 'Gather up the fragments left over, that nothing may be lost.' So they gathered them up and *filled twelve baskets* with *fragments* from the five barley loaves, left by those who had eaten. When the people saw the sign which he had done, they said, 'This is indeed the prophet who is come into the world!'

These two accounts have slightly more in common than the minimum of words and expressions necessary in order to tell the same story. John contains details which Mark does not include, for example, that Passover was at hand, the names of two of the disciples (Philip and Andrew), barley loaves, and the comment of the crowd at the end of the story. Similarly, Mark includes details which John does not record.

After this, John says that Jesus withdrew again to the hills by himself, because he perceived 'that they were about to come and take him by force to make him king' (6¹⁵)—another detail which is only in this Gospel; Mark says 'he made his disciples get into the boat and go before him to the other side, to Bethsaida, while he dismissed the crowd' (Mark 6⁴⁵).

Then follows in John, in Mark, and in Matthew, but not in Luke, the story of Jesus walking on the water:

Mark 6⁴⁷⁻⁵²	*John* 6¹⁶⁻²³
And *when evening came*, the boat was out on the sea, and he was alone on the land. And he saw that they were distressed in rowing, for the *wind* was against them. And about the fourth watch of the night he came to them, walking on the sea. He meant to pass by them, but when *they saw* him *walking on the sea* they thought it was a ghost, and cried out; for they all saw him, and *were terrified*. But immediately he spoke *to them* and *said*, 'Take heart, *it is I; have no fear*.' And he got *into the boat* with them and the wind ceased. And they were utterly astounded, for they did not understand about the loaves, but their hearts were hardened.	*When evening came*, his disciples went down to the sea, got into a boat, and started across the sea to Capernaum. It was now dark, and Jesus had not yet come to them. The sea rose because a strong *wind* was blowing. When they had rowed about three or four miles, *they saw* Jesus *walking on the sea* and drawing near to the boat. They *were frightened*, but he *said to them, 'It is I; do not be afraid.'* Then they were glad to take him *into the boat*, and immediately the boat was at the land to which they were going.

Once again, the two accounts share rather more than the minimum of words that are needed in order to tell the same story.

Mark goes on to describe the healings at Gennesaret, whereas John gives an account of the scene in the synagogue at

Capernaum (6^{25-59}), followed by a discussion between Jesus and the disciples (6^{60-71}) which has only very slight parallels in the Synoptic Gospels (Mark 8 $^{27\text{ff.}}$, etc.).

There are three points which it is important for our present purpose to notice in John's account of the scene in the synagogue. First, there are a number of references to the Old Testament: the crowd refers to the manna in the wilderness, and quotes from the scriptures (6^{31}); Jesus quotes from Isaiah (6^{45}). Secondly, Jesus makes certain claims for himself, using a formula to which we have already referred (see above, p. 1):

'I am the bread of life' (6^{35});
'I am the living bread which came down from heaven' (6^{51}).

Thirdly, the climax of the scene is the claim of Jesus in verses 53 ff. and notice in particular verse 54:

'He who eats my flesh and drinks my blood has eternal life.'

That is to say, from being a discussion about bread it becomes a discussion about food and drink, flesh and blood. What Jesus says leads many of his disciples to take offence at him and leave him ($6^{60\text{ ff.}}$).

The question we must now ask is, How did John compose this chapter? What were his sources, and how did he make use of them?

(a) There are clearly some similarities between John and Mark (and the other Synoptists); but they are not so close as to prove beyond doubt that there is literary dependence; that is to say, they are not as close as, for example, the agreements in the wording of this story between Mark, Matthew, and Luke. Two views are possible: (1) that John knew and drew upon one or more of the Synoptic Gospels; and (2) that he had independent access to traditions similar to those which the Synoptists had used. The former is the opinion of Hoskyns, Barrett, and Lightfoot; the latter of Gardner-Smith, Bultmann, and Dodd. (A third theory is also possible, but it would be very difficult to maintain it in view of other considerations: that the Synoptists drew upon John. It would be very difficult to explain why changes were made in the direction from John to Mark; it is not so difficult to explain them in the reverse order.)

(b) As well as the Synoptic material (in its pre-Gospel form or in its final form) John had a considerable knowledge of the

Old Testament, and was able to quote from it, as in 6³¹, ⁴⁵, but also in more elusive ways—for example, that the loaves were of barley (6⁹, ¹³) is probably a detail which has come in, not from historical reminiscence, but from a similar story in the Old Testament, in which Elisha fed a hundred men with twenty loaves of barley (2 Kings 4⁴²ᶠᶠ·).

(c) Another source on which John draws is the teaching and practice of the Church. There is a clear example of this in the chapter we are considering: the movement of the discussion from bread to the flesh and blood of the Son of man, which must be eaten and drunk (verse 53), can be most easily understood if it is taken as a reference to the Eucharist.

(d) However, the Synoptic material, the Old Testament and Christian worship do not account for the whole of Chapter 6 without remainder. There are, for example, the sayings of Jesus such as that in verse 38:

'I have come down from heaven',

and in verse 62:

'What if you were to see the Son of man ascending where he was before?'

No sayings of this kind are attributed to Jesus in the Synoptic Gospels, and the Old Testament does not provide a completely adequate background for this idea of one who is to descend from heaven and ascend there again. Some scholars, however, say that there are parallels in the Jewish Wisdom literature; while others find parallels in Hellenistic mythology; and others again in Jewish Gnostic sources.

(e) There may be a further factor in the making of Chapter 6, namely the contemporary Church situation. John says that there were disciples who took offence at the saying about the flesh and blood of the Son of man (verses 60 ff.). We know from the Johannine Letters that there were at that time many who had left the Church because they refused to acknowledge 'the coming of Jesus Christ in the flesh' (2 John⁷: cp. 1 John 2¹⁸ᶠᶠ·, 4¹ᶠᶠ·). It may be that this situation is reflected in the account of the withdrawal of disciples from Jesus which is described at the end of Chapter 6.

This study of Chapter 6 shows that in order to understand this Gospel we must be prepared to ask the following questions concerning any one section of it:

- (a) Has John used Synoptic material here?
- (b) Is there any Old Testament passage which he has in mind at this point in his Gospel?
- (c) Is there any aspect of the worship and experience of the Church or of the Christian life which explains what John is saying here?
- (d) Is there anything in the thought of the Jewish and pagan backgrounds of the author and his readers which is relevant?
- (e) Is there any allusion here to the historical situation in which this Gospel was written?

3. *The Authorship of the Gospel*

(a) *External Evidence*

One of the earliest surviving pieces of evidence for authorship is in the writings of Irenaeus. He had lived in the east *c.* A.D. 130; he moved to the west, and was consecrated Bishop of Lyons *c.* A.D. 178; and he died *c.* A.D. 200. He says that, after the writing of the other gospels,

John, the disciple of the Lord, who had even rested on his breast, himself also gave forth the gospel, while he was living at Ephesus in Asia. *Adv. Haer.* III. i. 1. (quoted in Euseduis, *Hist. Eccl.* v. viii. 4; Loeb trans.).

Moreover Irenaeus also says that when he was a boy in lower Asia, he had seen Polycarp (*c.* A.D. 69–155) the Bishop of Smyrna, and that he could remember that Polycarp had talked about 'John and . . . the others who had seen the Lord' (Irenaeus to Florinus, quoted by Eus. *Hist. Eccl.* v. xx. 4 f.). There is thus a direct link between Irenaeus, Polycarp, and John who, Irenaeus says, was the author of the Gospel.

Other Christian writers of this period and later held the same opinion about the authorship of the Gospel, with two exceptions: some heretical teachers, called by their opponents the Alogi (*c.* A.D. 170) said that the author was Cerinthus, a heretic who lived *c.* A.D. 100 (Epiph. *Pan.* li. 2–3); and Ephrem Syrus (*c.* A.D. 306–73) said that it was written at Antioch (though it is not clear whether Ephrem meant 'written' as opposed to 'published').

Although the testimony of Irenaeus appears very strong

indeed, it has been disputed, because to many scholars it seems impossible that the Fourth Gospel could have been written by John the son of Zebedee. We shall consider their reasons for this later; here, however, we must notice the following points in connection with Irenaeus' statement:

1. Irenaeus himself says that he was a boy at the time when he heard Polycarp in Asia. (It has been calculated by some scholars that he would not have been more than fifteen years old at the time of Polycarp's death. See W. G. Kümmel, *Introduction to the New Testament* (London, 1966), p. 170.)

2. Irenaeus was about fifty years old when he wrote *Against Heresies* in A.D. 180. He was thus describing what he remembered from thirty-five years before (*c.* A.D. 145) of what Polycarp, who was then about seventy-six, had said about events which must have happened at least forty-five years before that. (Cp. a man of fifty in 1960 discussing what he remembered from a conversation he had had in 1925, concerning events which happened in 1880.)

3. It can be shown that Irenaeus was certainly mistaken on a similar subject: he maintained that Papias, Bishop of Hierapolis, was 'a hearer of John', but this is not in fact what Papias himself says (Barrett, *The Gospel according to St. John* (London, 1955), pp. 87 f.).

4. There is some evidence from Papias, who wrote *c.* A.D. 140, that there were two people called John: the Apostle, and another, known as the Elder (or the Presbyter). Papias says:

If ever anyone came who had followed the presbyters, I inquired into the words of the presbyters, what Andrew or Peter or Philip or Thomas or James or John or Matthew, or any other of the Lord's disciples, had said, and what Aristion and the presbyter John, the Lord's disciples, were saying (quoted by Eus. *Hist. Eccl.* III. xxxix. 4; Loeb trans.).

This has been understood to imply that John the Elder was a different person from John the Apostle, the son of Zebedee; and it has been suggested that Irenaeus misunderstood Polycarp; that he thought Polycarp was referring to the Apostle whereas in fact he was referring to the Presbyter.

There is, therefore, a loophole in the apparently strong evidence which we have from Irenaeus; but we should only use it if the internal evidence required us to do so.

(b) Internal evidence

The Gospel itself contains two kinds of evidence bearing on the question of authorship: on the one hand there are those passages which make, or have been taken to make, explicit statements concerning the author of the book; on the other, there are those passages which reveal the identity of the author by implication.

Three passages have been held to make an explicit statement concerning the author of the Gospel:

1. And the Word became flesh and dwelt among us, full of grace and truth; and we have beheld his glory . . . (1¹⁴).

It has been said that by using the first person plural in this verse ('us', 'we'), the author claims that he was an eye-witness of the events which he records. But this is not certain, and a number of scholars say that the first person plural here refers to Christians as a whole, without necessarily making any claim for the author or defining his status in relation to the things he records.

2. He who saw it [sc. the piercing of the side of Jesus on the cross] has borne witness—his testimony is true, and he knows that he tells the truth—that you also may believe (19³⁵).

It is not completely certain who is meant by 'He who saw it' though most commentators understand this as a reference to 'the disciple whom he [Jesus] loved' mentioned a few verses earlier (19²⁶). But even if this is so, it still does not necessarily follow from this verse that that disciple is said to be the author of the Gospel, since all that is stated here is that this man 'saw it' and 'has borne witness'; it is not said that he wrote the Gospel; in fact, on the contrary, it could be (and has been) held that the author is here speaking of the beloved disciple as some one other than himself.

3. This is the disciple who is bearing witness to these things, and who has written these things; and we know that his testimony is true (21²⁴).

Here there is no doubt that 'This is the disciple' refers to the beloved disciple who was mentioned in the immediately preceding verses (20-3); nor is there any doubt that the beloved disciple is here said to be the author of 'these things', though it is not completely clear what this means. The first person plural in the last sentence of this verse is possibly the 'we' of the Christian congregation as a whole, as in 1¹⁴.

Thus it is only in Chapter 21 that there is an explicit and undeniable claim that this Gospel, or part of it, was written by the beloved disciple; and even about this there are certain qualifications which need to be made. First, 'has written these things' could mean 'has caused these things to be written', as in 19¹⁹⁻²². Secondly, 'these things' need not necessarily refer to the Gospel as a whole but only to Chapter 21. Thirdly, Chapter 21 is thought by some to be an addition to the Gospel, which seems to end satisfactorily at 20³⁰ f· (see note on p. 207 below).

The internal explicit evidence that the Gospel was written by the beloved disciple thus in the end consists of one verse in a chapter which for various reasons is thought by some scholars not to be part of the original book. Nevertheless, one would not resort to such arguments if it were not that other considerations weigh heavily against the view that this Gospel was written by an eye-witness. What these considerations are will appear when we turn to the implicit evidence.

Before we do so, however, there is another problem which can be most conveniently dealt with at this point. We saw that 21²⁴ may be taken to mean that the Gospel was written by the beloved disciple. Is this the same as to say that it was written by John the son of Zebedee? That is, does 'the disciple whom Jesus loved' mean John the Apostle?

The facts are as follows:

(a) The expression '[the disciple] whom [Jesus] loved' (Gk. ὃν ἠγάπα) occurs four times in the Gospel: 13²³, 19²⁶, 21⁷, ²⁰.

(b) A very similar expression, using a different Greek verb, occurs once, at 20² (Gk. ὃν ἐφίλει).

(c) In 18¹⁵ f· there are references to 'another disciple' who followed Jesus, with Peter, to the house of the high priest.

The first question with arises is, Do these expressions refer to one, two, or three individuals? It can be argued that the Greek verbs used in the first and second expressions (ἀγαπᾶν and φιλεῖν) are used interchangeably elsewhere in this Gospel (e.g. in 3³⁵ and 5²⁰ John says 'The Father loves the Son': in the former the verb is ἀγαπᾶν, in the latter it is φιλεῖν, and there is no difference in meaning). It seems likely therefore that there is no distinction between the disciple referred to in the first group of passages and the disciple mentioned in 20². Again, on many occasions when 'the disciple whom Jesus loved' is mentioned, Peter is also present and is in some way contrasted with him (see 13²³ ᶠ·, 20²ᶠᶠ·, 21⁷, ²⁰ᶠᶠ·). This is what happens in 18¹⁵ᶠᶠ· also: 'the other disciple' is known to the high priest, and to 'the maid who kept the door' and who said to Peter 'Are you not also one of this man's disciples?' It seems likely, therefore, that by 'the other disciple' here, is meant 'the disciple whom Jesus loved'; that is to say that all six passages refer to one individual.[1]

The second question is, Who was the disciple who is referred to in this way? One suggestion, first made sixty years ago, and still popular in some quarters, is that the beloved disciple was Lazarus. The evidence on which this theory is based is that in Chapter 11 John says three times that Jesus loved Lazarus; and it is relevant to note that the two Greek verbs, ἀγαπᾶν and φιλεῖν, are used interchangeably here, as we saw also above: in 11³, ³⁶ φιλεῖν; in 11⁵ ἀγαπᾶν. The difficulties of this theory are, first, that when Lazarus is mentioned in 12⁹ᶠᶠ·, he is mentioned by name; if the Evangelist is prepared to use the name 'Lazarus' there, why not also in Chapters 13, 18, 19, 20, and 21? And secondly, Lazarus is nowhere said to be a disciple of Jesus.

A second suggestion is that the beloved disciple is John the Elder, the disciple mentioned by Papias (see above, p. 9). However, the other Gospels do not mention a second John.

Thirdly, it is suggested that he is an imaginary figure, the creation of the Evangelist, the ideal disciple, who is close to Jesus and who shares his mind, believing in him and following him.

Fourthly, the most popular view is that by the beloved disciple, the Evangelist means John the Apostle, the son of Zebedee. If this were not so, John the Apostle would not be mentioned at all in Chapters 1–20, unlike Simon Peter, Andrew, Philip, Nathanael, Thomas, Judas (not Iscariot), and Judas Iscariot. Furthermore in Chapter 21 the following are introduced: Simon Peter, Thomas, Nathanael, the sons of Zebedee, 'and two others of his disciples'; and one of these is

---

[1] It is sometimes said that the beloved disciple is one of the two (the other is Andrew) who are mentioned in 1³⁵ᶠᶠ·, but there is nothing in the text of the Gospel to say so; this conclusion is only reached by a comparison of this passage with the Synoptic Gospels (e.g. Mark 1¹⁶ᶠᶠ·).

the beloved disciple (see verses 2, 7). This does not prove that the Evangelist identified the beloved disciple with the Apostle John, but that he did so is consistent with the evidence; it is also what Irenaeus seems to have thought, and what other early writers took the Evangelist to mean.

Perhaps the best solution to this problem lies in combining the third suggestion with the fourth: the beloved disciple is an idealized character based on the son of Zebedee. There would be partial parallels to such a treatment of a historical character in other New Testament writings from about this time; for example, the authors of the Letter to the Ephesians and of the Pastoral Epistles treated the figure of Paul in this way, and so perhaps did the author of Matthew's Gospel, the Apostle Matthew. Moreover, it would not be difficult to find the reason why the author of John's Gospel did this; he was writing a Gospel which he may have thought of as displacing earlier Gospels, certainly supplementing them, and in some ways offering a different account and interpretation of the ministry of Jesus from theirs; he contrasts Peter (the source of the earlier tradition, according to Papias) with the beloved disciple (whom he regards as his own authority), and claims for him a greater understanding of Jesus than Peter's.

If this is the solution (and it must be said that no solution o this problem is more than a hypothesis), then it will follow tha the writer of the Gospel was not John the Apostle, but some body else writing in his name. And this would agree with two other aspects of the problem: first, it seems unlikely that anybody would refer to himself as 'the disciple whom Jesus loved'; secondly, the internal implicit evidence confirms the view that the Gospel was not written by any one of the Apostles. We must now consider this part of the evidence.

In some respects, the contents of this Gospel do not return an unambiguous answer to the question, Was it written by an Apostle, and therefore an eye-witness of the events which it describes? On the one hand, it can be argued that the Evangelist is acquainted with a number of places which are not mentioned in the Synoptic Gospels; that he is accurate in his information about Jewish practices in Palestine during the time before the fall of Jerusalem in A.D. 70; and that he includes in his stories details which can only be historical. On the other hand, it is not possible to prove that a later writer, one who was not himself an eye-witness, but who had access to earlier stories, could not have written exactly what the Evangelist has written.[1]

The question is rather, Does the Evangelist write as one who is recording events in which he has taken part, or does he write in some other way? and the answer to this question cannot be in doubt. He shows no interest whatsoever in reproducing the words and phrases of Jesus which he spoke in Galilee and Jerusalem; there is no distinction at all in this Gospel between the language of Jesus and the language of the Evangelist; the sayings of Jesus as we find them in the Synoptic Gospels never appear in John, apart from a very few cases of isolated logia; there are none of the parables, and there is none of the preaching of the kingdom of God and repentance. If the Evangelist had heard Jesus talking in the flesh, it did not influence the way he wrote when he composed his Gospel. In this Gospel, Jesus speaks in the style of the Evangelist.

Again, we can see that John is not always describing historical events, from the fact that he records conversations of which there were apparently no other witnesses: e.g. Jesus and Nicodemus, Jesus and the Samaritan Woman, Jesus and Pilate in the Praetorium. The artificiality of these conversations becomes clear when they are looked at in detail; they all follow the same pattern, and it is a pattern which is frequently used elsewhere in the Gospel: Jesus makes a statement, which at first is misunderstood and then clarified in order that the truth may be expressed more clearly.

So we can say that although it cannot be proved that the Gospel was not written by the Apostle John, it can nevertheless be shown that if he was the author of it, his knowledge of Jesus in the days of his flesh has not contributed to the writing of the book as much as we should have expected. In spite of the passages in which the author says emphatically that he is describing what happened (e.g. $19^{35\,f\cdot}$, $20^{30\,f\cdot}$, $21^{24\,f\cdot}$) his main concern is to bear witness to what he believes about Jesus; and for this purpose he has, to some extent at least, forsaken straightforward narration of historical fact. We shall consider this further in sections 5 and 6 of this Introduction.

[1] For the possibility of historical inaccuracies in this Gospel, see the notes in the Commentary on the following passages: 1^{24}, 4^9, 6^1, $9^{22\,f\cdot}$, 10^{31}, 12^{42}, 16^2, $18^{28,\,31}$.

1. Rylands Papyrus 457; second century (see p. 16)

4. *The Date and Place of Origin of the Gospel*

A papyrus fragment (**p.** 52) which was found in Egypt and
is now in the John Rylands Library at Manchester (Rylands
Papyrus 457, containing John 18$^{31-3, 37, 38}$) must be dated not
later than the middle of the second century; and it is possibly
even earlier than that. Of similar date is Egerton Papyrus 2 (a
fragment of an unknown Gospel, which seems to show knowledge of John) also found in Egypt. Hence, John was known in
Egypt, and was copied by the middle of the second century at
the latest; it must have been written before that—perhaps
A.D. 140 is the latest possible date of writing.

It is more difficult to fix with certainty the earliest possible
date; some scholars maintain that John used Mark (which it
is thought was written *c.* A.D. 70); some that he also used Luke
(written perhaps *c.* A.D. 80–90); but as we have seen, others
think that he is independent of the Synoptic Gospels. The
expression 'put out of the synagogue' (9^{22}, 12^{42}, 16^{2}) may reflect
a situation which arose *c.* A.D. 85–90 (see note on 9^{22}). If this
is so, we should arrive at the period A.D. 90–140 for the writing
of the Gospel (e.g. Barrett, p. 108 f.) which some scholars
narrow down to A.D. 90–100 (e.g. Kümmel, op. cit., p. 175).

Three places of origin have been suggested: we saw that
Irenaeus and all the other early writers, with one exception,
said that the Gospel was published in Ephesus; and that the
exception, Ephrem Syrus, said that it was written in Antioch.
Some modern writers have suggested Alexandria as the home
of the Gospel but, though this would fit in with the discovery
of early papyri of John in Egypt, this is not generally accepted.
Ephesus or Antioch is the usual view. The former is traditional;
the latter would explain some similarities between John and
the letters of Ignatius of Antioch (*c.* A.D. 110).

5. *The Literary Character of the Gospel*

This Gospel is a highly developed literary work, and a
review of some of the methods and techniques which the
Evangelist has used will be useful at this point: it will show
what kind of book this Gospel is, and what kind of man wrote it.

2. Egerton Papyrus 2; second century (see p. 16)

First, the book has a clear plan. It is divided into two main parts: Chapters 1–12 describe the Ministry of Jesus; Chapters 13–21 are an account of the supper, the passion, and the resurrection. The division between these two main parts is marked by the retrospective summaries in 12$^{36-50}$, and by the opening of Chapter 13 which indicates that a new section starts at this point.

Within the first part of the Gospel it is possible to find the pattern in which the material has been arranged. The usual arrangement is narrative-material first, followed by conversation; the narratives describe the signs which Jesus did; the conversations introduce the discourses of Jesus. Thus Chapters 1–12 can be set out as follows:

	1	Prologue and Introduction
I.	2	Signs
	3^1–4^{42}	Discourses
II.	4^{43}–5^9	Signs
	5^{10} ff.	Discourse
III.	6$^{1-21}$	Signs
	6^{22} f.	Discourse
IV.	7, 8	Discourse
V.	9$^{1-12}$	Sign
	9^{13}–10^{42}	Discourses
VI.	11$^{1-44}$	Sign and Discourse
VII.	11^{45}–12^{36a}	Sign and Discourse
	12^{36b} ff.	Epilogue

In the second part of the Gospel, this pattern is reversed: the discourse is placed first, the narrative second.[1]

13–17	The last Discourse
18–21	The Passion and Resurrection

There is no difference between John and the Synoptists in this respect: like John, they have arranged their material according to a pattern, and not in the chronological order in which the events happened. There is also a close similarity between John's method of arrangement and Matthew's: both alternate sections describing the deeds of Jesus with those recording his words. The difference between John and the Synoptists lies in the extent to which he has imposed his own style and idiom upon the material.

[1] On the other hand, it could be argued that the foot-washing in 13^{1} ff. acts as the sign which introduces the discourse in 13^{12} ff..

We have already referred to this (above, p. 14), but another illustration of the point may be allowed here. At 3^{15} and 3^{30} the translators of the RSV note in the margin that some interpreters hold that the next section should be included in the quotation marks which they use to indicate the direct speech of Jesus, while they themselves treat these verses as the author's own comments. This uncertainty arises because there is no difference between the style and language of the Evangelist and the style and language of Jesus in this Gospel. It would be true to say that all the characters in the Fourth Gospel speak in the same style and that in every case it is the style of the Evangelist. The Synoptists were compilers of tradition; John on the other hand is an author. The material has passed through his mind, and it has been changed in the process.

Moreover, it is possible to detect recurring devices which he uses; and the frequency with which they occur in the Gospel suggests strongly that they are part of the author's technique, not the record of an eye-witness reporting what happened.

One of the most frequent of these devices is the sequence Ambiguity, Misunderstanding, Clarification. There is a clear example of it in Chapter 2: in answer to a question put to him by the Jews, Jesus says 'Destroy this temple, and in three days I will raise it up' (2^{19}). The Ambiguity here lies in the meaning of 'this temple', by which the Jews think he means the temple of Herod, but John says that they have misunderstood the saying, because (and this is the Clarification) 'he spoke of the temple of his body' (2^{21}). The Clarification in this case is provided by the Evangelist; in some of the other instances, Jesus himself gives the explanation of the ambiguous saying. There is an example of this in the next chapter: Jesus says to Nicodemus 'Unless one is born anew [mg., 'from above'], he cannot see the kingdom of God' (3^3); Nicodemus misunderstands this as if it meant that a man must be born a second time in a physical sense; Jesus then explains 'born anew' as 'born of water and the Spirit' (3^5).

For further examples see:

$4^{10\,ff.}$	water
$4^{32\,ff.}$	food
$6^{33\,ff.}$	bread
$8^{31\,ff.}$	free
$8^{38\,ff.}$	Father

11$^{11\,\text{ff.}}$	sleep
11$^{23\,\text{ff.}}$	resurrection
13$^{8\,\text{ff.}}$	washing
14$^{4\,\text{ff.}}$	way
14$^{7\,\text{ff.}}$	seeing
14$^{21\,\text{ff.}}$	manifestation
16$^{16\,\text{ff.}}$	little while

In each of these John uses the full sequence: Ambiguity, Misunderstanding, Clarification; but there are other occasions on which the Clarification is omitted, and the reader is left to supply it for himself. For instance, in Chapter 7 Jesus says to the Jews that he will go to him who sent him, and that they will seek him and will not find him; where he is they cannot come. The Jews ask one another where he means to go: 'Does he intend to go to the Dispersion among the Greeks, and teach the Greeks? What does he mean by saying, "You will seek me and you will not find me" and "Where I am you cannot come"' (7$^{33\,\text{ff.}}$). John does not go on to tell the reader what Jesus' saying did in fact mean; either he thinks that the reader can understand for himself that Jesus is referring to his death; or he is leaving the explanation until later (see 13$^{33\,\text{ff.}}$).

Another example of an unclarified Misunderstanding comes in 8$^{21\,\text{f.}}$: Jesus has said 'Where I am going, you cannot come', and the Jews think he means that he will kill himself. But John does not explain what the saying means.

These two passages are interesting for another reason: in both of them, the Misunderstanding is in a sense true, but not in the sense in which the Jews think. It is true that Jesus will go to the Dispersion and teach the Greeks: he will do it through the mission and work of the disciples. It is true that Jesus will lay down his life. But in neither case will it happen in the way that the Jews suppose. This is Johannine Irony, and there are many examples of it in the Gospel. One of the clearest is the statement of Caiaphas to the Sanhedrin: 'It is expedient for you that one man should die for the people', by which Caiaphas means that it is better that one man should die rather than that the rest of the people should do so (he continues, 'and that the whole nation should not perish'): in this sense he is wrong, both morally (the end does not justify the means) and historically (the death of Jesus did not save the Jews from the war of A.D. 66–70 and its consequences). John, however, sees another meaning in what the high priest says: 'he prophesied that Jesus should die for the nation . . .' that is, on their behalf, as the good shepherd who lays down his life for the sheep ($11^{49\,ff.}$, 18^{14}; cp. $10^{11\,ff.}$).

For some further examples of Irony in this Gospel, see:

$2^{9\,f.}$	You have kept the good wine until now.
4^{12}	Are you greater than our father Jacob?
7^{27}	We know where this man comes from.
7^{42}	The Christ is to come from Bethlehem.
7^{52}	No prophet is to rise from Galilee.
11^{16}	Let us also go, that we may die with him.
11^{36}	See how he loved him!
12^{19}	Look, the world has gone after him.
13^{37}	I will lay down my life for you.
18^{31}	It is not lawful for us to put any man to death.
18^{38}	I find no crime in him (see also $19^{4,\,6}$).
19^5	Here is the man!
19^{14}	Here is your King!
$19^{19\,ff.}$	Jesus of Nazareth, the King of the Jews.

Irony is a technique much used by dramatists, and this Gospel will be understood best if it is regarded as drama. For instance, in the account of the trial before Pilate, John uses what has been called by one commentator 'the device of two stages' (see notes on $18^{28\,ff.}$ and cp. the use of the same device in $4^{28\,ff.}$, Jesus and the Samaritans). Notice also how at the beginning of Chapter 4, John 'sets the scene' for the conversation with the Samaritan woman, mentioning the field that Jacob gave to Joseph, and Jacob's well, both of which will be referred to in the dialogue ($4^{5\,f.}$, $^{10\,f.}$). John adopts (as we have already seen, p. 14) the 'God's eye view', describing conversations for which he probably had no evidence; that is to say, he uses a dramatic convention whereby incidents which happened in private are presented to an audience (in this case, the readers of the Gospel) without any sense of incongruity.

John's Gospel is therefore a developed literary work akin to drama. Devices and techniques have been used, such as Ambiguity, Misunderstanding, Irony, the double stage, the God's eye view. Characters are brought on to play their part; but when they have fulfilled their role in the plot, they disappear, often without further mention, because the reader is not intended to be interested in them for their own sake, but in the development of the theme (notice in particular how nothing more is heard of the Greeks who enter at 12²⁰ asking to see Jesus).

It will follow from this that we can only put questions of a certain kind to this Gospel. It is not legitimate to ask about the connection between the 'scenes' (e.g. between Chapters 5 and 6—see above, p. 3). The events are tableaux, and they follow one another without any causal link. Nor is it legitimate to ask questions about the motives and intentions of the minor characters: they are there to carry the plot along, and this is their only function. The same is true also in some respects of the picture of Jesus: he is there for what he says and does, and he is not described as a man; there is no attempt to portray his personality, and any use of this Gospel for such a purpose is both illegitimate and fruitless. The only questions which may be asked are those which are in accordance with the Evangelist's purpose; and in order to understand that, we must consider the message of this Gospel.

6. *The Message of the Gospel*

The message of this Gospel is both simpler and more complex than that of the Synoptic Gospels. It is more complex in that it makes use of ideas which come from a wider and more 'international' background than those used by the Synoptists: e.g. the two worlds, above and below; the Word through whom all things were made; the descent and ascent of the Son of man; rebirth from above. These ideas, and others like them, can be traced back into earlier Jewish and pagan circles; whereas the background of the Synoptic Gospels is almost entirely Palestinian. But, on the other hand, John's Gospel can be regarded as a simplification of the Synoptic Gospels: part of their purpose is to show Jesus as the teacher who proclaims the way into the kingdom of God which is coming; the Synoptists are concerned to give the answers which Jesus would give to practical questions arising for disciples of Jesus. John, on the other hand, has none of the ethical teaching; he is only concerned with faith in Jesus.

For example, Mark records a story in which a man asks Jesus 'What must I do to inherit eternal life?' Jesus first reminds him of the commandments: 'Do not kill, Do not commit adultery, Do not steal, Do not bear false witness, Do not defraud, Honour your father and mother.' The man says 'Teacher, all these I have observed from my youth'; then Jesus says to him, 'You lack one thing; go, sell what you have, and give to the poor, and you will have treasure in heaven; and come, follow me' (Mark 10[17.ff.]). In John, the answer to what is in effect the same question is much simpler; when the Jews ask 'What must we do, to be doing the works of God?' [i.e. the works which God requires of us in order that we may have eternal life], Jesus replies 'This is the work of God, that you believe in him whom he has sent' (6[28 f.]). The whole of the teaching of Jesus as it is recorded in this Gospel is narrowed down to one point, and this point is that Jesus is the one to be believed, because he is the Word of God, the one whom God has sent to give life to the world.

The teaching of Jesus in John is not a distortion of what is given as his teaching by the Synoptists, but a concentration on one part of what was present in the earlier tradition, to the exclusion of everything else. The one element in the tradition on which John concentrates is that which is involved when Jesus says 'Follow me'. John takes up the idea that Jesus associated disciples with himself, as his followers, and promised them eternal life in the kingdom of God as the reward for such following; and he works out the implications of such a relationship in his own terms.

In order to appreciate this, we must first notice an aspect of John's style to which we have already referred—his use of synonymous expressions (see above on $\dot{a}\gamma a\pi\hat{a}\nu$ and $\phi\iota\lambda\epsilon\hat{\iota}\nu$, p. 11). He has a passion for saying the same thing in different words. In order to give one example, it is clear that he is saying the same thing twice in 6[35]:

He who comes to me shall not hunger, and he who believes in me shall never thirst;

that is to say, 'to come' to Jesus is a synonym for 'to believe' in him. Other synonyms for believing in John are 'following' him (as in the Synoptic Gospels), 'abiding in' him, 'loving' him, 'keeping his word', 'receiving' him, 'having' him, 'seeing' him. All these expressions are used by John to describe the relationship between the disciple and Jesus, and this relationship, as

John sees it, is the whole of the message which his book is written to convey.

That is to say, John has taken up the historical fact that disciples followed Jesus believing that in doing so they would enter eternal life, and he has worked out the theological implications of this. If Jesus is regarded in this way (John is saying), if he is the one who makes unconditional demands upon his followers, and offers them eternal rewards, then we must say of him that he is the one through whom we receive all the gifts of God which we seek; he is our maker and our Saviour. Thus the quotation from 6[35] (which was used to illustrate the parallelism between 'coming' and 'believing') begins:

'I am the bread of life.'

Many of the other 'I am' sayings are of this kind, in that a claim made by Jesus is followed immediately by a promise to the believer; e.g.

'I am the light of the world; he who follows me will not walk in darkness, but will have the light of life' (8[12]).

'I am the door; if anyone enters by me, he will be saved' (10[9]).

'I am the resurrection and the life; he who believes in me, though he die, yet shall he live, and whoever lives and believes in me shall never die' (11[25 f.]).

'I am the way, and the truth, and the life; no one comes to the Father, but by me' (14[6]).

'I am the vine, you are the branches. He who abides in me, and I in him, he it is that bears much fruit' (15[5]).

John's teaching about Jesus (i.e. his Christology) is the working out of the implications of the faith by which Christians live.

If we look now at the 'I am' sayings quoted above, we shall see again John's use of synonymous expressions to describe discipleship: 'come', 'follow', 'enter', 'believe', 'abide'. In exactly the same way, the words which are used of Jesus are all used to point to one and the same thing: that he is 'the Saviour of the world' (4[42]). All the 'I am' sayings and all the titles of Jesus which John uses ('the Christ', 'the Word', 'the Lord', 'the King of Israel', 'the Son of God', 'the Son of man') express this one idea: Jesus is the one through whom God has sent salvation into the world.

Thus, for all his variety of expression, and for all the

apparent complexity of his thought, John's message is extremely simple; he writes his Gospel, as he says himself, 'that you may believe that Jesus is the Christ, the Son of God, and that believing you may have life in his name' (20^{31}).

7. An Evaluation of John's Gospel

The Gospel was written somewhere around the turn of the first century; it expressed Christian faith in terms which could be understood by a man of that time, whether he was a Jew or a Greek. The difficulty we have today in deciding whether the background of the Evangelist was Greek or Jewish is some evidence of his achievement: he made use of terms with which either could feel at home. (The best example of this is his choice of Logos (Word), which could be understood either in the light of the Old Testament background (Genesis 1; Ps. 33^6, etc.), or of Stoicism.)

We cannot be certain whether the Evangelist's intention was to refute false teachers, or to propagate the faith; we cannot be certain for whom he wrote—orthodox Christians, heretical Christians, or non-Christians. But it seems that the book was not at first accepted by orthodox Christian writers; it is uncertain whether Ignatius of Antioch used it, or Justin Martyr; the earliest certain allusions to it are in the Homily *On the Passion* by Melito of Sardis, *c.* A.D. 160–70.

John's Gospel must be the only book in the New Testament of which we have fragments of the text that are earlier than the first quotations from it in Christian writers. The reason for this may be that in the first half of the second century, John's Gospel made more appeal to the Gnostics than to the orthodox, and seemed to favour their point of view rather than that of their opponents.

From the time of Irenaeus, however, the Gospel was used by the orthodox against the heretics; and in the doctrinal controversies of the following centuries appeal was more frequently made to it than to the Synoptics. Clearly, if the dispute was over the pre-existence of Christ, or the relationship between the first and second Persons of the Trinity, or the divinity of the Holy Spirit, John would be more useful than Matthew, Mark, or Luke.

And in general Christian practice, this Gospel has always been popular: we need think only of the recitation of part of the Prologue in the Mass, the eucharistic devotion which has been based on Chapter 6, the Christian iconography of the Good Shepherd, the *Stabat Mater*.

Nevertheless the Gospel has certain limitations, and it is important to see what they are. Like all other Christian literature in the New Testament and later, this Gospel was written in response to a particular situation; and the demands of the situation imposed restrictions on the author and left their mark on what he wrote.

First, the Evangelist's decision to write theology in dramatic form has had the result that the picture of Jesus which emerges from this Gospel, when it is taken by itself, is less historical than that which we find in the Synoptic Gospels. Even in the Synoptics, there is a contradiction between the view of Jesus which the Evangelists impose on the material they have received, and that which is contained in the material they use. For example, the Synoptists write as if Jesus knew beforehand in detail all that was to happen to him and foretold his Passion and Resurrection to the disciples, and their failure; whereas the material which they use (e.g. Gethsemane, the flight of the disciples, the story of Peter's betrayal) forces us to ask whether Jesus can have been as explicit about the future as they say. This process of 'supernaturalizing' Jesus has gone further in John: here the Lord speaks constantly about himself, as one who has come from God; he proclaims himself, not the kingdom of God. And his manner of dealing with people, as it appears in John, can hardly be historical. As Professor Burkitt said: 'There is an argumentativeness, a tendency to mystification, about the utterances of the Johannine Christ which, taken as the report of actual words spoken, is positively repellent.'[1] If the reader does not normally notice this, it is perhaps because he reads John with the Synoptists' picture of Jesus (or his own) at the back of his mind.

Secondly, we noticed the use which the Evangelist makes of Ambiguity, and contrived Misunderstanding. This way of writing had become so much a part of him, that he was almost incapable of making any unambiguous statement whatsoever.

[1] F. C. Burkitt, *The Gospel History and its Transmission* (Edinburgh, 1906), p. 227.

An example of this tendency in his writing is the mystery with which he has surrounded 'the disciple whom Jesus loved'. But again and again as one studies his Gospel, one says 'If that is what you meant, why did you not say it more plainly?'

Thirdly, as we have seen, John concentrates on Christology, making explicit in his own way what was implicit from the earliest days, bringing out the significance of Jesus' command, 'Follow me'; and omits most of the teaching of Jesus found in the Synoptic Gospels (e.g. the Sermon on the Mount). This itself is a loss. But notice that there is one exception to this general tendency, namely, the command to love ($13^{34\ f.}$, $15^{22\ f.}$). And even here, love (Gk. $\dot{a}\gamma\dot{a}\pi\eta$) has begun to be diluted or narrowed down. In the teaching of Jesus in the Synoptics, the nature of love is seen most clearly in the command to love your enemies; that is to say, the love which is commanded by Jesus is to be such as to overcome every obstacle which self-interest puts in its way, and be free from any kind of limitation. In John, on the other hand, there is no mention of this; love is only love for 'one another', that is, for the other members of the community, for one's 'friends' (15^{13}); $\dot{a}\gamma\dot{a}\pi\eta$ is reduced to $\phi\iota\lambda\alpha\delta\epsilon\lambda\phi\dot{\iota}\alpha$.[1]

Fourthly, John has set his Gospel in a framework of ideas which is very different from that of the Synoptists; theirs was the apocalyptic imagery of the imminent end of the world and the coming of the Son of man in glory; John's framework is the pre-existent Word of God, who descends from the Father into the world, and returns to the Father bringing the elect with him. The advantage of John's way of thinking over the Synoptists' is that it avoids the difficulty of the delay in the coming of the end; but it remains a first-century mythology, foreign to the twentieth-century reader.

One of the many unsolved problems which this Gospel raises is whether it was written to replace other Gospels, or to supplement them. The latter is the ancient and traditional view; yet it is difficult to imagine a situation in which an Evangelist wrote a Gospel to be read alongside another; and if Matthew's use of Mark and Luke's were any guide in this matter, the more likely view would be that those who wrote Gospels intended them to stand on their own, replacing any

[1] See A. Nygren, *Agape and Eros* (ET by P. S. Watson) (London, 1953), p. 153 ff.

earlier work of the same kind. Yet, whatever John's intention was, the value of his Gospel lies in supplementing the Synoptics by pointing to the theological and, in particular, the Christological problem which they raise. That is to say, its role is subsidiary to that of the Synoptic Gospels: it shows the reader what questions he must ask about Jesus; whereas they, in preserving the tradition of the words and deeds of Jesus in a more historical form, bear witness to what he said and what he did.

THE GOSPEL ACCORDING TO
JOHN

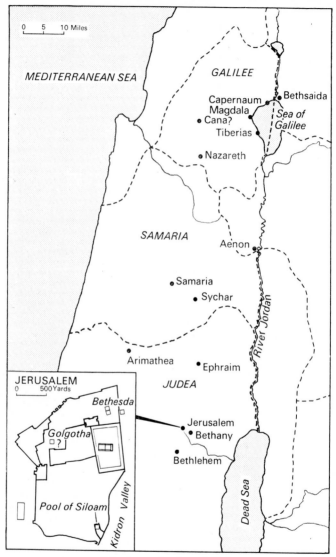

3. Palestine at the time of Christ

4. The Eastern Mediterranean

THE GOSPEL ACCORDING TO
JOHN

1 IN the beginning was the Word, and the Word was with God,
2 and the Word was God. He was in the beginning with God;

1: 1–18 *The prologue*

John, like the Synoptic Gospels, begins with an introduction, or prologue, not with an account of the first public action of Jesus. Mark's introduction took the form of a description of the Baptist and his work; Matthew began with the descent of Jesus from Abraham and the story of his birth; Luke introduced his Gospel with a formal literary preface (Luke 1^{1-4}) followed by accounts of the birth of the Baptist and of Jesus.

Like Mark, John has no birth stories, but, unlike Mark, he begins, not with the Baptist, but with the pre-existence of Jesus as the Word; though notice that the Baptist is mentioned as early as v. 6.[1]

The Prologue is written mainly in a poetic style, and this marks it off from the rest of the Gospel and gives rise to a number of questions: Is it a hymn which the Evangelist is quoting with alterations, and to which he has made additions in prose (so, e.g. J. Jeremias, *The Central Message of the New Testament* (London, 1965), pp. 71 ff.)? Or is it an addition to the original Gospel, a 'preface to the second edition', written by the Evangelist as a summary of the Gospel, and as an explanation of the meaning of the book (so e.g. J. A. T. Robinson, *NTS* ix (1962–3), pp. 120 ff.)? Or is it the author's 'overture', in which he announces his themes in advance? What is certain is that the prologue is both distinct from the rest of the Gospel in style and vocabulary (e.g. 'The Word' is used in this Gospel as a title of Jesus only in vv. 1 and 14; 'grace' is only used in vv. 14 and 16 f.), and yet at the same time connected with it, in that it treats of the same themes as the Gospel (e.g. light and life).

[1] On the question whether John knew any of the birth stories, see note on 7^{41 f.} below.

3 all things were made through him, and without him was not
4 anything made that was made. In him was life,^a and the life
5 was the light of men. The light shines in the darkness, and
the darkness has not overcome it.

    ^a Or *was not anything made. That which has been made was life in him*

    The purpose of the Prologue as it now stands is to introduce
the reader to Jesus, the subject of the book, as the Word who
existed with God before the creation of the world; who was
the agent of God in the making of all things; and who is the
Life of everything and the Light of every man. This eternal
being became flesh and lived as a man. He was rejected by his
own people, the Jews: but, through the testimony borne to him
by another man, John (the Baptist), there are those who believe
in him as the only Son from the Father, and thus receive from
him the gift of God which makes them members of God's family.

1   *In the beginning* means before creation, from eternity; there is an
allusion here to Gen. 1¹. *the Word* (Gk. ὁ Λόγος): the title is used without explanation, and we cannot be certain from what environment it
came, or what it meant to the first readers of the Gospel. The most
likely suggestion is that it comes from a Jewish Hellenistic background,
and that it referred to a supernatural being; other Jews referred to
the Law and Wisdom in a similar way. Therefore, Christians who
spoke of Jesus as the Word were saying that he held the highest place
in the order of things, second only to God himself. *the Word was with
God*: cp. Wisdom, who says 'I was beside him [i.e. God], like a master
workman' (Prov. 8³⁰). *the Word was God*: i.e. *the Word* shared all the
attributes and powers of God.

2   This verse repeats, in the poetic manner, two of the statements
which had been made in the previous verse.

3   This verse consists of two lines of antithetic parallelism, and it
expresses the belief that the Word was the agent through whom God
made everything, and thus that everybody is answerable to him.

4   The Word is the *life* of creatures, and the *light of men*: i.e. their true
existence is not in themselves, but in God; and their blessedness consists in acknowledging this. RSV margin gives an alternative translation of vv. 3 and 4, for which there is some support both among the
early Christian writers and among present-day scholars.

5   The mention of light and men in v. 4 recalls an aspect of the world
to which reference has not yet been made, namely, its opposition to

6 There was a man sent from God, whose name was John.
7 He came for testimony, to bear witness to the light, that all
8 might believe through him. He was not the light, but came
   to bear witness to the light.
9 The true light that enlightens every man was coming into
10 the world. He was in the world, and the world was made

God. This opposition is now spoken of as *the darkness*. The *light* of the
Word continues to shine in the darkness, because God does not forsake
his rebellious creation, and the *light* is more powerful than the *darkness*,
which neither overcomes it nor understands it (the word translated
overcome, Gk. κατέλαβεν, is ambiguous and can mean both 'welcome'
and 'understand').

6   The prologue now turns from the general activity of the Word
to the particular events which will be described in the Gospel.
The beginning of these events was the appearance of *John* the Baptist
(cp. Mark 1[1f.]), *a man sent from God* as the O.T. prophets had been
(e.g. Jer. 25[4]).

7   John's function was entirely *to bear witness to the light* (i.e. the Word,
see v. 4), in order that everybody might recognize him, believe in him,
and be saved. The need for such a witness is not completely apparent
yet, though v. 5 may have hinted at it; it will, however, become more
clear when we are told in v. 14 that 'the Word became flesh', i.e. that
the eternal being who is the creator and Saviour lived as a man. To
recognize him demands faith, and faith requires testimony. The words
testimony and *to bear witness* translate two Greek words which have the
same root (μαρτυρία, μαρτυρεῖν).

8   The Evangelist emphasizes the distinction between the witness (i.e.
the Baptist) and *the light* (i.e. the Word, Jesus Christ). Possibly he does
this because he knows of the existence of followers of the Baptist who
have not yet beccme Christians at the time when he is writing his
Gospel (cp. Acts 19[1 ff.]). For the same emphasis on the inferiority of
the Baptist to Jesus, see also vv. 20, 20 and 3[25 ff.].

9   *The true light* is the Word, in contrast with all the false saviours of
the pagan world, and even with his witness, John the Baptist. He
enlightens every man, in the sense that he is the Saviour and judge of the
world.

10   *The world* (Gk. ὁ κόσμος) in this Gospel means both (*a*) the universe
which God has created and which is therefore fundamentally good
(e.g. 3[16 f.]) and (*b*) mankind which has disobeyed God (e.g. 17[9]). Both
these aspects of the world are present in this verse: (*a*) *the world was
made through him*; (*b*) *the world knew him not*—i.e. refused to acknowledge
him as its life and light.

11 through him, yet the world knew him not. He came to his
12 own home, and his own people received him not. But to all
who received him, who believed in his name, he gave power
13 to become children of God; who were born, not of blood nor
of the will of the flesh nor of the will of man, but of God.

14   And the Word became flesh and dwelt among us, full of
grace and truth; we have beheld his glory, glory as of the only
15 Son from the Father. (John bore witness to him, and cried,
'This was he of whom I said, "He who comes after me ranks
16 before me, for he was before me." ') And from his fulness
17 have we all received, grace upon grace. For the law was given

---

11   *his own home . . . his own people*: these expressions may refer to mankind in general, or to Israel in particular, or to both. Men reject the
Word, because they live in the darkness of sin.

12   Nevertheless, there were those who believed, and they were admitted into the new existence of salvation which is here described as
becoming *children of God*.

13   Salvation is compared to rebirth, and it is the act of God, not of
man. The Evangelist will expound this idea further in Chapter 3.

14   The coming of the Word into the world (v. 9) is now described more
fully in the words *The Word became flesh, and dwelt among us*, i.e. the
Word appeared as a man of weakness and humiliation, but also, for
those who believed, as the Saviour; that is the meaning of *full of grace
and truth*. The words *flesh . . . full of grace and truth* contain the paradox
of the cross. *We* means the Christians, the believers, who have experienced the splendour and love of God through the coming of Jesus,
the only Son.

15   This verse fills out, in more detail, what was said in v. 7, 'he came
for testimony'. The testimony of John is that Jesus is superior to him
because, though he comes on the scene after John, he existed before
John; see v. 2, 'He was in the beginning with God'.

16   Along with the testimony of the Baptist, there is also the testimony
of Christians (*we*, cp. v. 14), that they have received the gifts of God
which sustain them in their new existence: *grace*, the word the Evangelist uses here to describe these gifts, is not used in this Gospel except
in the prologue (1[14, 16, 17]).

17   A contrast between the old dispensation (Judaism) and the new
(Christianity) in order to show the superiority of the latter. Here, for
the first time in the book, the personal name *Jesus* is introduced in

through Moses; grace and truth came through Jesus Christ.
18 No one has ever seen God; the only Son,[b] who is in the bosom
of the Father, he has made him known.

19   And this is the testimony of John, when the Jews sent
priests and Levites from Jerusalem to ask him, 'Who are
20 you?' He confessed, he did not deny, but confessed, 'I am
21 not the Christ.' And they asked him, 'What then? Are you

[b] Other ancient authorities read *God*

contrast with another name, *Moses*. *Christ* was originally a title, not
a name; the Greek word ($X\rho\iota\sigma\tau\acute{o}s$) means 'Anointed' and translates
the Hebrew word 'Messiah' (see v. 41).

18   Moses had asked to see the glory of God, but his request was not
granted (Exod. 33[12 ff.]). *the only Son*, that is, the Word, who was with
God in the beginning, and who is second only to the Father (this is
the meaning of *is in the bosom of the Father*), has both seen the Father
and revealed him to men. The remainder of the book will show how
he has done this.

1 : 19–28. *The testimony of John: the first day*

The 'text' for this section is 1[8]: 'He [sc. the Baptist] was not
the light, but came to bear witness to the light.' John defines
himself wholly in terms of the Christ to whom he bears witness,
and to whom he is utterly inferior. Jesus himself has not yet
appeared. John's testimony is given to 'the Jews', the opponents
of Jesus in this Gospel, and to 'the Pharisees', that section of the
Jews which, according to this Evangelist, led the opposition to
Jesus.

19   *And this is the testimony of John*: cp. 1[7] ('He came for testimony'). *The
Jews* is a characteristic Johannine term, expressing the opposition
between the Church and the Synagogue at the time when the Evangelist was writing. *Levites* were inferior to *priests*; they are only
mentioned in the N.T. here and at Luke 10[32] and Acts 4[36].

20   *I am not the Christ*: cp. 1[8] 'He was not the light'.

21   Some Jews believed that God would send *Elijah* and a *prophet* like
Moses before the end of the world (see Mal. 4[5 f.], Deut. 18[15 ff.]). The
Synoptic Gospels show that some Christians believed that the Baptist
was Elijah, see Matt. 17[9 ff.], Mark 9[9 ff.], Luke 1[17]. In this Gospel, however, this is denied, perhaps in order to concentrate attention upon
the testimony of John to Jesus, lest reflection upon the Baptist's own
place in the plan of God should distract from his function as a witness.

5. St. John the Baptist: detail from the Isenheim Altarpiece;
Grünewald, sixteenth century (see also plate 17)

Elijah?' He said, 'I am not.' 'Are you the prophet?' And he
22 answered, 'No.' They said to him then, 'Who are you? Let us
have an answer for those who sent us. What do you say about

6. The River Jordan

23 yourself?' He said, 'I am the voice of one crying in the
wilderness, "Make straight the way of the Lord," as the
prophet Isaiah said.'

---

22   Notice the contrast between John, who was 'sent from God' (1^6)
and his questioners who were *sent* by the Jews (1^{19}).
23   John's answer is a quotation from Isa. 40^3, a text which had also
been used of the Baptist in Mark 1^3. By using these words, John
confesses that he fulfils prophecy, but only in the preparatory and
subsidiary role of the Lord's herald.

24, 25   Now they had been sent from the Pharisees. They asked
          him, 'Then why are you baptizing, if you are neither the
   26   Christ, nor Elijah, nor the prophet?' John answered them,
          'I baptize with water; but among you stands one whom you
   27   do not know, even he who comes after me, the thong of
   28   whose sandal I am not worthy to untie.' This took place in
          Bethany beyond the Jordan, where John was baptizing.

          The next day he saw Jesus coming toward him, and said,

---

24   *The Pharisees* were the strictest Jews; in this gospel they are the most
      violent opponents of Jesus (see e.g. 9[40], 11[46 f.], 12[19, 42]). John's use of
      the term here suggests that he was not acquainted with the situation
      in Palestine in the period before the destruction of Jerusalem; the
      Pharisees could not have sent priests and Levites to John.
25   This is the first reference to baptizing in this Gospel; the Evangelist
      assumes that the reader knows that John baptized, and it was indeed
      a well-known fact, not only among Christians (cp. Synoptic Gospels
      and Acts), but also among Jews (e.g. Josephus, *Ant.* XVIII. v. 2 (116–19)).
26   *I baptize with water* prepares for the contrast which will be made in
      v. 33 ('he who baptizes with the Holy Spirit'). *one whom you do not know*:
      cp. v. 10 'the world knew him not'; the Jews are in the same position
      as the world—i.e. darkness, ignorance, unbelief.
27   See v. 15 for the same contrast between 'to come after' and 'to rank
      before'. To untie the thong of a sandal in order to take it off was the
      most humiliating service one person could render to another (D. Daube,
      The New Testament and Rabbinic Judaism (London, 1956), p. 266 f.).
28   Nothing is known of a *Bethany beyond the Jordan*, and this may be why
      the place-name has been changed in some manuscripts, etc., to
      Bethabara; in others to Betharaba. Another Bethany, two miles from
      Jerusalem, is mentioned at 11[1, 18], 12[1].

1: 29–34 *The testimony of John: the second day*
      The Baptist came to bear witness to the light, but the ques-
      tion would arise, How did the Baptist know that Jesus was the
      one to whom he was to bear witness? The answer which is
      given in this paragraph, is that God had given him a sign: the
      descent of the spirit would designate the coming one. These
      verses are the Johannine equivalent of the Synoptic account of
      the baptism of Jesus (Mark 1[9–11] and parallels); but notice that
      in this Gospel it is not said that Jesus was baptized by John.

29   *The next day*: the first of a series of notes of time (cp. 1[35, 41, 43], 2[1])

'Behold, the Lamb of God, who takes away the sin of the
30 world! This is he of whom I said, "After me comes a man who
31 ranks before me, for he was before me." I myself did not
know him; but for this I came baptizing with water, that he
32 might be revealed to Israel.' And John bore witness, 'I saw
the Spirit descend as a dove from heaven, and it remained on
33 him. I myself did not know him; but he who sent me to
baptize with water said to me, "He on whom you see the
Spirit descend and remain, this is he who baptizes with the
34 Holy Spirit." And I have seen and have borne witness that
this is the Son of God.'

---

which link together 1¹⁹–2¹¹. It has been suggested that the Evangelist
arranged this material as a week. *the Lamb of God*: the Greek word
which is translated *Lamb* (ἀμνός), is never used in the LXX for the
passover lamb, but it is used in Isa. 53⁷ of the servant of the Lord. The
Evangelist perhaps means to bring together in this word a number of
O.T. ideas and prophesies, including the idea of sacrifice; hence, *who
takes away the sin of the world*. And notice that it is not only Israel's sin
that he will remove, but the world's.

30   See 1¹⁵.
31   The Baptist could not have recognized Jesus without the sign which
God had given him (and so could not have revealed him to Israel),
because the Word had become flesh. According to the Synoptists, the
descent of the Spirit took place at the time of the baptism of Jesus by
John in the Jordan. This may be why John says *for this I came baptizing
with water, that he might be revealed to Israel*—i.e. the one and only purpose
of the Baptist's life and work, according to this Gospel, is to provide
the occasion for his faith and witness.

32   The Jews believed that there would be an outpouring of the Spirit
of God upon Israel in the last days (e.g. Joel 2²⁸ ᶠ·); Christians held
that this had begun when Jesus was baptized, and continued when
believers were baptized in his name (e.g. Acts 2³⁸).

33   This verse leads up to a climax in its conclusion: the ignorance of
John; the sign given to him by God; Jesus as the one *who baptizes with
the Holy Spirit*, and not like John with water (1²⁶).

34   The Baptist declares the completion of his ministry: he has *seen* (the
descent of the Spirit on Jesus), and he has *borne witness* (Behold, the
Lamb of God . . . 1²⁹). *the Son of God*: two MSS. and some versions

35 The next day again John was standing with two of
36 his disciples; and he looked at Jesus as he walked, and said,
37 'Behold, the Lamb of God!' The two disciples heard him say
38 this, and they followed Jesus. Jesus turned, and saw them
following, and said to them, 'What do you seek?' And they
said to him, 'Rabbi' (which means Teacher), 'where are you

---

have 'the Chosen One of God', and this is probably the correct text
here; cp. Isa. 42¹.

1: 35–42 *The testimony of John and Andrew: the third day*

The effectiveness of the Baptist's ministry is seen in the
events of the following day: two of his disciples hear him and
follow Jesus. At first they follow because of the testimony of
John, but when they have stayed with Jesus, even for a short
time, they become convinced through what they have seen
for themselves; and one of them, Andrew, in turn becomes
a witness, and brings his brother Simon to Jesus (cp. 4³⁹⁻⁴²
for a similar sequence of events). Notice how John uses words
in this paragraph which can be understood in two senses, e.g.
'follow', 'seek', 'stay', 'come', 'see'.

35 *The next day again*: see note on 1²⁹. *two of his disciples*: there is
another reference to disciples of John at 4¹. For references to disciples
of the Baptist elsewhere in the N.T. see Mark 2¹⁸, Luke 11¹, Acts
18²⁴–19⁷. There is no evidence apart from this paragraph that disciples
of the Baptist became disciples of Jesus during the ministry.
36 See note on 1²⁹.
37 *they followed Jesus*: the word 'follow' is used in two senses: first, the
literal sense, as in 11³¹ and 20⁶; second, the metaphorical sense, i.e. to
be a disciple of, as in 1⁴³, 8¹². Though the first sense is uppermost here,
the second is suggested.
38 *What do you seek?* Again, there may be an intentional ambiguity:
both, What are you looking for as you come behind me? and, What
do you seek in life? Cp. the characteristic Johannine expressions, to
seek one's own glory, and to seek the glory that comes from God (5⁴⁴,
7¹⁸, etc.). *Rabbi (which means Teacher)*: Jesus is addressed as Rabbi in
Mark and in Matthew; in the latter with a slightly sinister overtone,
because the speaker is Judas (Matt. 26²⁵⁻⁴⁹, cp. Matt. 23⁷ᶠᶠ.). In John,
it is an indication that the person addressing Jesus is in need of enlightenment—see 1⁴⁹, 3², 4³¹, 6²⁵, 9², 11⁸· ²⁸ (20¹⁶). *where are you staying?*

39 staying?' He said to them, 'Come and see.' They came and
saw where he was staying; and they stayed with him that
40 day, for it was about the tenth hour. One of the two who
heard John speak, and followed him, was Andrew, Simon
41 Peter's brother. He first found his brother Simon, and said
to him, 'We have found the Messiah' (which means Christ).
42 He brought him to Jesus. Jesus looked at him, and said, 'So
you are Simon the son of John? You shall be called Cephas'
(which means Peter^c).

c From the word for *rock* in Aramaic and Greek, respectively

---

(Gk. ποῦ μένεις;): possibly another question with a double meaning;
John uses the same Gk. word of the relationship between Jesus and the
Father (e.g. 15^{10}).

39   *Come and see*: both words are used metaphorically in this Gospel:
come = believe, e.g. 6^{35}; *see* = know, e.g. 14^9. *about the tenth hour*: i.e.
about 4 p.m.; the point seems to be that they spent a short time with
Jesus—about 2 hours; compare 'two days' (4$^{40, 43}$).

40   *Andrew, Simon Peter's brother*: for the Synoptic accounts of their call,
see Matt. 4$^{18–20}$, Mark 1$^{16–18}$, Luke 5$^{1–11}$. It is not possible to harmonize
the Johannine and the Synoptic narratives.

41   *first*: there are variant readings in the textual authorities, and the
translations would be (a) 'He first' (implying that the other disciple
did so later); (b) 'the first thing he did'; (c) 'in the morning'. (b) is
probably correct. *the Messiah (which means Christ)*: the Fourth Gospel
here seems to contradict the Synoptic Gospels, in which the messiah-
ship of Jesus is not mentioned until much later in the ministry; see
Mark 8$^{27ff.}$ and parallels. For the meaning of the title, see note on 1^{17}.

42   John portrays Jesus as the one who knows men and can foretell future
events; see, for example, 1$^{47ff.}$, 2$^{19, 21, 25}$, 4$^{17ff.}$, 5^6, 6$^{6, 64, 70f.}$, 11$^{4, 11f.}$,
12$^{23, 32f.}$, 13$^{1f., 10ff., 21ff., 36ff.}$, 16$^{31f.}$, 18$^{4, 32}$. John's purpose in stressing this
point is to show Jesus as the Revealer, and as the one who is wholly in
command of every situation. (On this, see R. Bultmann, *Theology of
the New Testament*, ii (London, 1955), pp. 42 f.)

Simon the son of John: cp. 21$^{15–17}$. The name of Simon's father is given
only in this Gospel. *You shall be called Cephas (which means Peter)*:
there is no evidence that the nickname, Rock (= Cephas in Aramaic; Petra, Petros in Greek) had ever been used before (J. Lowe, *Saint
Peter* (Oxford, 1956), p. 7). For the Synoptic account of the renaming
of Simon, see Matt. 16^{18}, Mark 3^{16}, Luke 6^{14}.

43 The next day Jesus decided to go to Galilee. And he found
44 Philip and said to him, 'Follow me.' Now Philip was from
45 Bethsaida, the city of Andrew and Peter. Philip found
    Nathanael, and said to him, 'We have found him of whom
    Moses in the law and also the prophets wrote, Jesus of
46 Nazareth, the son of Joseph.' Nathanael said to him, 'Can
    anything good come out of Nazareth?' Philip said to him,
47 'Come and see.' Jesus saw Nathanael coming to him, and

---

1 : 43–51 *The testimony of Philip and Nathanael: the fourth day*

In this paragraph, the initiative comes from Jesus, who calls
Philip to follow him. Philip finds Nathanael, just as Andrew
had found Simon; and he speaks to him about Jesus in
terms which will be shown to be inadequate. Jesus promises
Nathanael the vision of greater things: he will see *the Son of
man*, the link between men and God.

43 *The next day*: see note on 1²⁹. *Galilee*: so far, the scene has been
'Bethany beyond the Jordan' (1²⁸). *Philip*: in the Synoptic Gospels
he is only a name in the list of the twelve (Mark 3¹⁸ and parallels); in
John, he will be mentioned again at 6⁵ᶠᶠ·, 12²¹ᶠ·, 14⁸ᶠ·. *Follow me*: cp.
Mark 1¹⁷, 2¹⁴, and parallels.
44 *Bethsaida* is mentioned in the Synoptic Gospels as the scene of some
of the miracles, Matt. 11²⁰ᶠ·, Mark 8²² (and see John 12²¹). Mark 1²¹⁻²⁹
implies that the home of Andrew and Simon was at Capernaum, not
Bethsaida.
45 *Nathanael* means Gift of God; he is mentioned again at 21², but there
is no disciple of this name in the Synoptic Gospels. He has often been
identified with the Bartholomew mentioned in the Synoptic Gospels,
but there is no evidence for this or against it.
    The Evangelist intends his readers to see the inadequacy and
incompleteness of Philip's description of Jesus: he is the Son of God,
and not just the son of Joseph; he is from above, and not just from
Nazareth; he is more than the fulfilment of Old Testament promises.
46 Nathanael's answer may be understood either as a proverb or as an
objection based on the belief that the Messiah would come from
Bethlehem (cp. 7⁴²). *Come and see*: cp. 1³⁹.
47 For Jesus' knowledge, see note on 1⁴². 'Israel' was the name given
to Jacob (Gen. 35¹⁰); and of Jacob (which means *he supplants*) it was
said that 'he came with guile' and took away Esau's blessing (Gen.

said of him, 'Behold, an Israelite indeed, in whom is no
48 guile!' Nathanael said to him, 'How do you know me?' Jesus
answered him, 'Before Philip called you, when you were
49 under the fig tree, I saw you.' Nathanael answered him,
'Rabbi, you are the Son of God! You are the King of Israel!'
50 Jesus answered him, 'Because I said to you, I saw you under
the fig tree, do you believe? You shall see greater things than
51 these.' And he said to him, 'Truly, truly, I say to you, you

---

25^{26}, $27^{35\,f.}$). Jesus sees in Nathanael an Israelite who is genuine, and
not a man of guile like Jacob.

48   *when you were under the fig tree, I saw you*: the meaning of this is uncertain, but one suggestion is that under the influence of Susanna 52 ff.,
'Under what tree?' became a stock question, a proverbial expression
meaning 'Can you tell me all about it?' (C. F. D. Moule, *JTS*, N.S., v
(Oct. 1954), pp. 210 f.). The meaning of Jesus' answer would then be
that Jesus knew all about Nathanael before Philip found him.

49   *Rabbi*: see note on 1^{38}. *the Son of God* and *the King of Israel* may be
used here as equivalent expressions: see for example 2 Sam. 7^{14}, where
God says of the son of David, who is to be King of Israel 'I will be his
father, and he shall be my son.' John does not often use royal titles
of Jesus: see 6^{15}, 12^{13}, 18^{33-39}, $19^{14\,f.}$, $19^{ff.}$; he regards them as inadequate, or at least as open to misunderstanding.

50   The final object of faith is not the supernatural knowledge of Jesus,
any more than it is his *works* (see 10^{38}, 14^{11}); there are *greater things
than these*, i.e. Jesus himself, the mediator between God and Man.
See next verse.

51   *Truly, truly* (Gk. ἀμὴν ἀμήν, literally, Amen, amen): this expression
occurs twenty-five times in John and always double, whereas in the
Synoptic Gospels it is always single (e.g. Matt. $5^{18,\,26}$). It introduces a
pronouncement, and emphasizes its importance. There is apparently
no evidence for this introductory use of Amen in Jewish literature
before the time of Jesus (J. Jeremias, *The Prayers of Jesus* (London, 1967),
pp. 112 ff.). There is another reference here (cp. 1^{47}) to the story of
Jacob; see Gen. 28^{12}. The meaning of this verse is the same as that of
$1^{14,\,17,\,18}$: Jesus is the one in whom God's dealings with the world have
been made concrete and effective; he is the way to God (14^6) and the
door of heaven ($10^{7,\,9}$). The rest of the Gospel will show how this is so.
the Son of man: John uses this title twelve times (1^{51}, $3^{13\,ff.}$, 5^{27}, $6^{27,\,53,}$
^{62}, 8^{28}, $12^{23,\,34(bis)}$, 13^{31}), always in the words of Jesus (as in the Synoptic Gospels) except in 12^{34}, where the crowd uses it; but this is only

will see heaven opened, and the angels of God ascending and
descending upon the Son of man.'

2 ON the third day there was a marriage at Cana in Galilee,
2 and the mother of Jesus was there; Jesus also was invited to
3 the marriage, with his disciples. When the wine failed, the

---

an apparent exception, because the crowd is quoting the words of
Jesus. In eight of the passages where the title occurs, it is used with the
words ascend, descend, lift up, be glorified; that is to say it refers to
Jesus primarily as the mediator between God and man (who has come
down from heaven, and ascends or is glorified by being lifted up on
the cross). Of the other four passages, two refer to 'the food which the
Son of man will give to you', (6²⁷), which is his flesh and his blood (6⁵³);
one refers to judgement (5²⁷); and the other is the question of the crowd,
'Who is this Son of man?' (12³⁴).

2: 1–11 *The first sign*

The account of the miracle at Cana is linked to the previous
section by a further note of time, 'on the third day' (2¹: cp. 1²⁹,
³⁵, ⁴³); but it is also the beginning of the ministry of Jesus, 'the
first of his signs', in which he 'manifested his glory' (2¹¹). It
should, however, be noticed that the miracle is only partially
public (see v. 9). The story is thus a transitional stage between
the Introduction in Chapter 1, and the completely public
action of Jesus in Jerusalem in 2¹³ᶠᶠ.

The significance of this story is probably to be found in the
steward's remark, 'You have kept the good wine until now'
(2¹⁰). He says this to the bridegroom, supposing that he has
provided the wine; but the reader knows that its source is the
supernatural power of Jesus (and note that in 3²⁹ the Baptist
refers to Jesus as the bridegroom). As in Mark 2¹⁸⁻²² (where
Jesus refers to himself as the bridegroom), wine here stands
for the new relationship between God and men, which Jesus
has brought about—what in 1¹⁷ is called 'grace and truth'.
Similarly, 'the six stone jars . . . for the Jewish rites of purification' stand for the law which was given through Moses. In the
note at the end of this story, John says that Jesus 'manifested
his glory': cp. 1¹⁴ ('we have beheld his glory'). Thus, the statements made in the prologue are now being illustrated in the

4 mother of Jesus said to him, 'They have no wine.' And Jesus
said to her, 'O woman, what have you to do with me? My

7. The Marriage Feast at Cana: Scrovegni Chapel, Padua; *Giotto,*
fourteenth century

narrative. The wine which Jesus gives in place of the water of
purification is the new order of grace and truth, the gift of
eternal life which he is bringing into the world.

'The passage therefore is highly theological in character'
(Dodd, *HTFG*, p. 223); there is no parallel to it in the Synoptic
Gospels, but there are similar legends in pagan writers associated
with the god Dionysus. It may be that John has combined
such a legend with Mark 2[18 ff.], or that he has transformed a
parable of Jesus into a miracle-story.

1   *On the third day*: some scholars maintain that the days mentioned in
Chapter 1 and 2[1-11] make up a week, which is balanced by another
week at the end of the Gospel (see 12[1]). It has also been suggested that
the third day would suggest the resurrection of Jesus, when his glory
was finally manifested in his victory over death. *marriage*: a symbol
of the age to come (see Matt. 22[1 ff.], 25[1 ff.]: Rev. 19[7 ff.]) and thus a suitable

5 hour has not yet come.' His mother said to the servants, 'Do
6 whatever he tells you.' Now six stone jars were standing
there, for the Jewish rites of purification, each holding

---

occasion for the first sign of the new order. *Cana in Galilee*, according
to 21², was the home of Nathanael to whom the promise in 1⁵⁰ᶠ· was
made; the 'greater things' begin in his village, and in his presence (see
vv. 2, 11). *the mother of Jesus* is mentioned in this Gospel, here and at
2³, ⁵, ¹², 19²⁵⁻²⁷; her name (Mary) is not used. The reason for this may
be that just as the Baptist is of no importance in himself in this Gospel,
but only as a witness to Jesus, so she is of no significance in herself, but
only through her relationship to her son, and through him to his
disciples (see 19²⁶ᶠ·).

3   Twice later in the Gospel, people suggest to Jesus what he should
do, and in both cases he first refuses, and later complies (see 7¹ᶠᶠ·,
11¹ᶠᶠ·: cf. also 4⁴⁷ᶠ·); this is what happens here. John may be reminding
his readers in this way that Jesus acts only in obedience to his Father
(see e.g. 8²⁸ᶠ·).

4   *O woman*: in Greek apparently this mode of address would not imply
disrespect: see also 4²¹, [8¹⁰], 19²⁶, 20¹³, ¹⁵. *what have you to do with me?*:
an expression signifying the refusal of a request or command; see e.g.
2 Sam. 16¹⁰, 19²²; Mark 1²⁴, 5⁷. *My hour has not yet come*: the *hour* of
Jesus is his exaltation on the cross; see 12²³ᶠ·, 17¹. But what is the
meaning of Jesus' answer to his mother? It could be taken absolutely
literally, 'My moment for action has not yet come'; and there are
parallels to this in Hellenistic magical sources. John almost certainly
means more than that, however, as his use of the word 'hour' elsewhere in the Gospel shows. Possibly he means that Jesus and his
mother are not yet united in purpose and understanding, as they will
be when his hour comes and he is lifted up on the cross (see 19²⁵ᶠᶠ·).
Or, that the miracle for which she is (by implication) asking will be
an anticipation of the full manifestation of his glory in the crucifixion,
and must only be understood in this way.

5   His mother trusts him, in spite of the gulf which seems to separate
them (see note on previous verse), and she instructs *the servants* (Gk.
διακόνοις, literally 'waiters'; it is the word used for 'deacons', and
there may possibly be an allusion to the Eucharist in this miracle-
story) to obey him.

6   The Jews used water for ritual washing before meals (see Mark
7¹ᶠᶠ·). *stone jars* were used, rather than vessels made of earthenware,
because stone is non-porous, and therefore the jars themselves would
not become ritually unclean. *Six* may have a symbolic significance
in this Gospel, standing for imperfection: cp. Heb. 7¹⁹ ('the law made

7 twenty or thirty gallons. Jesus said to them, 'Fill the jars
8 with water.' And they filled them up to the brim. He said to
  them, 'Now draw some out, and take it to the steward of the
9 feast.' So they took it. When the steward of the feast tasted
  the water now become wine, and did not know where it came
  from (though the servants who had drawn the water knew),
10 the steward of the feast called the bridegroom and said to
   him, 'Every man serves the good wine first; and when men
   have drunk freely, then the poor wine; but you have kept the
11 good wine until now.' This, the first of his signs, Jesus did at
   Cana in Galilee, and manifested his glory; and his disciples
   believed in him.

12   After this he went down to Capernaum, with his mother
   and his brothers and his disciples; and there they stayed for
   a few days.

---

nothing perfect'). *twenty or thirty gallons*: the large quantity of water,
and thus perhaps the large quantity of wine (if all the water was
turned into wine—though this is not said) may symbolize the abun-
dance of the gift brought by Jesus; cp. the bread left after the feeding
of the five thousand (6¹³).

7 f.   The obedience of the servants is an act of faith; the steward would
    not thank them for giving him water to drink. *The steward of the feast*
    is not the bridegroom, but possibly the toast-master.

9   The ignorance of the steward is contrasted with the knowledge of
    the servants: those who obey Jesus know who he is (cp. 7¹⁷).

10   God's ways are not the ways of men: God has kept the best thing
    (eternal life) till the end (cp. Heb. 11³⁹ f.).

11   The miracle is called a *sign* (Gk. σημεῖον), i.e. a word or action
    which contains a deeper meaning than that which lies upon the
    surface. The deeper meaning here is the *glory* of the gift which came
    into the world with Jesus (cp. 1¹⁴, 'We have beheld his glory').

2: 12–25 *Jesus in Jerusalem: the first Passover*

    The first public action of Jesus is in Jerusalem, in the temple:
he has come to replace the Law, so he goes straight to the centre
of the worship which was regulated by the Law. There, he
removes the material used for sacrifices: he himself is the Lamb

13   The Passover of the Jews was at hand, and Jesus went up
14 to Jerusalem. In the temple he found those who were selling
     oxen and sheep and pigeons, and the money-changers at
15 their business. And making a whip of cords, he drove them
     all, with the sheep and oxen, out of the temple; and he poured

---

of God which makes other sacrifices obsolete. The Jews chal-
lenge him, and in a reply which they misunderstand he foretells
his death and resurrection. The disciples also do not understand the full significance of the action of Jesus in the temple,
until after the resurrection. John mentions other signs that
Jesus did at Jerusalem, and the faith which they elicited in
many people; but this faith was imperfect, as Jesus knew, and
so he did not entrust himself to them.

The Synoptists also record the cleansing of the temple, but
they place it at the end of the ministry (Mark 11[15ff.] and
parallels). Scholars are not agreed on the answer to two questions which arise here: Did John use any of the Synoptic
accounts? Is the Synoptic or the Johannine chronology to be
preferred?

12   *Capernaum* was on the shore of the lake; Cana (2[1]) was in the hills;
     hence, *down to Capernaum*. *his mother*: see note on 2[1]. *his brothers*
     (RSVCE 'brethren') are mentioned again in this Gospel at 7[1ff.], 20[17].
     There are references to them in the Synoptic Gospels (e.g. Mark 3[31],
     6[3], and parallels) and elsewhere, but there is no evidence how they
     were related to Jesus: some hold the view that they were cousins of
     Jesus, or the children of Joseph by a former marriage; others, that
     they were the younger children of Joseph and Mary. This visit to
     Capernaum may correspond to the period that Jesus spent there
     which is mentioned in the Synoptic Gospels (e.g. Mark 1[21–39]).
13   *The Passover of the Jews*: possibly John is contrasting the Old
     Testament type with its fulfilment in Christ. *Jesus went up to Jerusalem*:
     this feast could only be kept in the City.
14   *oxen and sheep and pigeons* were needed for the sacrifices, and also
     money-changers, because only Tyrian coinage could be used in the
     temple.
15   Only John says that Jesus drove out the animals; perhaps because
     he sees the significance of the story in the abolition of the Jewish
     sacrificial worship, whereas in the Synoptic Gospels the emphasis is
     on buying and selling in the temple.

out the coins of the money-changers and overturned their
16 tables. And he told those who sold the pigeons, 'Take these
things away; you shall not make my Father's house a house
17 of trade.' His disciples remembered that it was written,
18 'Zeal for thy house will consume me.' The Jews then said to
19 him, 'What sign have you to show us for doing this?' Jesus
answered them, 'Destroy this temple, and in three days I will
20 raise it up.' The Jews then said, 'It has taken forty-six years
to build this temple, and will you raise it up in three days?'
, 22 But he spoke of the temple of his body. When therefore he
was raised from the dead, his disciples remembered that he
had said this; and they believed the scripture and the word
which Jesus had spoken.

---

16   Cp. Mark 11¹⁷, 'My house shall be called a house of prayer for all
the nations. But you have made it a den of robbers' (Isa. 56⁷, and
Jer. 7¹¹). John may have the same O.T. passages in mind.
17   The quotation is from Ps. 69⁹, a psalm which Christians understood
as a prophecy of the passion of Christ. In John, as in the Synoptic
Gospels, the cleansing of the temple provokes the crucifixion; but
whereas this is stated historically by the Synoptists, John preserves the
connection with the passion through the quotation of the psalm.
18   Cf. Matt. 12³⁸ᶠ·, Mark 8¹¹, Luke 11²⁹ for requests for a miracle to
authenticate Jesus.
19   This is an ambiguous reply, referring both to the death and resurrection of Jesus, and to the destruction of the temple and its replace-
ment by the Church, i.e. the temple not made with hands (cp. Mark
14⁵⁸).
20   The Jews only understand the reference to the building, and John
mentions this in order to bring out the real meaning of the words of
Jesus. Herod began the rebuilding of the temple in 20 B.C. and it was
not completed until A.D. 63.
21   The body of Jesus can be thought of as a temple in three ways: (a)
the body as the temple of the soul; (b) the body of Jesus as the dwelling
place of the glory of God (1¹⁴); (c) the body of Christ as the Church
(cp. 1 Cor. 12²⁷, etc.).
22   The disciples' understanding comes after they have received the
Spirit (20²²). the scripture: possibly Ps. 69⁹ (see v. 17) or the Old
Testament as a whole, as the witness to Jesus (cp. 5³⁹).

23   Now when he was in Jerusalem at the Passover feast, many
        believed in his name when they saw the signs which he did;
24, 25 but Jesus did not trust himself to them, because he knew all
        men and needed no one to bear witness of man; for he him-
        self knew what was in man.

3:      NOW there was a man of the Pharisees, named Nicodemus,
 2   a ruler of the Jews. This man came to Jesus[d] by night and
        said to him, 'Rabbi, we know that you are a teacher come from
        God; for no one can do these signs that you do, unless God

        d Greek *him*

---

23   Faith based on signs (i.e. miracles) is preliminary to faith in Jesus,
        but by itself it is inadequate: see note on 1^{50}.
24   Cp. the sequence of events in 6^{1-15}, where the crowd see the sign of
        bread, and are about to make Jesus king by force; but he withdraws.
        For Jesus' knowledge, see note on 1^{42}.

3: 1–21 *Jesus and Nicodemus: rebirth*

In Chapter 2, John described two of Jesus' signs; he will next
write passages of dialogue, in which the meaning of these signs
is explained. Nicodemus, for example, who is the first to enter
into such a dialogue with Jesus, speaks as a leader of the Jews,
and also as one of those whose imperfect faith was mentioned
in 2^{23}; and the subject of the discussion is entry into the new
order. Jesus says that there must be a completely new beginning, a rebirth through the Spirit. Nicodemus' final words here
are 'How can this be?', and the passage continues without any
further comment from him; we seem, in fact, to be overhearing
the controversy between the Church and the Synagogue in the
last quarter of the first century, rather than a discussion between Jesus and a rabbi before the crucifixion (e.g. notice how
Jesus speaks in the first person plural, and addresses Nicodemus
in the plural ($3^{11\ f.}$).

The Jews have rejected the demand for a new beginning,
and have not believed the one who both descended from
heaven and ascended into heaven. He had been given to them
for their healing, like the bronze serpent in the wilderness; but

3 is with him.' Jesus answered him, 'Truly, truly, I say to you, unless one is born anew,*e* he cannot see the kingdom of God.'
4 Nicodemus said to him, 'How can a man be born when he is old? Can he enter a second time into his mother's womb and

e Or *from above*

---

by rejecting him, they have rejected eternal life, and condemned themselves to death.

1   *Pharisees*: see note on 1²⁴. *a ruler of the Jews* probably means a member of the Sanhedrin.
2   *by night*: elsewhere in John, *night* always stands for ignorance and evil and unbelief (9⁴, 11¹⁰, 13³⁰, 21³). There may be that sense here too, and in 19³⁹. See also note on 'darkness', 6¹⁶ ᶠ·. *Rabbi*: see note on 1³⁸. *we know that you are a teacher come from God*: the Evangelist means this to be understood as an inadequate statement of faith; it is based on the *signs* which Jesus has done (cp. 2²³); to say that *God is with him*, is less than to say that he is the Word of God. Nicodemus speaks in the plural, and is perhaps to be taken as the representative of those Jews who were sympathetic to Christian claims, but would not break with their past: John may have known people who held this point of view in Asia, and may have written his Gospel with them in mind.
3   *unless one is born anew* (mg. *from above*): the Greek word (ἄνωθεν) can mean either 'once again' or 'from heaven' (for the latter meaning see 3³¹, 19¹¹). There is no need to decide which it means here, because John intended it to be taken in both senses: conversion is both a new start and an act of God. The idea of rebirth is not found in Jewish literature, but there is a similar image in the saying concerning becoming like children in Matt. 18³, and it was an accepted idea in certain Hellenistic religious writings. The Evangelist is thus developing a Christian theme by means of Hellenistic parallels, and urging it upon his Jewish contemporaries. *see the kingdom of God*: *see* means 'enjoy' —cp. Ps. 34¹² (quoted in 1 Pet. 3¹⁰), and also v. 5. *the kingdom of God*, though frequently used in the Synoptic Gospels, is used only here and in v. 5 in John: it is a term which comes from Jewish apocalypticism, with which John does not seem to have had much sympathy.
4   Partial misunderstanding by an interlocuter, in order to disclose the real meaning of Jesus, is a characteristic device of John (see Introduction, pp. 19 f.). Nicodemus takes the demand for birth over again literally, and sees its impossibility; this throws light on what is really meant, namely, a new beginning which is made by God, a birth 'from above'.

5 be born?' Jesus answered, 'Truly, truly, I say to you, unless
  one is born of water and the Spirit, he cannot enter the king-
6 dom of God. That which is born of the flesh is flesh, and that
7 which is born of the Spirit is spirit.*f* Do not marvel that I said
8 to you, "You must be born anew."*e* The wind*f* blows where it
  wills, and you hear the sound of it, but you do not know
  whence it comes or whither it goes; so it is with every one
9 who is born of the Spirit.' Nicodemus said to him, 'How can
10 this be?' Jesus answered him, 'Are you a teacher of Israel,
11 and yet you do not understand this? Truly, truly, I say to
  you, we speak of what we know, and bear witness to what we

e Or *from above*
f The same Greek word means both *wind* and *spirit*

---

5   *born of water and the Spirit* is a reference to baptism, through which
     the disciples are initiated into the new order (see 1³³). References to
     the Sacraments are infrequent in John, and some commentators think
     that they have been added by an editor (e.g. R. Bultmann, *Theology
     of the New Testament*, ii (London, 1955), pp. 58 f.).
6   There are two kinds of existence—*flesh* and *spirit*: a return to the
     womb, if it were possible, would only involve another birth into the
     life of weakness and sin. Baptism, however, being an act of God, can
     be described as birth by *the Spirit*, and it initiates a man into the
     higher order.
7   This fact of experience, that like is born of like, ought to be clear
     to Nicodemus; so he should not be astonished at the demand which
     Jesus is making for rebirth from God.
8   The Greek word ($\pi\nu\epsilon\hat{v}\mu\alpha$), like the Hebrew word (*ruach*), means
     spirit, breath, or wind. The unknown source and destination of the
     wind is a parable of the reborn man, who has his origin and destiny
     in the unseen God (cp. 1¹³).
9   Nicodemus' incomprehension exhibits the bankruptcy of a Judaism
     which has left the living God out of account: cp. 19¹⁵.
10   Israel's existence is a sign of the power of God. Nicodemus, as a
     teacher of Israel, should have known this.
11   *Truly, truly*: see note on 1⁵¹. Jesus speaks on behalf of the Church
     (for *we*, cp. 1¹⁴, ¹⁶). The Church bears witness to the power of God in
     the life, death, and resurrection of Jesus, and the Jews (*you*, plural) do
     not believe.

12 have seen; but you do not receive our testimony. If I have told you earthly things and you do not believe, how can you
13 believe if I tell you heavenly things? No one has ascended into heaven but he who descended from heaven, the Son of
14 man.*g* And as Moses lifted up the serpent in the wilderness,
15 so must the Son of man be lifted up, that whoever believes in him may have eternal life.'*h*

16   For God so loved the world that he gave his only Son, that whoever believes in him should not perish but have eternal
17 life. For God sent the Son into the world, not to condemn the world, but that the world might be saved through him.
18 He who believes in him is not condemned; he who does not

g Other ancient authorities add *who is in heaven*
h Some interpreters hold that the quotation continues through verse 21

---

12   *earthly things* possibly refer to vv. 6a and 8a, which are parables of *the heavenly things*, i.e. rebirth and the mysterious activity of the Spirit. *you* is still plural in this verse.

13   The post-resurrection point of view becomes even more clear in this verse, especially if we follow the RSV mg., as we probably should, and include the final words: 'who is in heaven.' The meaning of the verse in the context is that Jesus alone has *descended* and *ascended*, and is now in heaven, and he is the revealer of God. For *Son of man* see 1^{51} and note.

f.   See Num. 21$^{8\,f.}$. *the Son of man* must be lifted up on the cross, like the bronze serpent on the pole, and exalted (the Greek word ὑψοῦν has this double sense), in order that men may be saved from the death which is otherwise inevitable. For *must* (Gk. δεῖ): cp. Mark 8^{31}. It is scarcely worth asking whether the inverted commas should close after v. 15, or after v. 21 (see RSV mg.): the historical situation (Jesus and Nicodemus) was left behind as early as v. 11 (see also Introduction, p. 19).

16   The crucifixion is necessary (v. 14), because of the love of God for the world; but faith is necessary also, on the part of those who would enter life, and this faith is not present in the Jews of whom John is writing here.

7 f.   The sole purpose of God in sending his Son into the world was salvation. But, because faith is required and is not always present, condemnation follows for the unbelievers.

believe is condemned already, because he has not believed in
19 the name of the only Son of God. And this is the judgment,
that the light has come into the world, and men loved dark-
20 ness rather than light, because their deeds were evil. For
every one who does evil hates the light, and does not come
21 to the light, lest his deeds should be exposed. But he who
does what is true comes to the light, that it may be clearly
seen that his deeds have been wrought in God.

22   After this Jesus and his disciples went into the land of

---

19 ff.   The unbeliever refuses to *come to the light* (i.e. to believe on Jesus)
because he is afraid of exposure. The believer comes to it, and his
goodness is thereby revealed as the work of God in him. That is to
say, the only thing a man can call his own is his sin, and he can either
cling to it in darkness, or allow his goodness to be disclosed as God's
work. Sin is, in fact, the desire to have something of one's own, and
so, in the nature of things, the only private possession which it is possible
to have is sin itself.

3: 22–36 *The final witness of John*

According to the Synoptists Jesus' public work began after
the arrest of the Baptist (Mark 1[14] and parallels), but according
to the Fourth Evangelist their ministries overlapped; both
John and Jesus were baptizing in Judea, and this gave rise to
a controversy which provides the Evangelist with an occasion
for the final witness of the Baptist to the superiority of Jesus:
Jesus, he says, is the bridegroom; he himself is only the 'best
man'. Jesus' importance will grow; his own work is temporary.
Jesus is the Lord over the world; he is a part of it. Jesus brings
knowledge of God, and this is not received except by some who
accept it as God's message, because they believe that Jesus is
fully empowered by God's spirit, and is the beloved Son of
the Father, to whom the Father has given full authority.
To believe and obey the Son, is to enter into eternal life;
the alternative is death.

22   *went into the land of Judea* is slightly odd, since the previous events
have presumably taken place in Jerusalem (see 2[13, 23]), which is in

23 Judea; there he remained with them and baptized. John also
    was baptizing at Aenon near Salim, because there was much
24 water there; and people came and were baptized. For John
    had not yet been put in prison.

25   Now a discussion arose between John's disciples and a Jew
26 over purifying. And they came to John, and said to him,
    'Rabbi, he who was with you beyond the Jordan, to whom
    you bore witness, here he is, baptizing, and all are going to
27 him.' John answered, 'No one can receive anything except
28 what is given him from heaven. You yourselves bear me
    witness, that I said, I am not the Christ, but I have been sent
29 before him. He who has the bride is the bridegroom; the
    friend of the bridegroom, who stands and hears him,

Judea. *he . . . baptized*: here and in 3^{26}, 4^1, Jesus is said to have baptized. This is denied in 4^2, and it is not said that he did so in any
other Gospel.

23   *Aenon near Salim*: the sites are not known for certain (see e.g. W. F.
Albright, *The Archaeology of Palestine* (Harmondsworth, 1960), p. 247).

24   Contrast Mark 1^{14} and parallels. For the Synoptists' account of
his imprisonment and death, see Mark $6^{14\mathrm{ff.}}$ and parallels.

25   *a Jew*: some of the MSS. and ancient versions read 'Jews', and a
number of scholars have conjectured that the original text read 'Jesus'.
purifying: cp. 2^6. The point may be that neither John nor the Jews can
administer the purification which Jesus alone can provide: cp. 1^{29}
('the Lamb of God, who takes away the sin of the world').

26   The Baptist is addressed as *Rabbi* only here. *to whom you bore witness*:
the report made to the Baptist recalls his testimony to Jesus, but
without understanding of its import—namely, that Jesus is he who
baptizes with the Holy Spirit (1^{33}). It should not be surprising that
all are going to him.

27   A man can only be what God has determined that he should be, and
in the Baptist's case this was that he should be a witness (cp. 1^7).

28   See $1^{15, 20, 30}$.

29   The *bride* refers to the people going to Jesus (cp. Eph. $5^{21\mathrm{ff.}}$). Jesus,
therefore, is the bridegroom (see above, p. 48); John is the friend of
the bridegroom, i.e. the best man (cp. Judg. 14^{20}). The Baptist's joy
consists in doing God's will.

rejoices greatly at the bridegroom's voice; therefore this joy
30 of mine is now full. He must increase, but I must decrease.'[i]
31   He who comes from above is above all; he who is of the
earth belongs to the earth, and of the earth he speaks; he who
32 comes from heaven is above all. He bears witness to what he
33 has seen and heard, yet no one receives his testimony; he
who receives his testimony sets his seal to this, that God is
34 true. For he whom God has sent utters the words of God,
35 for it is not by measure that he gives the Spirit; the Father
36 loves the Son, and has given all things into his hand. He who
believes in the Son has eternal life; he who does not obey
the Son shall not see life, but the wrath of God rests upon
him.

[i] Some interpreters hold that the quotation continues through verse 36

---

30   There is less need for a witness as more people believe in Jesus. On
the problem of the inverted commas here (RSV mg.) see note after
$3^{14f.}$: the same considerations apply.

31   *He who comes from above* (Gk. ἄνωθεν, as in $3^{3, 7}$) means Jesus. *is above
all*: i.e. is greater than all men, including the Baptist. *he who is of the
earth* in this context means John the Baptist. *belongs to the earth*: i.e.
is inferior to Jesus. *of the earth he speaks*: the meaning of this may be
that the Baptist has not the revelation which Jesus has and gives
(cp. 3^{12}).

32   *He bears witness to what he has seen and heard* means Jesus, who reveals
what he has received from the Father (cp. 3^{11}), namely, that he is the
bringer of life. *yet no one receives his testimony* (cp. $1^{10f.}$): those who do
receive it (see next verse) do so by the gracious power of God upon
them.

33   To believe in Jesus is to believe and accept what God says as true:
see next verse.

34   The Spirit rests upon Jesus in its fullness, and not in fragmentary
gifts, as in the case of the prophets (cp. Heb. $1^{1f.}$).

35   The thought moves back and up to the love of God, as in $3^{16ff.}$, but
whereas there it was God's love for the world, here it is his love for
the Son, and his entrusting to him the work of salvation.

36   As in $3^{16ff.}$ the passage ends with a statement of the division between
faith and unbelief, life and death.

4 NOW when the Lord knew that the Pharisees had heard that
   Jesus was making and baptizing more disciples than John
2 (although Jesus himself did not baptize, but only his disciples),
4 he left Judea and departed again to Galilee. He had to pass
5 through Samaria. So he came to a city of Samaria, called
   Sychar, near the field that Jacob gave to his son Joseph.
6 Jacob's well was there, and so Jesus, wearied as he was with
   his journey, sat down beside the well. It was about the sixth
   hour.
7   There came a woman of Samaria to draw water. Jesus said

4: 1–42 *Jesus in Samaria*

Jesus goes from Judea to Galilee through Samaria. This
provides the Evangelist with the setting for a conversation
which will recapitulate some of the points already made. Thus,
the theme of the first sign (water into wine) is expressed here in
terms of living water which is superior to that of Jacob's well;
and the promise made in the second sign (the temple destroyed
and raised up) is repeated when Jesus says that the hour is
coming when worship will be confined neither to the Samaritan
temple on Mount Gerizim nor to Jerusalem. Jesus speaks of his
work and that of his disciples as sowing and reaping a harvest;
and the result of his visit to Samaria is indeed a harvest—many
believe, and confess their faith in the words, 'This is indeed the
Saviour of the world'.

1   *Pharisees*: see note on 1²⁴. *more disciples than John*: cp. 3²⁶, ³⁰. For
Jesus baptizing, see note on 3²².
2   This verse contradicts 3²², ²⁶ and 4¹, and interrupts the context.
Some scholars think it has been added by an editor.
3   See 3²² and 4¹ᶠ·.
4   The shortest route was through Samaria, and the journey took
three days.
5   *Sychar*: possibly the modern Askar; but one ancient version has
'Sychem', i.e. Shechem, the modern Balatah, and W. F. Albright thinks
this is correct (*The Archaeology of Palestine* (Harmondsworth, 1960),
p. 247). See Gen. 33¹⁸ᶠ·, 48²², for the land which Jacob gave to Joseph.
6   The gift of Jacob, and his *well*, will play a part in the conversation
that follows (see vv. 12 ff.); that is why they are mentioned. *It was
about the sixth hour*: the same words come again at 19¹⁴. R. H. Lightfoot

8 to her, 'Give me a drink.' For his disciples had gone away
9 into the city to buy food. The Samaritan woman said to him,
'How is it that you, a Jew, ask a drink of me, a woman of
10 Samaria?' For Jews have no dealings with Samaritans. Jesus
answered her, 'If you knew the gift of God, and who it is that
is saying to you, "Give me a drink," you would have asked
11 him, and he would have given you living water.' The woman
said to him, 'Sir, you have nothing to draw with, and the well
12 is deep; where do you get that living water? Are you greater
than our father Jacob, who gave us the well, and drank from
13 it himself, and his sons, and his cattle?' Jesus said to her,
14 'Every one who drinks of this water will thirst again, but
whoever drinks of the water that I shall give him will never
thirst; the water that I shall give him will become in him a

---

thought that this was significant (*St. John's Gospel* (Oxford, 1956),
p. 122); Jesus can only give the Samaritans the gift of which he will
be speaking in v. 14, by dying for them. See also the next note.
7   Cp. 'I thirst' (19²⁸) and see note on previous verse.
8   See vv. 31 ff.
9   *For Jews have no dealings with Samaritans.* Some authorities omit these
words, but they are probably part of the original text. The translation
however should be, 'Jews and Samaritans do not use vessels in common' (cp. NEB). This seems to reflect a regulation, the date of which
(*c.* A.D. 65) is later than the ministry of Jesus (D. Daube, *The New
Testament and Rabbinic Judaism* (London, 1956), pp. 373 ff.).
10   *the gift of God* (contrast the gift of Jacob, v. 5) and *living water* (an
ambiguous term, meaning both running water and the water that gives
life) stand for salvation and eternal life; because the speaker, whom
the woman does not yet know, is 'the Saviour of the world' (see v. 42).
11   The woman's misunderstanding (see note on 3⁴) draws attention
to the source of the *living water*, i.e. God.
12   An example of Johannine irony: Jesus is greater than Jacob, as he
is also greater than Moses (1¹⁷), the temple (2¹⁹ ff.), and the Baptist
(3²⁷ ff.); the water he gives will not be drunk by *cattle*.
13 f.   The gift of Jesus is compared to a permanent supply of water. For
a similar idea: cp. Ps. 1³ 'He is like a tree planted by streams of
water'; also Isa. 49¹⁰, Ecclus. 24²¹.

15 spring of water welling up to eternal life.' The woman said to
   him, 'Sir, give me this water, that I may not thirst, nor come
   here to draw.'

16   Jesus said to her, 'Go, call your husband, and come here.'
17 The woman answered him, 'I have no husband.' Jesus said
18 to her, 'You are right in saying, "I have no husband"; for
   you have had five husbands, and he whom you now have is
19 not your husband; this you said truly.' The woman said to
20 him, 'Sir, I perceive that you are a prophet. Our fathers
   worshiped on this mountain; and you say that in Jerusalem is
21 the place where men ought to worship.' Jesus said to her,
   'Woman, believe me, the hour is coming when neither on
   this mountain nor in Jerusalem will you worship the Father.
22 You worship what you do not know; we worship what we
23 know, for salvation is from the Jews. But the hour is coming,

---

15   The woman does not yet understand the gift (note *nor come here to
draw*) because she does not yet know the giver: cp. v. 10). See 6³⁴ for
a similar misunderstanding leading on to the revelation of Jesus as
the Saviour.

ff.   The subject of the conversation now moves from the gift to the
speaker (i.e. Jesus) by way of the status of the one who is addressed.
call your husband: some commentators take this as an example of Jesus'
knowledge of individuals (see on 1⁴²), and understand the husband
literally (so, e.g., Bernard); others (e.g. Hoskyns) as a reference to
the mixed nations of Samaria, and their many gods (see 2 Kgs.
17²⁴ ff.).

9 f.   Some think that the woman is turning the conversation away from
herself and her personal life to less embarrassing matters; others see
here a natural sequence of thought: Jesus' insight shows that he is a
prophet, therefore he can answer the question, Which is the correct
place to worship God, Mount Gerizim or Jerusalem?

21   *Woman*: see note on 2⁴. *the hour*: see note on 2⁴; Christian worship
will not be confined to special places.

22   Although 'Christ is the end of the law' (Rom. 10⁴), he does not
abolish the Law as a witness, but fulfils it. *salvation* thus comes *from the
Jews* to the Gentiles.

23   *the hour is coming, and now is*: see 5²⁵ for the same words. The
meaning is that the order which is to be established by the death and

and now is, when the true worshippers will worship the
Father in spirit and truth, for such the Father seeks to wor-
24 ship him. God is spirit, and those who worship him must
25 worship in spirit and truth.' The woman said to him, 'I know
that Messiah is coming (he who is called Christ); when he
26 comes, he will show us all things.' Jesus said to her, 'I who
speak to you am he.'

27   Just then his disciples came. They marvelled that he was
talking with a woman, but none said, 'What do you wish?'
28 or, 'Why are you talking with her?' So the woman left her
water jar, and went away into the city, and said to the
29 people, 'Come, see a man who told me all that I ever did.
30 Can this be the Christ?' They went out of the city and were
coming to him.

---

resurrection of Jesus is anticipated beforehand in his ministry, because
he is present. *the true worshippers will worship the Father in spirit and
truth*: there will be a new worship of God, different both from that of
the Jews and from that of the Samaritans; it will belong to the world
above, the realm of God and reality, and not to the earthly copies,
whether in Jerusalem or on Mount Gerizim (cp. Heb. *passim*, e.g. 9²³ ff.).
such the Father seeks to worship him: the initiative of salvation and of
worship lies with God.

24   *God is spirit*: i.e. he belongs to the realm above, and not to the lower
realm; in order to worship him, one must enter this realm (cp. 3³ ff.).
25 f.   The woman confesses faith in the coming Messiah, and Jesus
reveals himself to her as such; the second part of her ignorance mentioned in 4¹⁰ has now been dispelled.

27   'To converse in public with a woman was regarded by the Rabbis
as at least suspicious' (Hoskyns, *The Fourth Gospel* (London, 1940),
p. 269). 'It is not for disciples to question the actions of their Master'
(Barrett, p. 201).

28   *water jar*: the same word as in 2⁶ where it stood for the Law; does
John mean that the woman leaves the old order, now that the Messiah
has come?

29   Cp. the faith and witness of the first disciples, 1⁴¹, ⁴⁵, ⁴⁸ f.. *Come, see*:
cp. 1³⁹, ⁴⁶.

30   See on v. 35 f.

31 Meanwhile the disciples besought him, saying, 'Rabbi,
32 eat.' But he said to them, 'I have food to eat of which you
33 do not know.' So the disciples said to one another, 'Has any
34 one brought him food?' Jesus said to them, 'My food is to do
35 the will of him who sent me, and to accomplish his work. Do
you not say, "There are yet four months, then comes the
harvest"? I tell you, lift up your eyes, and see how the fields
36 are already white for harvest. He who reaps receives wages,
and gathers fruit for eternal life, so that sower and reaper
37 may rejoice together. For here the saying holds true, "One
38 sows and another reaps." I sent you to reap that for which
you did not labour; others have laboured, and you have entered
into their labour.'

39 Many Samaritans from that city believed in him because
of the woman's testimony, 'He told me all that I ever did.'

---

31 See v. 8 for the disciples going to buy food. *Rabbi*: see note on 1[38].
2 ff. The answer of Jesus causes the disciples to misunderstand him, and
he then explains what he means (cp. 4[10ff.]): He lives by his obedience
to the will of God, which is that he should be the Saviour of the
world; he has been engaged in this work in his conversation with the
woman (cp. 19[28 ff.]).
35 *the fields are already white for harvest* because the Samaritans are
coming to him across them (see v. 30). For the work of Jesus as the
gathering of a harvest, see e.g. Matt. 9[37].
36 *He who reaps receives wages*: see 1 Cor. 3[14] for the same expression, in
Gk., for the reward of the minister of Christ. *gathers fruit for eternal
life*: i.e. the believers who receive eternal life. *so that sower and reaper
may rejoice together*: it is not clear who is meant by the *sower* (John the
Baptist? Jesus?) or by the *reaper* (Jesus? the woman? the disciples?).
37 Various biblical sources for the saying have been suggested, e.g.
Job 31[8], Mic. 6[15]; others think that it is a Greek proverb.
38 It is not at all clear what this verse means. A possible interpretation
is: Jesus will send his disciples (cp. 20[21]) to reap the harvest of salvation
for which others (Old Testament prophets? the Baptist? Jesus himself?) have laboured. (See O. Cullmann, *The Early Church* (London,
1956), pp. 185 ff.; and the criticism by J. A. T. Robinson in *Twelve
New Testament Studies* (London, 1962), pp. 61 ff.)
39 See note on v. 29.

40 So when the Samaritans came to him, they asked him to stay
41 with them; and he stayed there two days. And many more
42 believed because of his word. They said to the woman, 'It is
   no longer because of your words that we believe, for we have
   heard for ourselves, and we know that this is indeed the
   Saviour of the world.'

43,44   After the two days he departed to Galilee. For Jesus himself testified that a prophet has no honour in his own country.
45 So when he came to Galilee, the Galileans welcomed him,

---

40   Cp. 1³⁹. The brief stay of *two days* reminds the reader that the work
in Samaria is only an anticipation of the world-wide mission of the
Church after the resurrection.

41 f.   Faith by means of the testimony of another gives place to first-hand
knowledge of Jesus through his word.   *the Saviour of the world* is the
climax and conclusion of this section (1¹⁹–4⁴²), which is a miniature
Gospel within the Gospel. Note how it matches the Baptist's testimony
at the beginning, 'Behold, the Lamb of God, who takes away the sin
of the world!' (1²⁹) and that this confession is appropriate in the mouth
of those who were not themselves Jews.

4: 43–54 *Jesus heals the official's son at Capernaum*

Jesus continues his journey to Galilee and is welcomed there.
He returns to Cana, the scene of his first sign, and is visited by
an officer of Herod Antipas who asks him to go to Capernaum
to heal his son who is near death. At first he is unwilling, but
finally he assures the officer that his son will recover. The man
takes Jesus at his word and returns, to be met by his servants
with news of the boy's recovery which began at the moment
when Jesus spoke to him. He and his household therefore
become believers.

This story may be John's version of the healing of the
centurion's servant (Matt. 8⁵⁻¹³, Luke 7¹⁻¹⁰).[1] If so, then the
officer is a Gentile, and this would be in line with the other
recorded healing of a Gentile by Jesus; he never meets them,
but always cures them from a distance (see also Matt. 15²¹⁻²⁸,
Mark 7²⁴⁻³⁰). Possibly the Evangelists are recording Jesus' own

---

[1] A similar story is told about a son of Gamaliel II in *Berakoth*, 34b
(Barrett, p. 208).

having seen all that he had done in Jerusalem at the feast, for they too had gone to the feast.

46 So he came again to Cana in Galilee, where he had made the water wine. And at Capernaum there was an official whose
47 son was ill. When he heard that Jesus had come from Judea to Galilee, he went and begged him to come down and heal
48 his son, for he was at the point of death. Jesus therefore said to him, 'Unless you see signs and wonders you will not
49 believe.' The official said to him, 'Sir, come down before my
50 child dies.' Jesus said to him, 'Go; your son will live.' The

---

limitation of his ministry to Israel, and foreshadowing the healing of the Gentiles by his word preached by his apostles after his resurrection (see 12$^{20ff.}$).

If this is an account of the healing of a Gentile, it follows on appropriately after the confession 'this is the Saviour of the world' (4^{42}). The recovery of the boy is described by means of the verb 'to live', and the faith of the officer is emphasized. Thus the story also illustrates the saying in 3^{16} ('For God so loved the world that he gave his only Son, that whoever believes in him should not perish but have eternal life').

43 *the two days*: cp. 4^{40}. *to Galilee*: cp. 4^3.
44 Cp. Matt. 13^{57}, Mark 6^4, Luke 4^{24}; and note that in the Synoptists *his own country* is Nazareth or Galilee; in John it is Jerusalem or Judea.
45 Cp. 2^{23} and see the note.
46 Cp. 2$^{1-11}$. *Capernaum* has been previously mentioned in 2^{12}; it is the scene of the similar miracle in Matt. 8$^{5ff.}$, Luke 7$^{1ff.}$. *official* (Gk. βασιλικός): either a relative of the royal family, or one who served a king (in this case, Herod Antipas).
47 For the request for a miracle, cp. 2^3, (7^3?), 11^3. *came down*: see note on 2^{12}. *at the point of death*: contrast Lazarus (11^{17}).
48 Jesus rebukes those whose faith is dependent on signs: see 2$^{23ff.}$ and 4^{45}.
49 The officer pleads for his son: he is not concerned about questions of faith, but faith is implicit in his coming to Jesus, and will become explicit through the granting of his request; see v. 53.
50 *will live*: the same verb (Gk. ζῆν) was used in Num. 21$^{8f.}$ (LXX)

man believed the word that Jesus spoke to him and went his
51 way. As he was going down, his servants met him and told
52 him that his son was living. So he asked them the hour when
he began to mend, and they said to him, 'Yesterday at the
53 seventh hour the fever left him.' The father knew that was
the hour when Jesus had said to him, 'Your son will live';
54 and he himself believed, and all his household. This was now
the second sign that Jesus did when he had come from Judea
to Galilee.

5 AFTER this there was a feast of the Jews, and Jesus went up
to Jerusalem.

('every one who is bitten, when he sees it [the bronze serpent] shall
live'), cp. 3¹⁴ᶠ·.
51   *going down*: see note on 2¹².
52   *the seventh hour*: i.e. 1 p.m.
53   *he himself believed, and all his household*: the expression is used in Acts
of conversion to Christianity (e.g. Acts 18⁸).
54   See 2¹⁻¹¹.

5: *The Father and the Son*

Jesus returns to Jerusalem at the time of a Jewish feast, and
heals a cripple on a sabbath. This again (cp. 2¹⁸ᶠᶠ·) provokes
the opposition of the Jews, but Jesus says that God, who is his
Father, has never stopped working, even on the sabbath, and
that this is why he himself heals on that day. This claim to a
special relationship to God incurs the opposition of the Jews,
who want to kill Jesus.

This situation provides John with the setting for a long
uninterrupted speech by Jesus to the Jews (vv. 19–47). The
theme of it is the relationship between the Father and the Son,
and this relationship is considered under four heads: giving
life, judging, bearing witness, and receiving glory. The speech
is in part at least a refutation of the charge that Jesus was
'making himself equal with God' (5¹⁸), and this is answered in
the following negative statements which are the framework of
the speech:

2   Now there is in Jerusalem by the Sheep Gate a pool, in
3   Hebrew called Beth-zatha,*j* which has five porticoes. In

    j Other ancient authorities read *Bethesda*, others *Bethsaida*

'The Son can do nothing of his own accord' (5^{19}).
'I can do nothing on my own authority' (5^{30}).
'If I bear witness to myself, my testimony is not true' (5^{31}).
'I do not receive glory from men' (5^{41}).

As the speech develops, we come to see that it is not in fact
the arrogance of Jesus, as the Jews thought, that makes them
want to kill him, but exactly the opposite. They can only
believe in one who makes claims for himself; Jesus comes to
them as the one who is sent by the Father, and who is nothing
in himself. It is the absence of self-assertion that offends. There
are a number of possible points of contact between the account
of the healing in 5^{1-18} and the conflicting stories in Mark 2^{1}-3^{6}.
There are also similarities and contrasts between $5^{1\text{ff.}}$ and $9^{1\text{ff.}}$.

1   Some commentators hold that there has been a dislocation of the
text at this point, and that Chapter 6 should follow here, immediately
after Chapter 4 (e.g. J. H. Bernard, *The Gospel according to St. John*
(Edinburgh, 1928), pp. xvii f., A. Guilding, *The Fourth Gospel and
Jewish Worship* (Oxford, 1960), pp. 45 ff.): others do not think it
necessary to rearrange the order (e.g. Barrett, pp. 18 ff.; Lightfoot,
pp. 7 ff.; see also Introduction, pp. 3, 22). *a feast of the Jews*: some
MSS. have 'the feast of the Jews': if that were the correct reading,
the feast referred to would be Passover, or Tabernacles (so Barrett,
p. 209); but the correct reading is probably *a feast* (RV, RSV, NEB),
and the question is, Which feast does John mean? The following suggestions have been made: Pentecost, Purim, New Year (Guilding,
pp. 69 ff.; Lightfoot, p. 148; B. F. Westcott, *The Gospel according to St.
John* (London, 1908), i, pp. 204 ff.; Bernard, p. 225). If John meant
New Year, then a number of features in the discourse ($5^{19\text{ff.}}$) could
be understood as allusions to the ideas connected with this feast
(see notes on vv. 21, 22, 31).

2   Archaeological research has revealed the double pool, north of the
temple court, with its five porches; and the copper scroll from
Qumran has established the original name as *Bethesda* (RSV mg.).
See J. Jeremias, *Expository Times*, lxxi, 8 (May, 1960), pp. 227 f.; and
The Rediscovery of Bethesda (Louisville, 1966).

3a The sick represent mankind in need of healing; the miracle is a sign
of the life which Jesus has brought to the world.

5 these lay a multitude of invalids, blind, lame, paralysed.[k] One
6 man was there, who had been ill for thirty-eight years. When
Jesus saw him and knew that he had been lying there a long

[k] Other ancient authorities insert, wholly or in part, *waiting for the moving of the water; [4]for an angel of the Lord went down at certain seasons into the pool, and troubled the water: whoever stepped in first after the troubling of the water was healed of whatever disease he had*

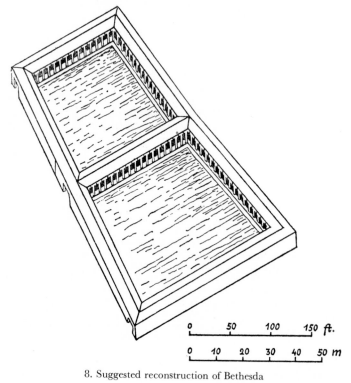

8. Suggested reconstruction of Bethesda

3b-4   These words are not present in the best witness for the original text of John; they were probably added later by a scribe to explain the man's words in v. 7.

9. One of the cisterns at the Pool of Bethesda

5   Some commentators see a parallel between the *thirty-eight years* of
the man's illness and the time of the Israelites' wanderings in the
desert (Deut. 2¹⁴; Guilding, p. 83); others take it as a simple statement
of fact (e.g. Bernard, Barrett).

6   For Jesus' knowledge, see note on 1⁴². *Do you want to be healed?*:
see note on next verse.

7 time, he said to him, 'Do you want to be healed?' The sick
man answered him, 'Sir, I have no man to put me into the
pool when the water is troubled, and while I am going
8 another steps down before me.' Jesus said to him, 'Rise, take
9 up your pallet, and walk.' And at once the man was healed,
and he took up his pallet and walked.

10   Now that day was the sabbath. So the Jews said to the man
who was cured, 'It is the sabbath, it is not lawful for you to
11 carry your pallet.' But he answered them, 'The man who
healed me said to me, "Take up your pallet, and walk." '
12 They asked him, 'Who is the man who said to you, "Take up
13 your pallet, and walk"?' Now the man who had been healed
did not know who it was, for Jesus had withdrawn, as there
14 was a crowd in the place. Afterward, Jesus found him in the
temple, and said to him, 'See, you are well! Sin no more,
15 that nothing worse befall you.' The man went away and told

---

7   The insertion (vv. 3b–4) explains what was believed about the
healing properties of the pool.
        Is the sick man's reply genuine, or is it an excuse? On the latter
view, C. H. Dodd says 'The man might have been healed long ago,
perhaps, if he had stepped down into the pool. Precisely; and that is
why the first word of Jesus is, "*Have you the will* to become a healthy
man?" The reply is a feeble excuse. The man has not the will' (*IFG*,
pp. 319 f.).

8 f.   The words of Jesus here are very similar to Mark 2[11] (the account
of the healing of the paralytic).

10   *Now that day was the sabbath*: this will be important in what follows;
see vv. 10, 16, 18. It is introduced after the account of the healing, as
in 9[14].
        See Mishnah, *Shabbath*, vii. 2, which forbids 'taking ought from one
domain into another on the sabbath'.

11 ff. The man lays the responsibility for his breach of the law upon his
unknown healer: cp. 9[12]. *there was a crowd in the place*: cp. Mark 2[2, 4].

14   *Jesus found him*: cp. 9[35]. *Sin no more*: possibly another allusion to the
Marcan story; see Mark 2[5 ff.]. On the relationship between sin and
sickness, see note on 9[1 f.].

15   Contrast the blind man in Chapter 9.

16 the Jews that it was Jesus who had healed him. And this was
why the Jews persecuted Jesus, because he did this on the
17 sabbath. But Jesus answered them, 'My Father is working
18 still, and I am working.' This was why the Jews sought all
the more to kill him, because he not only broke the sabbath
but also called God his Father, making himself equal with
God.

19 Jesus said to them, 'Truly, truly, I say to you, the Son can
do nothing of his own accord, but only what he sees the
Father doing; for whatever he does, that the Son does like-
20 wise. For the Father loves the Son, and shows him all that he
himself is doing; and greater works than these will he show
21 him, that you may marvel. For as the Father raises the dead

---

16   This verse is mistranslated in RSV; the tenses of the verbs are
imperfect, not aorist, and the second *this* is plural (Gk. ταῦτα). Cp.
NEB, 'It was works of this kind done on the Sabbath that stirred the
Jews to persecute Jesus'.

17   There is evidence that first-century rabbis held that God continues
his creative and kingly work on the sabbath, in spite of Gen. 2² ᶠ·. Jesus'
answer to the Jews is that he does what his Father does.

18   *sought all the more to kill him*: cp. Mark 3⁶. *called God his Father*:
'. . . There is no evidence so far that in Palestinian Judaism of the first
millennium anyone addressed God as "my Father". But Jesus did just
this' (J. Jeremias, *The Central Message of the New Testament* (London,
1965), p. 17). *making himself equal with God*: this is what the Jews
wrongly supposed, not what John believes, as the speech which follows
shows.

19   *Truly, truly*: see note on 1⁵¹. *the Son can do nothing of his own accord*:
i.e. the Son is not 'equal with God' in the sense that he can act
independently; all initiative is with the Father, and the Son is wholly
his imitator.

20   The obedience and dependence of the Son upon the Father is
matched by the love of the Father for the Son, and his complete
revelation to him of all that he does: cp. 15⁹, ¹⁴ ᶠ·. The Father does more
than heal the sick—he raises the dead: see v. 21. *that you may marvel*:
in all the other places in John where this word (Gk. θαυμάζειν) is used,
it signifies unbelief or misunderstanding (3⁷, 4²⁷, 5²⁸, 7¹⁵, ¹²). The

and gives them life, so also the Son gives life to whom he
22 will. The Father judges no one, but has given all judgment to
23 the Son, that all may honour the Son, even as they honour the
Father. He who does not honour the Son does not honour the
24 Father who sent him. Truly, truly, I say to you, he who hears
my word and believes him who sent me, has eternal life; he
does not come into judgment, but has passed from death to
life.

25 'Truly, truly, I say to you, the hour is coming, and now is,
when the dead will hear the voice of the Son of God, and
26 those who hear will live. For as the Father has life in himself,

---

unbelief of the Jews is the fulfilment of scripture and in accordance
with the will of God: see 12$^{37-41}$.

21 *the Father raises the dead and gives them life*: this is part of the work
which God does on the sabbath; see v. 17. Resurrection is also one
of the main ideas associated with the New Year festival (Guilding,
p. 76). *to whom he will*: the Son determines to whom he will give life,
just as Jesus chose the sick man from out of the multitude, vv. 3 ff.;
cp. 15^{16}, for Jesus' choice of disciples.

22 Judgement is the other part of God's sabbath work (see v. 17). And
it is another of the New Year festival themes (Guilding, ibid.).

23 There are sayings in the Synoptic Gospels which 'equate' Jesus and
the Father, e.g. Matt. 10^{40} ('he who receives me receives him who sent
me'). This is the idea behind the saying in this verse; because of the
Father's delegation of judgement to the Son, the Son is to be given
equal honour with the Father; and it is now impossible to honour the
Father without honouring the Son equally: cp. 14^6 ('no one comes to
the Father, but by me').

24 *Truly, truly*: see note on 1^{51}. The themes of life (v. 21) and judgement
(v. 22), are combined in this saying; the believer receives Christ's
benefits now: cp. Mark 2^{10} ('the Son of man has authority on earth to
forgive sins').

25 *the hour is coming, and now is*: see note on 4^{23}. *the dead will hear the
voice of the Son of God, and those who hear will live*: the reference is
partly to the healings of Jesus which reach a climax in the raising of
Lazarus (11$^{43 f.}$), but also in the faith of Christians and their life
through faith: cp. Eph. 2$^{1 f.}$ ('You he made alive, when you were dead
through the trespasses and sins in which you once walked').

26 The life-giving power of the Son is a gift which he has received from
the Father (cp. v. 22).

27 so he has granted the Son also to have life in himself, and
has given him authority to execute judgment, because he is
28 the Son of man. Do not marvel at this; for the hour is coming
29 when all who are in the tombs will hear his voice and come
forth, those who have done good, to the resurrection of life,
and those who have done evil, to the resurrection of judgment.

30 'I can do nothing on my own authority; as I hear, I judge;
and my judgment is just, because I seek not my own will but
31 the will of him who sent me. If I bear witness to myself, my
32 testimony is not true; there is another who bears witness to
me, and I know that the testimony which he bears to me is
33 true. You sent to John, and he has borne witness to the truth.
34 Not that the testimony which I receive is from man; but I
35 say this that you may be saved. He was a burning and shining
lamp, and you were willing to rejoice for a while in his light.
36 But the testimony which I have is greater than that of John;

---

27   *the Son of man*: this expression was used in Dan. 7[13], and became
a technical term for the judge to come at the end of the world. In the
Synoptic Gospels it is used of Jesus (e.g. Mark 2[10], quoted on v. 24
above). See also note on 1[51].

28 f.   *Do not marvel at this*: see note on v. 20. Again (as in v. 25) the reference is partly to the raising of Lazarus (note 11[17, 44]) but also to the
final judgement of the unbelievers, at the end of the world.

30   This verse repeats the thesis of v. 19, and applies it to judgement.

31   Witness is the third theme of the New Year festival (Guilding, p. 76)
and this is applied to Jesus in the same way that the other two themes
(the giving of life, and judging) have been applied.

32   *there is another*: i.e. the Father.

33   The Father works through others, e.g. the Baptist who 'came for
testimony, to bear witness to the light, that all might believe through
him' (1[7]).

34   The NEB brings out the meaning of this verse more clearly: 'Not
that I rely on human testimony, but I remind you of it for your own
salvation'; cp. 1[7], quoted in previous note.

35   John was a *lamp*, and not the light itself (1[8]). The Jews accepted him
as a prophet (cp. Mark 11[32]) but not as a witness to Jesus.

36   The miracles of Jesus also are signs that God is with him: cp. 3[2].

for the works which the Father has granted me to accomplish, these very works which I am doing, bear me witness that the
37 Father has sent me. And the Father who sent me has himself borne witness to me. His voice you have never heard, his
38 form you have never seen; and you do not have his word abiding in you, for you do not believe him whom he has sent.
39 You search the scriptures, because you think that in them you have eternal life; and it is they that bear witness to me;
40,41 yet you refuse to come to me that you may have life. I do not
42 receive glory from men. But I know that you have not the love
43 of God within you. I have come in my Father's name, and you do not receive me; if another comes in his own name, him
44 you will receive. How can you believe, who receive glory from one another and do not seek the glory that comes from
45 the only God? Do not think that I shall accuse you to the

---

37   The witness of the Father in the scriptures has been misunderstood by the Jews.

38   Only those who have the testimony or *word* of God abiding in them can believe in Jesus, the Word become flesh.

39 f.   The Jews treat the scriptures as a self-contained system which gives life to those who obey it; whereas the function of the scriptures is to bear witness to Jesus, who is the life-giver. To *come* here = believe (cp. 1³⁹).

41   Jesus does not depend on the praise of men (cp. v. 34).

42   The Jews have no love for God, but do their pious works 'before men in order to be seen by them' (Matt. 6¹).

43   Like is known by like; they can appreciate self-assertion, but not the obedience and self-denial of Jesus.

44   The attitude which depends on the praise of men amputates the mind so that it cannot believe in God (cp. Matt. 6¹⁻²¹).[1]

45 f.   At the last judgement Moses will condemn them for not having believed the one of whom he wrote (see v. 39). They have set their hope on Moses in the sense described in v. 39: cp. also Luke 16³¹ ('If they do not hear Moses and the prophets, neither will they be convinced if some one should rise from the dead').

[1] Compare the saying of Macarius, *Verba Seniorum*, x. 34 (trans. in H. Waddell, *The Desert Fathers* (London, 1936), p. 143).

Father; it is Moses who accuses you, on whom you set your
46 hope. If you believed Moses, you would believe me, for he
47 wrote of me. But if you do not believe his writings, how will
you believe my words?'

6 AFTER this Jesus went to the other side of the Sea of Galilee,
2 which is the Sea of Tiberias. And a multitude followed him,

10. The Sea of Galilee

6: 1–15 *Jesus feeds the crowd*

The story of the feeding of the five thousand is told by all
four Evangelists, but whereas most scholars agree that Matthew
and Luke are dependent on Mark, there is no general agreement whether this is so with John also (see Introduction, p. 6).

His account differs from theirs, both in what it adds and in
what it omits; and it is used later as the 'text' for a dialogue
between Jesus and those who had eaten the bread, in the
Synagogue at Capernaum, 6²⁵⁻⁵⁹.[1]

There are four points in the story which John picks out for
his reader's attention now, before he goes on to the dialogue:

---

[1] It is perhaps worth noticing that in Matthew and Mark also, the feeding
miracles become the subject of a conversation between Jesus and his
disciples (Matt. 16⁵⁻¹², Mark 8¹⁴⁻²¹).

because they saw the signs which he did on those who were
3 diseased. Jesus went up into the hills, and there sat down with
4 his disciples. Now the Passover, the feast of the Jews, was
at hand. Lifting up his eyes, then, and seeing that a multitude

---

(a) The feeding takes place at the time of the Passover: this
would suggest to his readers the ideas connected with Moses
and the manna, the death of Jesus, which took place at Passover, and perhaps the institution of the Eucharist; (b) The
disciples can think of no way of dealing with the situation, and
they themselves play no part in the miracle, apart from making
the people sit down, and gathering up the remains; (c) Jesus is
completely in control of the situation: he knows what he will
do, he ignores the remarks of the disciples, he gives them their
instructions, and he alone distributes the food to the crowd;
(d) The people had followed Jesus because they had seen his
cures, and now they take the feeding as evidence that he is the
prophet like Moses, and attempt to make him king by force.

In the light of these four points, it might be true to say that
John wishes his readers to see the feeding as a sign of the salvation which Jesus has brought to the world: he is the fulfilment
of the ideas associated with the Passover; he deals with a
situation which to others seems impossible; he deals with it
alone, but so adequately that there is no lack; and his action is
misunderstood by those who have an inadequate faith.

1   See pp. 3, 22, 67 for the impossibility of the itinerary, and for the
suggestion that Chapter 6 should follow Chapter 4.   *the Sea of Galilee,
which is the Sea of Tiberius*: the city of Tiberias was founded in A.D. 26,
and named after the Emperor Tiberius. 'It is doubtful whether the
name "Sea of Tiberias" would have come into general use as early
as the ministry of Jesus' (Barrett, p. 227).
2   John does not mean that the *multitude* believed; their attempt to
force him to be king (6[15]) and the scene in the synagogue (e.g. 6[41, 52])
show that this is not the case (see also notes on 2[23] and 6[14]).
3   *into the hills*: literally 'to the mountain'. *sat down with his disciples*:
possibly John means that Jesus sat down to teach (cp. Matt. 5[1 f.]),
contrast 7[37] and see note on 8[2] in Additional Note, p. 214.
4   'The Passover is mentioned here not for chronological but for
theological reasons' (Barrett, p. 228).

5 was coming to him, Jesus said to Philip, 'How are we to buy
6 bread, so that these people may eat?' This he said to test him,
7 for he himself knew what he would do. Philip answered him,
  'Two hundred denarii[l] would not buy enough bread for
8 each of them to get a little.' One of his disciples, Andrew,
9 Simon Peter's brother, said to him, 'There is a lad here who
  has five barley loaves and two fish; but what are they among
10 so many?' Jesus said, 'Make the people sit down.' Now there
  was much grass in the place; so the men sat down, in number
11 about five thousand. Jesus then took the loaves, and when he
  had given thanks, he distributed them to those who were
12 seated; so also the fish, as much as they wanted. And when
  they had eaten their fill, he told his disciples, 'Gather up

  [l] The denarius was worth about seventeen pence

---

5 f.   *Philip*: see note on 1[43ff.]. John explains that Jesus' question did not
        arise out of uncertainty (see note on 1[42]) but was put in order to *test*
        Philip, and to reveal his unbelief.

7   *Two hundred denarii*: the same sum is mentioned in Mark 6[37], and
        is used by some scholars as evidence for John's use of Mark (e.g.
        Barrett). 'The denarius was a day's wage for a labourer' (RSVCE
        mg.). Philip's answer shows that he cannot conceive any way of
        feeding the crowd, except by buying bread; and that the amount of
        bread necessary would be beyond their means.

8   *Andrew, Simon Peter's brother*: cp. 1[40].

9   *five barley loaves and two fish*: cp. Mark 6[38] ('five [loaves] and two
        fish'). John adds *barley*, and though some commentators take this to
        be the reminiscence of an eye-witness, others see it as an allusion to
        2 Kgs. 4[42 ff.], and think that the *lad* may be a recollection of Elisha's
        servant (the word (Gk. παιδάριον) is used of him in 2 Kgs. 4[38, 41]
        LXX; R. H. Strachan, *The Fourth Gospel, its Significance and Environment*
        (London, 1946), p. 179; Barrett, p. 229).

10   Cp. Mark 6[39, 44].

11   *when he had given thanks*: i.e. said 'the grace' or blessing before bread
        —'Blessed art thou, O Lord our God, King of the Universe, who
        bringest forth bread from the earth.'

2 f.   Cp. Mark 6[42] and 2 Kgs. 4[44]. John emphasizes the quantity of
        bread left over: Jesus' salvation is abundant. See D. Daube, *The New
        Testament and Rabbinic Judaism* (London, 1956), pp. 36–51.

13 the fragments left over, that nothing may be lost.' So they
gathered them up and filled twelve baskets with fragments
14 from the five barley loaves, left by those who had eaten. When
the people saw the sign which he had done, they said, 'This
is indeed the prophet who is to come into the world!'

15   Perceiving then that they were about to come and take him
by force to make him king, Jesus withdrew again to the hills
by himself.

---

14   *saw the sign*: cp. 2^{23}, 6^2. *the prophet*: see Deut. $18^{15\text{ff}\cdot}$, and above, 1^{21};
the statement of the multitude is meant to be understood as an in-
adequate declaration of faith.

15   *to make him king*: the Christian belief is that Jesus was made king by
God, and that this happened through his death and resurrection. It is
noticeable how the title 'King of the Jews' is used almost exclusively
in the passion narratives in all four Gospels. *to the hills*: see note
on 6^3.

6: 16–21 *Jesus walks on the lake*

    The story of Jesus walking on the lake follows the feeding-
miracle in Matthew, Mark, and John (Luke does not record
it); and again the question can be asked, Did John use Mark
(as Matthew certainly did), or had he independent access to
the tradition? A more profitable question, however, is Why
did John include this miracle? He makes very little use of it in
the dialogue which follows (in 6^{25} the people ask when Jesus
reached Capernaum) whereas usually John refers back to the
signs, in the conversations which follow them. It is hardly
satisfactory to say that John includes this miracle simply because it was in Mark, his source; there are many other
miracles in Mark which John has not reproduced; John does
not seem to have been a slave to tradition. A suggestion which
is worth considering is that the pattern of events in the two
signs is reproduced in the second part of the chapter; thus:

Bread	6^{1-13}	6^{25-40}
Misunderstanding	$6^{14\,\text{f}.}$	6^{41-59}
Separation of Jesus from his disciples	6^{16-19}	6^{60-66}
Jesus' disclosure of himself to them	$6^{20\,\text{f}.}$	6^{66-71}
and their faith		

(Cp. Dodd, *IFG*, pp. 344 f.).

16 When evening came, his disciples went down to the sea,
17 got into a boat, and started across the sea to Capernaum. It
18 was now dark, and Jesus had not yet come to them. The sea
19 rose because a strong wind was blowing. When they had
rowed about three or four miles,*m* they saw Jesus walking on
21 the sea and drawing near to the boat. They were frightened,
but he said to them, 'It is I; do not be afraid.' Then they
were glad to take him into the boat, and immediately the
boat was at the land to which they were going.

22 On the next day the people who remained on the other side
of the sea saw that there had been only one boat there, and

m Greek *twenty-five* or *thirty stadia*

---

16 f.   *Capernaum*: previously mentioned at 2^{12}, 4^{46}; it will be the scene of the second part of this chapter (see vv. 24, 59). *It was now dark*: literally, 'Darkness had now arrived'; for darkness as a symbol of ignorance and unbelief see 1^5, 8^{12}, $12^{35, 46}$, (20^1). Cp. 'night', for which see note on 3^2.

19 f.   The maximum width of the lake is 7 miles; therefore John is in agreement with Mark's statement that the boat was in the middle of the sea (Mark 6^{47}). *They were frightened*: John does not explain why; contrast Mark 6^{49}. This is the only reference to fear on the part of the disciples in John (Lightfoot, p. 157).

20   *It is I; do not be afraid*: the same words as in Mark 6^{50}. Some commentators take *it is I* (literally, 'I am'), to mean divine self-revelation (Hoskyns, p. 327, Dodd, *IFG*, p. 345), others in the weaker sense of identification (Bernard, p. 187, Barrett, p. 234).

21   *they were glad*: this translation presupposes a misreading of an Aramaic source; taken literally the Greek means 'they wished'. Barrett translates 'They wished to take him into the boat, but found immediately that they had reached the shore', and compares Ps. 107^{30} ('he brought them to their desired haven', p. 234; so also Hoskyns, p. 327; Lightfoot, p. 157).

6: 22–59 *Jesus in the synagogue at Capernaum*

The people who had been fed (6^{1-14}) now find Jesus in Capernaum on the other side of the lake, and John reports a discussion between him and them which takes place in the synagogue. They ask him how he reached the opposite shore,

that Jesus had not entered the boat with his disciples, but
23 that his disciples had gone away alone. However, boats from
Tiberias came near the place where they ate the bread after
24 the Lord had given thanks. So when the people saw that
Jesus was not there, nor his disciples, they themselves got
into the boats and went to Capernaum, seeking Jesus.

25   When they found him on the other side of the sea, they
26 said to him, 'Rabbi, when did you come here?' Jesus answered them, 'Truly, truly, I say to you, you seek me, not because

---

but he rebukes them for their unbelief: they do not understand
the meaning of the loaves, or believe in the one who fed them.
Because they have not perceived the sign, they ask for another,
and quote the example of Moses and the manna. Jesus says
that he is the real bread from heaven which has come to give
life to the world.

The crowd, which John now refers to as 'the Jews' (thus
underlining their unbelief and opposition to Jesus), acts like
Israel in the wilderness, and 'murmurs', that is, complains and
objects. Jesus says that they cannot believe; they will die, like
their ancestors who ate the manna. He also shows what it will
cost him to give life to the world: the living bread is his flesh;
he must die in order that others may live.

The reader is now in a position to see what the outcome
will be: the Jews, because they do not believe, will kill Jesus;
he will give himself to death, and thus make himself available
to those who believe, for them to receive his life. The way that
this is described (eating his flesh, drinking his blood) will be
understood by the Christian reader as a reference to the
Eucharist.

22   See vv. 16 f. for departure of the disciples to Capernaum.
23   *Tiberias* was on the west side of the lake (see note on 6[1], and see Map
on p. 30).
24   *seeking Jesus*: their motive is to be understood from vv. 14, 15, 26.
25   *Rabbi*: see note on 1[38].
26   *Truly, truly, I say to you*: see note on 1[51]. *not because you saw signs* means
here that they had not perceived the significance of the miracle: cp.
v. 36 and contrast v. 14. Their motive is purely material: cp. 4[15].

27 you saw signs, but because you ate your fill of the loaves. Do
   not labour for the food which perishes, but for the food which
   endures to eternal life, which the Son of man will give to you;
28 for on him has God the Father set his seal.' Then they said to
   him, 'What must we do, to be doing the works of God?'
29 Jesus answered them, 'This is the work of God, that you
30 believe in him whom he has sent.' So they said to him, 'Then
   what sign do you do, that we may see, and believe you? What
31 work do you perform? Our fathers ate the manna in the
   wilderness; as it is written, "He gave them bread from
32 heaven to eat." ' Jesus then said to them, 'Truly, truly, I say
   to you, it was not Moses who gave you the bread from

---

27   *the food which perishes* means ordinary bread; *the food which endures to
      eternal life* means the gift which Jesus can give to them (cp. 4¹³f.). *the
      Son of man*: see note on 1⁵¹. *will give*: i.e. through his death and resur-
      rection. *on him has God the Father set his seal*: i.e. authorized him, by
      giving him the Spirit, which he in turn will give to the believer.

28   *to be doing the works of God*: literally 'to be working the works of God';
      the verb is the same word as 'labour' in v. 27 (Gk. ἐργάζεσθαι).

29   The work which God wills is faith in Jesus as the agent of God; but
      they cannot do this, unless God gives them faith (see next verse and
      vv. 36, 44 f.).

30   Their unbelief is demonstrated by their demand for a sign: the sign
      has been given already; and to ask for a sign is in itself to declare one's
      unbelief in advance.

31   They cite the manna (Exod. 16) as an example of a sign, and it is
      not a random example: it is partly suggested by the feeding miracle
      and by the Passover season (v. 4); but also by the comparison between
      Jesus and Moses (e.g. v. 14); and it was believed that there would be
      a further gift of manna in the last days. If Jesus is the one whom God
      has sent, where is the bread from heaven? (cp. 2 Baruch 29⁸, 'And it
      shall come to pass at that self-same time that the treasury of manna
      shall again descend from on high, and they will eat it in those years,
      because these are they who have come to the consummation of time').
      For the quotation *He gave them bread from heaven to eat*, see Neh. 9¹⁵;
      Ps. 78²⁴.

32   *Truly, truly, I say to you*: see note on 1⁵¹. There is a double antithesis:
      Not Moses, but the Father; the real bread was not given then, but it
      is given now.

heaven; my Father gives you the true bread from heaven.
33 For the bread of God is that which comes down from heaven,
34 and gives life to the world.' They said to him, 'Lord, give us this bread always.'

35   Jesus said to them, 'I am the bread of life; he who comes to me shall not hunger, and he who believes in me shall never
36 thirst. But I said to you that you have seen me and yet do not
37 believe. All that the Father gives me will come to me; and
38 him who comes to me I will not cast out. For I have come down from heaven, not to do my own will, but the will of
39 him who sent me; and this is the will of him who sent me, that I should lose nothing of all that he has given me,

---

33   An alternative, and possibly better, translation would be 'he who comes down . . .'; in any case, the reference is to Jesus.
34   Cp. the Samaritan woman's request at 4^{15} and see the note there.
35   *I am the bread of life*: Jesus had commanded them to labour for the food which endures (v. 27), and had explained that this labour is belief in the one whom God has sent (v. 29). Thus, the food is the one sent by God, and there is no way of obtaining the food other than by faith in Jesus. The Jews for whom John wrote thought of the Law and Wisdom as *bread of life*: John is saying that Jesus is all that the Jews hoped for from the revelation of God in the Old Testament, and more. This is the first of the sayings in the form *I am the* . . . (Gk. ἐγώ εἰμι, see also $6^{41, 48, 51}$, 8^{12}, $10^{7, 9, 11, 14}$, 11^{25}, 14^{6}, $15^{1, 5}$). *he who comes . . . and he who believes* . . .: parallel sentences of identical meaning. Contrast what Wisdom says: 'Those who eat me will hunger for more, and those who drink me will thirst for more' (Ecclus. 24^{21}).
36   *I said to you*: see v. 26; they have seen without perceiving (cp. Mark 4^{12}).
37   *come* = believe, as in v. 35: the believers (the elect) are the gift of the Father to the Son, and he will keep them safe for eternal life (see, e.g. $17^{6, 12}$).
38   *I have come down from heaven*: cp. the manna, vv. 31, 33. *not to do my own will*: cp. 4^{34}, 5^{30}.
39   The will of the Father is that the Son should give life to the elect. *raise it up at the last day*: although the emphasis on the future is much less in John than in the Synoptists, it has not disappeared completely (cp. $5^{28 f.}$).

40 but raise it up at the last day. For this is the will of my
Father, that every one who sees the Son and believes in him
should have eternal life; and I will raise him up at the
last day.'

41   The Jews then murmured at him, because he said, 'I am
42 the bread which came down from heaven.' They said, 'Is not
this Jesus, the son of Joseph, whose father and mother we
know? How does he now say, "I have come down from
43 heaven"?' Jesus answered them, 'Do not murmur among
44 yourselves. No one can come to me unless the Father who
sent me draws him; and I will raise him up at the last day.
45 It is written in the prophets, "And they shall all be taught by
God." Every one who has heard and learned from the Father

---

40   Contrast v. 36: there it was seeing without believing; here, seeing
and believing.
41   *The Jews*: John uses this expression (Gk. οἱ ᾿Ιουδαῖοι) to refer to
people outside Judea, only in this chapter (cp. v. 52); see note on
1[19]. *murmured*: the word recalls the story of the manna (e.g. Exod.
16[2]). The change from *people* (Gk. ὄχλος, literally 'crowd') in vv. 22,
24 to *the Jews*, coincides with their adoption of the role of their
ancestors—viz. murmurers, i.e. those who complain against God and
his ways. *I am the bread which came down from heaven*: see above vv.
33, 35.
42   For the objection, cp. Matt. 13[55], Mark 6[3], Luke 4[22]. Cp. also 1[45].
They suppose that his human parentage disproves his claim to
heavenly origin. Do John and his readers know the stories of the
virginal conception, and is the Jewish objection thus a false assertion?
He is not the son of Joseph; they do not know his Father. Cp. 8[19]
('You know neither me nor my Father').
43   *Do not murmur among yourselves*: see note on v. 41.
44   To *come* to Jesus (i.e. to believe in him, cp. v. 35) is possible only
when God makes it so; the Father *draws* the believer to the Son (cp.
the idea of the Father giving the disciples to Jesus, v. 39). *and I will
raise him up at the last day*: see note on v. 39.
45   The quotation is from Isa. 54[13]. The teaching of God is the witness
of the Father mentioned in the previous chapter (5[37f.]), which creates
faith in the disciples.

46 comes to me. Not that any one has seen the Father except
47 him who is from God; he has seen the Father. Truly, truly,
48 I say to you, he who believes has eternal life. I am the bread
49 of life. Your fathers ate the manna in the wilderness, and they
50 died. This is the bread which comes down from heaven, that
51 a man may eat of it and not die. I am the living bread which
    came down from heaven; if any one eats of this bread, he will
    live for ever; and the bread which I shall give for the life of
    the world is my flesh.'

52   The Jews then disputed among themselves, saying, 'How
53 can this man give us his flesh to eat?' So Jesus said to them,
    'Truly, truly, I say to you, unless you eat the flesh of the Son
54 of man and drink his blood, you have no life in you; he who

---

46   Cp. 1¹⁸: Jesus, not Moses, is the one who has seen God, and now
       makes him known (cp. v. 32).
47   *Truly, truly, I say to you*: see note on 1⁵¹. *he who believes*: vv. 44–46
       have been about faith. *has eternal life*: unlike the Jews, who murmur
       in unbelief, and who will die, like their ancestors (see v. 49).
48   See v. 35; the saying is repeated, partly to explain what is meant by
       'believe' in the previous verse: Jesus is talking about faith in himself—
       there is no other life-giving faith; partly to contrast Jesus with the
       manna mentioned in the next verse.
49   See vv. 31, 47.
50   Jesus is superior to the manna, and Christianity to Judaism; the
       believer never passes out of the sphere of life. Is there perhaps a refer-
       ence back at this point to the 'second miracle' in vv. 12 f., the abun-
       dance of food left over?
51   The last part of this verse introduces a new development in the
       dialogue: Jesus identifies the bread with his *flesh*—i.e. his humanity
       (cp. 1¹⁴). *I shall give* perhaps refers to the Eucharist; the tenses have
       been present until this verse.
52   The question of *the Jews* (see above on v. 41) draws attention to the
       saying of Jesus by repeating it.
53   *Truly, truly, I say to you*: see note on 1⁵¹. At this point (cp. v. 51) the
       reference to the Eucharist becomes more clear, and this explains the
       introduction of the sayings about *blood*. *the Son of man*: see note on 1⁵¹.
54   *he who eats my flesh and drinks my blood has eternal life*: cp. 6⁴⁷ ('he
       who believes has eternal life'). The implication which John may have

eats my flesh and drinks my blood has eternal life, and I will
5 raise him up at the last day. For my flesh is food indeed, and
6 my blood is drink indeed. He who eats my flesh and drinks
7 my blood abides in me, and I in him. As the living Father
sent me, and I live because of the Father, so he who eats me
8 will live because of me. This is the bread which came down
from heaven, not such as the fathers ate and died; he who
9 eats this bread will live for ever.' This he said in the synagogue, as he taught at Capernaum.

0   Many of his disciples, when they heard it, said, 'This is a
1 hard saying; who can listen to it?' But Jesus, knowing in

---

wished his readers to draw from these statements is that there can be
no valid participation in Christ in the Eucharist, apart from faith.
and I will raise him up at the last day: see note on v. 39.
5   *indeed* (Gk. ἀληθῶς): that is, 'truly'; i.e. belonging to the heavenly
sphere.
6   *abides in me, and I in him*: the idea of mutual indwelling is frequently
used to this Gospel; it expresses complete communion or fellowship
in all possible and appropriate aspects, e.g. here, the obedience of the
believer to Christ, and the care and love of Christ for the believer.
7   The relationship between the Father and the Son (see 5[19ff.]) will
be reproduced in the relationship between the Son and the believer.
8   This verse summarizes and concludes the whole dialogue which
began in v. 25; notice in particular vv. 31 f., 49 ff.
9   It is characteristic of John to insert explanations of time and place
later in the narrative than one might have expected: cp. 1[28], 5[9], 8[20],
9[14] (10[22]?). This is the only account of Jesus teaching in a synagogue
in the narrative part of the Fourth Gospel (cp. 18[20]); the Synoptists
(e.g. Mark 1[21, 39], 3[1], 6[2]) refer to such occasions more frequently.

: **60–71** *Faith and unbelief*

We hear no more of 'the Jews' in this chapter; like Nicodemus in Chapter 3, once they have played their part, they
move off the stage; on to it come the disciples. Mark had
described the reactions of those who had heard the word, in
the explanation of the parable of the sower and the seed (Mark
4[14–20]; note Mark 4[17], 'they stumble', RSV mg.); John too says

himself that his disciples murmured at it, said to them, 'Do
62 you take offence at this? Then what if you were to see the
63 Son of man ascending where he was before? It is the spirit

11. Reconstruction of a synagogue

that many disciples took offence and left Jesus because they had
no faith. On the other hand, just as in Mark there is mention
of 'good soil', so also in John there are the twelve who confess,
through Peter (cp. Mark 8²⁹), their faith in Jesus as the bringer
of eternal life. And yet, even among the twelve, there will be
defection: Jesus knows that Judas will betray him.

It has been suggested that John has in mind the situation in
the life of the Church at the time when he was writing, and
that we can see what that situation was from the Johannine
Letters. Some, who had apparently been members of the
community, had left it, because they did not believe that Jesus
Christ had come in the flesh; and the writer of the Letters says
that they are antichrists (see 1 John 2¹⁸ ff., 4¹ ff.; 2 John 7). It may
be therefore that the withdrawal of many disciples from Jesus
here in the Gospel (v. 66) because of the 'hard saying', namely
that they must eat his flesh and drink his blood (v. 60), is a

that gives life, the flesh is of no avail; the words that I have
54 spoken to you are spirit and life. But there are some of you
that do not believe.' For Jesus knew from the first who those
were that did not believe, and who it was that should betray
55 him. And he said, 'This is why I told you that no one can
come to me unless it is granted him by the Father.'

66 After this many of his disciples drew back and no longer
67 went about with him. Jesus said to the twelve, 'Will you also

---

retrojection into the account of the ministry of events which
were happening at the time when the Evangelist was writing.

60   The *hard saying* is the demand that they must eat the flesh of the Son
of man and drink his blood (v. 53); it is *hard* in the sense that they
cannot see how this can be done; *listen to it*, means 'fulfil it', 'obey it'.

61   *knowing in himself*: see note on 1⁴² for Jesus' supernatural knowledge.
murmured: see note on v. 41; the *disciples* (not the twelve, see vv. 66 f.
below) take up the same attitude as 'the Jews' (vv. 41, 43). *Do you take
offence at this?* (Gk. τοῦτο ὑμᾶς σκανδαλίζει;) literally, 'Does this make
you stumble?'

62   This verse can be taken in two ways: (*a*) If they are offended at the
demand that they should eat his flesh and drink his blood, how much
more will they be offended when (without faith) they see him crucified
and thus (though they will not know this) *ascending where he was before?* (*b*)
If they were to see his death and ascension (and believe on him), then
they would not be offended at his demand that they should eat his
flesh and drink his blood. Perhaps John intended the saying to be
understood in both ways: faith will make it possible to listen to the
hard saying, and not to take offence at the crucifixion.

3 f.   Cp. 3⁶. The *Spirit* (capital S, not as RSV) will be given to the faithful, after the ascension of the Son of man (see 7³⁹), and then they will
understand his words, which are at present unintelligible and offen-
sive, because of their unbelief.   For the supernatural knowledge of
Jesus, see note on 1⁴², and cp. v. 71 below.

65   Cp. v. 44. The defection of faithless disciples will illustrate the
teaching that faith is a gift from God: cp. 1 John 2¹⁹.

66   *After this* (Gk. ἐκ τούτου): the meaning may be 'Because of this'; i.e.
because of their lack of faith: see v. 65.   *drew back and no longer went
about with him*: cp. 1 John 2¹⁸ᶠᶠ·.

67   Cp. Jesus' question and Peter's answer in Mark 8²⁹.

68   *the words of eternal life*: the revelation which Jesus has brought gives
life to the faithful.

68 go away?' Simon Peter answered him, 'Lord, to whom shall
69 we go? You have the words of eternal life; and we have
believed, and have come to know, that you are the Holy One
70 of God.' Jesus answered them, 'Did I not choose you, the
71 twelve, and one of you is a devil?' He spoke of Judas the son
of Simon Iscariot, for he, one of the twelve, was to betray
him.

7 AFTER this Jesus went about in Galilee; he would not go
2 about in Judea, because the Jews[n] sought to kill him. Now
3 the Jews' feast of Tabernacles was at hand. So his brothers

[n] Or Judeans

---

69   *we have believed, and have come to know*: the two expressions are synonymous. *the Holy One of God*: the same title was used in Mark 1[24];
John uses it here instead of 'the Christ' (Mark 8[29]), perhaps because
it was less Jewish in connotation.
70 f.   The faith of the disciples is dependent on the choice of them by
Jesus; this choice, however, does not guarantee salvation: one of the
twelve is a devil (cp. 13[2, 27], 14[30]; 1 John 2[18]).

7: 1–9 *Jesus and his disbelieving brothers*

The time of the next scene is autumn (the feast of Tabernacles) and Jesus is in Galilee because the Jews in Judea are
seeking to kill him. But even in Galilee he is in the midst of
unbelief—the unbelief of his brothers. They advise him to go
to Judea in order to show himself to the world and thus attain
his object, which is to be known and believed. But he refuses to
go there for the purpose which they suggest, and when eventually he does go, he goes in secret.

John says that the brothers of Jesus did not believe in him;
they speak here as representatives of the world, and they argue
in a worldly way: if Jesus is what he claims to be, then let him
seek publicity. Jesus, on the other hand, is from God, and not
of the world; his actions are always determined by the will of
God. Therefore he rejects the advice of his brothers (see also
2[4], 11[3 f.], and cp. Mark 8[33], 'Get behind me, Satan! For you
are not on the side of God, but of men').

said to him, 'Leave here and go to Judea, that your disciples
4 may see the works you are doing. For no man works in secret
if he seeks to be known openly. If you do these things, show
5 yourself to the world.' For even his brothers did not believe
6 in him. Jesus said to them, 'My time has not yet come, but
7 your time is always here. The world cannot hate you, but it

---

This controversy between Jesus and his brothers, or between
those who live by faith and those who do not, arises from two
opposed attitudes to action: for the unbeliever, the only question that needs to be asked is whether an act is such as to fulfil
an intention effectively; for the believer, however, all human
action must be related to the will of God, and must be fulfilled
by God if it is to be effective (cp. 12²⁴, 'Unless a grain of wheat
falls into the earth and dies, it remains alone; but if it dies, it
bears much fruit').

1   In this Gospel, Galilee is to some extent associated with faith, while
Judea and Jerusalem are places of unbelief; 'Whereas the signs in
Galilee are in each case fruitful and forthwith produce belief, the
signs in Jerusalem in each case lead at once to controversy, the
presence of opponents being strongly emphasized' (R. H. Lightfoot,
Locality and Doctrine in the Gospels (London, 1938), p. 149).

2   For the *feast of Tabernacles*, see Lev. 23³³ᶠ·. It was originally an
agricultural festival, celebrated at the time of the grape-harvest; under
the influence of Jewish faith, the idea of living in booths after the
Exodus was added. See Guilding, pp. 92 ff.

3 f.   *his brothers* (RSVCE, 'his brethren'): see note on 2¹². With these
disbelieving brothers, contrast the disciples, the true brethren of the
Lord, 19²⁷, 20¹⁷. We may compare the temptations in Matt. 4¹ᶠᶠ·,
Luke 4¹ᶠᶠ·, and the Pharisees' request for a miracle (Mark 8¹¹ᶠᶠ·, etc.).

5   The brothers of the Lord did eventually believe—1 Cor. 9⁵, 15⁷;
Acts 1¹⁴, etc.; James 1¹; Jude¹; hence some of the textual authorities
add 'at that time'.

6   Jesus always acts in obedience to the Father (cp. e.g. 8²⁹), and the
Father will show him when the time has come to go to Jerusalem.
There is no such 'limitation' for the unbeliever.

7   The brothers of Jesus, being unbelievers, belong to the world, and
the world loves its own (cp. 15¹⁹); it hates Jesus, because he exposes
its wickedness.

8 hates me because I testify of it that its works are evil. Go to
   the feast yourselves; I am not^o going up to this feast, for my
9 time has not yet fully come.' So saying, he remained in
   Galilee.

10   But after his brothers had gone up to the feast, then he also
11 went up, not publicly but in private. The Jews were looking
12 for him at the feast, and saying, 'Where is he?' And there was
   much muttering about him among the people. While some
   said, 'He is a good man,' others said, 'No, he is leading the
13 people astray.' Yet for fear of the Jews no one spoke openly of
   him.

14   About the middle of the feast Jesus went up into the

<hr>

o Other ancient authorities add *yet*

<hr>

8   The word *yet* (RSV mg.) was probably inserted to avoid the contra-
     diction between this verse and v. 10.

7: 10–24 *Jesus goes to Jerusalem and teaches in the temple*

     Jesus goes to Jerusalem, but not in the way or with the
     motives that his brothers had proposed. He comes into a
     situation of confusion and disagreement concerning himself,
     and claims that he is the emissary of God, and that his teaching
     is the word of God. The Jews cannot believe him, because they
     do not believe in God, or in the Law of Moses which points to
     Jesus; if they had understood the relationship between the
     sabbath and circumcision in the Law, they would not have
     been offended at the healing of the lame man on the sabbath.

10   *not publicly, but in private* (Gk. οὐ φανερῶς ἀλλὰ ὡς ἐν κρυπτῷ): contrast
     v. 4, in secret . . . openly (Gk. ἐν κρυπτῷ . . . ἐν παρρησίᾳ).
11   John always uses the term *the Jews* to denote people who do not
     believe. *were looking for him* (Gk. ἐζήτουν), that is, to kill him (cp. v. 19).
12 f. *muttering*: from the same root as the word translated 'murmured' in
     6⁴¹ (see also 6⁴³, ⁶¹, 7³²). *the people* (literally, 'the crowds') are divided
     in their reaction to the claims of Jesus, but even those who have the
     beginnings of faith are afraid to express it, because of the Jewish
     leaders (see 9²², 12⁴²).
14   The feast of Tabernacles lasted eight days: see Lev. 23³³⁻³⁶.

15 temple and taught. The Jews marvelled at it, saying, 'How is
it that this man has learning,[p] when he has never studied?'
16 So Jesus answered them, 'My teaching is not mine, but his
17 who sent me; if any man's will is to do his will, he shall
know whether the teaching is from God or whether I am
18 speaking on my own authority. He who speaks on his own
authority seeks his own glory; but he who seeks the glory of
him who sent him is true, and in him there is no falsehood.
19 Did not Moses give you the law? Yet none of you keeps the
20 law. Why do you seek to kill me?' The people answered, 'You
21 have a demon! Who is seeking to kill you?' Jesus answered
22 them, 'I did one deed, and you all marvel at it. Moses gave

[p] Or *this man knows his letters*

---

15 f.   *marvelled* (Gk. ἐθαύμαζον): better 'were scornful'; see note on 5²⁰.
The Jews correctly perceive that the teaching of Jesus is not, like theirs,
the fruit of their study of the law (cp. Mark 1²²); this provides the cue
for Jesus' claim that his teaching is from God.

17   Only the man who is devoted to the will of God, and thus released
from self-will, can recognize Jesus as the Revealer sent by God; in
other men pride prevents understanding (cp. 8⁴⁷).

18   Jesus is entirely devoted to God; he seeks God's glory, and he
speaks on God's authority; he is authentic, but incomprehensible to
the Jews who as unbelievers are not open to the possibilities of God,
but 'receive glory from one another' (5⁴⁴).

19   The Jews are without excuse: in the law they have the will of God,
yet they desire to kill Jesus. 'Jesus has exposed the desire of the Jews
to kill Him, and has characterized their intention as the violation of
the Law of Moses' (Hoskyns, p. 358).

20   Demons are mentioned in this Gospel only here and in 8⁴⁸⁻⁵²,
10²⁰ ᶠ·: in each of these passages, the Jews say that Jesus is possessed by
a demon, whereas the truth is that it is the Jews themselves who are
of the devil (cp. 8⁴⁴).

21   *I did one deed*: i.e. the healing of the lame man in Chapter 5.   *you all
marvel at it* (Gk. θαυμάζετε): see notes on 5²⁰, 7¹⁵ ᶠ·.

22   This verse refers to the rabbinic regulation that the law of circumcision on the eighth day takes precedence over the sabbath law
(*Shabbath*, xviii. 3; xix. 2). *from the fathers* means 'from the time of the
patriarchs' (e.g. Gen. 17⁹ᶠᶠ·).

you circumcision (not that it is from Moses, but from the
23 fathers), and you circumcise a man upon the sabbath. If on
the sabbath a man receives circumcision, so that the law of
Moses may not be broken, are you angry with me because on
24 the sabbath I made a man's whole body well? Do not judge
by appearances, but judge with right judgment.'

25   Some of the people of Jerusalem therefore said, 'Is not this
26 the man whom they seek to kill? And here he is, speaking
openly, and they say nothing to him! Can it be that the
27 authorities really know that this is the Christ? Yet we know
where this man comes from; and when the Christ appears,

---

23   The argument is that since the healing of the whole body is greater
than circumcision, therefore it is not an infringement of the sabbath
law to heal a man on the sabbath. As the Jews circumcise on the
sabbath in obedience to Moses, so Jesus heals on the sabbath in
obedience to the Father.

24   Superficially, Jesus has broken the sabbath; but the *right judgment*
is that he has fulfilled the will of God. This can only be known by
faith, and this saying invites the Jews to believe in Jesus.

7 : 25–36 *The partial faith of the crowd and the unbelief of the Jewish
leaders*

The inhabitants of Jerusalem express surprise that their
leaders permit Jesus to speak openly, and raise the question
whether the authorities themselves now believe that he is the
Christ. They then bring forward an objection to this: the
Messiah was expected to appear out of obscurity, whereas Jesus
is known to have come from Nazareth. This provides a further
occasion for Jesus to claim that his origin is from God, and that
he is the one sent by God; and this claim in turn produces on
the one hand a further attempt to kill Jesus, and on the other
an imperfect faith in him. Jesus then predicts his departure to
God, and this is misunderstood by the Jews.

27 f.   *we know where this man comes from*: see 1[45 f.], 7[41]. This is an example of
judging 'by appearances' (7[24]); in fact Jesus has come from God,
but the crowd do not know it, because they do not believe in him.

28 no one will know where he comes from.' So Jesus proclaimed, as he taught in the temple, 'You know me, and you know where I come from? But I have not come of my own accord;
29 he who sent me is true, and him you do not know. I know
30 him, for I come from him, and he sent me.' So they sought to arrest him; but no one laid hands on him, because his hour
31 had not yet come. Yet many of the people believed in him; they said, 'When the Christ appears, will he do more signs than this man has done?'

32 The Pharisees heard the crowd thus muttering about him, and the chief priests and Pharisees sent officers to arrest him.
33 Jesus then said, 'I shall be with you a little longer, and then I
34 go to him who sent me; you will seek me and you will not

29   Only Jesus knows his own origin, and the believer to whom he reveals it.

30   *his hour* is the appointed time for his departure to the Father (13¹), and this cannot be hastened or anticipated by attempts to arrest him sooner.

31   This faith is imperfect, because, as John says, it is based only on the number of signs which Jesus has done: see notes on 1⁵⁰, 2²³.

32   *muttering*: see note on 7¹² ᶠ·. *the chief priests* combine with the *Pharisees* to arrest Jesus, in order to put an end to the suggestion made in v. 26, and to destroy the beginnings of faith mentioned in the previous verse (v. 31). In fact, however, their attempts are useless: on the one hand 'his hour had not yet come'; and when it does come, their destruction of Jesus will have the opposite result to that which they intend (cp. 8²⁸, 12³²).

33   Jesus says that he is to be with them a little longer, and that his departure will not be simply his death, but his glorious return to the Father who sent him.

34   'The opportunity for the search for the Messiah *while he may be found* (Isa. lv. 6) is therefore severely limited. When it is passed the desire of the Jews to find the Messiah must remain unsatisfied, for He has gone into heaven, whither they cannot follow him' (Hoskyns, p. 363). Note the contrast between the present seeking to kill him (7¹⁹, ²⁵) and the future seeking for his mercy. *where I am*: not 'where I shall be'; he is always out of their reach, because he dwells with the Father; they can only *come* to him by faith.

35 find me; where I am you cannot come.' The Jews said to one
another, 'Where does this man intend to go that we shall not
find him? Does he intend to go to the Dispersion among the
36 Greeks and teach the Greeks? What does he mean by saying,
"You will seek me and you will not find me," and, "Where I
am you cannot come"?'

37   On the last day of the feast, the great day, Jesus stood up
and proclaimed, 'If any one thirst, let him come to me and
38 drink. He who believes in me, as^q the scripture has said, "Out
39 of his heart shall flow rivers of living water."' Now this he

q Or *let him come to me, and let him who believes in me drink. As*

---

35   The saying of Jesus leads to a misunderstanding on the part of the
Jews, which is, ironically, a true prophecy. He will indeed go to the
Greeks because he will send his apostles to them, and he will teach
the Greeks through their ministry: see 12$^{20\text{ff}}$.

36   The words of Jesus are repeated in order to emphasize their importance, as in 16$^{16-19}$.

7: 37–52 *The proclamation of Jesus and the failure of the Jews to
apprehend him*

At the end of the feast of Tabernacles, Jesus declares publicly
that he is the giver of the Spirit, which he speaks of in terms of
water. His self-disclosure creates differences of opinion among
the crowd: some say that he is the prophet, some the Messiah;
while some object that the Messiah is to be a descendant of
David, and to come from Bethlehem, whereas Jesus is a
Galilean. The temple police, who had been sent to arrest him,
return and explain why they have not done so: they have been
impressed by the authority of Jesus' teaching. They are rebuked
by the Pharisees for siding with the crowd; and when Nicodemus speaks up for following the correct procedure of hearing
the evidence before forming a judgement, he is accused of
being another Galilean. The passage as a whole shows the
inability of the Jews either to understand Jesus, or to silence
him (see note on 1^5).

37 f.   There is some doubt whether *the last day of the feast*, means the
seventh day, or the closing festival on the eighth day (see Lev. 23$^{33-36}$).
Some commentators punctuate these verses as in RSV text (e.g.

said about the Spirit, which those who believed in him were
to receive; for as yet the Spirit had not been given, because
Jesus was not yet glorified.

40   When they heard these words, some of the people said,
41 'This is really the prophet.' Others said, 'This is the Christ.'
42 But some said, 'Is the Christ to come from Galilee? Has not
the scripture said that the Christ is descended from David,
and comes from Bethlehem, the village where David was?'
44 So there was a division among the people over him. Some of
them wanted to arrest him, but no one laid hands on him.

Lightfoot, Barrett), others as RSV mg. (e.g. Guilding; cp. NEB
text, 'If anyone is thirsty let him come to me; whoever believes in me,
let him drink'). If the former punctuation is adopted, *the scripture*
which is quoted in v. 38 refers to the believer; if the latter, it may refer
either to the believer, or to Christ, or to both. One of the ceremonies
of the seven days of the festival was the drawing of water from the pool
of Siloam, and the pouring out of it in the temple. 'It seems probable
that this feature of the festival suggested the form of the saying here
ascribed to Jesus' (Barrett, p. 271; cp. Guilding, pp. 104 ff.). *Out of
his heart shall flow rivers of living water*: this is not an exact quotation
from the O.T., the passage closest to it is perhaps Zech. 14[8] ('On that
day living waters shall flow out from Jerusalem': this chapter of the
book of Zechariah was read during the feast of Tabernacles).

39   In rabbinic interpretation, water is understood as a symbol of the
Spirit; and cp. 1 Cor. 12[13] ('we were . . . all made to drink of one
Spirit'). *for as yet the Spirit had not been given*: literally 'Spirit was not
yet'; i.e. was not yet made available as he was after the glorification
(that is, the death and resurrection) of Jesus (cp. 16[7]).

40   For the prophecy of the coming of the Spirit, see Joel 2[28 f.]. Jesus'
claim to be the giver of the Spirit leads some people to think of him
as *the prophet*: see 1[21], 6[14].

41 f.   While others go further and say he is the Messiah himself, a third
group objects that he has not fulfilled the prophecies concerning the
Son of David (e.g. Ps. 89, Mic. 5[2]). John is probably aware of the
tradition behind the birth stories in Matthew and Luke in which these
prophecies are fulfilled, but he regards them as unimportant; the
important truth is that Jesus is from God: see 7[27ff.].

43   *division* (Gk. σχίσμα: cp. 9[16], 10[19]) is always the result of Jesus'
revelation of himself.

44   Cp. 7[30].

45   The officers then went back to the chief priests and Pharisees, who said to them, 'Why did you not bring him?'
46 The officers answered, 'No man ever spoke like this man!'
47 The Pharisees answered them, 'Are you led astray, you also?
48 Have any of the authorities or of the Pharisees believed in
49 him? But this crowd, who do not know the law, are accursed.'
50 Nicodemus, who had gone to him before, and who was one of
51 them, said to them, 'Does our law judge a man without first
52 giving him a hearing and learning what he does?' They replied, 'Are you from Galilee too? Search and you will see that no prophet is to rise from Galilee.'[r]

[r] Other ancient authorities add 7⁵³–8¹¹ either here or at the end of this gospel or after Luke 21³⁸, with variations of the text:

7⁵³–8¹¹   ⁵³They went each to his own house, ¹but Jesus went to the Mount of Olives. ²Early in the morning he came again to the temple; all the people came to him, and he sat down and taught them. ³The scribes and the Pharisees brought a woman who had been caught in adultery, and placing her in the midst ⁴they said to him, 'Teacher, this woman has been caught in the act of adultery. ⁵Now in the law Moses commanded us to stone such. What do you say about her?' ⁶This they said to test him, that they might have some charge to bring against him. Jesus bent down and wrote with his finger on the ground. ⁷And as they continued to ask him, he stood up and said to them, 'Let him who is without sin among you be the first to throw a stone at her.' ⁸And once more he bent down and wrote with his finger on the ground. ⁹But when they heard it, they went away, one by one, beginning with the eldest, and Jesus was left alone with the woman standing before him. ¹⁰Jesus looked up and said to her 'Woman, where are they? Has no one condemned you?' ¹¹She said, 'No one, Lord.' And Jesus said, 'Neither do I condemn you; go, and do not sin again.'

45   See 7³² for the sending of the temple police to arrest Jesus.
46   On the significance of the failure of the police to arrest Jesus, see notes on 18¹⁻¹¹.
47   This verse refers back to v. 12, the only other passage where *lead astray* (Gk. πλανᾶν) is used in this Gospel.
48 f.   The argument of the Pharisees is that the police should rely on the opinion of their employers and betters, who have not believed, and not on the facts of the case (contrast the point of view of Nicodemus, vv. 50 f.), or on the views of the crowd who do not keep the Law, and are therefore cursed by God (cp. Deut. 27²⁶ quoted in Gal. 3¹⁰).
50   See 3¹ ff. for the previous appearance of Nicodemus, and cp. 19³⁹ ff..
51   For the instruction in the law to 'inquire diligently' into the facts, see e.g. Deut. 17⁴.
52   They will not allow Nicodemus to make his point, but attribute a

12   Again Jesus spoke to them, saying, 'I am the light of the
      world; he who follows me will not walk in darkness, but will

false motive to him—that he himself is a Galilean, and thus that he
is blinded by local patriotism. In fact there was a prophet from Galilee,
Jonah of Gath-Hepher in Galilee (2 Kgs. 14^{25}), and there is evidence
that the rabbis believed that prophets had come from every tribe in
Israel. Perhaps John intends his readers to understand that the Jews,
in their anger, deny their Jewish faith: cp. 19^{15} ('We have no king but
Caesar'). *Search*: the word is used only twice by John, here and in 5^{39}
('You search the scriptures').

7^{53}–8^{11}, the story of the woman taken in adultery, is not part of the
original text of John's Gospel, and is found at this point in only a few
of the MSS., etc. See below, Additional Note, pp. 213 ff.

8: **12–59** *The Son of God and the children of the devil*

This section consists entirely of discussion between Jesus and
the Jews in the treasury of the temple; the only narrative
element is in the final verse where John says 'they took up
stones to throw at him; but Jesus hid himself, and went out of
the temple' (8^{59}). The debate begins with the second I AM
saying—'I am the light of the world'—but the meaning of this
saying will not be considered until the following chapter, where
the saying is repeated (9^{5}) and the claim is symbolically
demonstrated by the gift of sight to a blind man; here it is not
so much that Jesus is 'the light' that is being disputed, as that
he claims to be something at all. John continues to use 'the
Jews' as the spokesmen for unbelief, and he shows here how
unbelief cannot make anything of Jesus, cannot attend to what
he says, or receive it, but can only react in anger, and attempt
to destroy Jesus. They object that he is bearing witness to himself (8^{13}) and that he speaks of a Father who bears witness to
him but cannot be produced to testify (8^{19}). They misunderstand him when he says that he is going away (8^{21}), that he can
make them free (8^{32}), that he can give them the status of sons
of Abraham and of God (8$^{39, 41}$), that he can save them from
death (8^{51}).

The discussion as a whole illustrates the statement which
Jesus makes in 8^{47}, 'He who is of God hears the words of God;
the reason why you do not hear them is that you are not of
God'. It is a frustrating discussion, because it takes place

13 have the light of life.' The Pharisees then said to him, 'You
   are bearing witness to yourself; your testimony is not true.'

14 Jesus answered, 'Even if I do bear witness to myself, my
   testimony is true, for I know whence I have come and whither
   I am going, but you do not know whence I come or whither

15 I am going. You judge according to the flesh, I judge no one.

---

between the Son of God and the children of the devil, the light
of the world and the darkness. Jesus says at one point that the
devil 'was a murderer from the beginning' (8^{44}), and so the
inevitable outcome of the meeting is that his children attempt
to kill Jesus. In the next chapter, however, we shall be shown
how 'the light shines in the darkness' (1^5).

12   *them*: not the crowd, which is not mentioned in this chapter, but
      the Jewish leaders. The terms which John uses now are 'the Pharisees'
      (v. 13) and 'the Jews' (vv. 22, 31, 48, 52, 57): John uses these titles
      because he is describing the fundamental conflict between faith and
      unbelief.   *I am the light of the world*: see note on 6^{35} for other sayings in
      this form. One of the ceremonies of the feast of Tabernacle was the
      illumination of the court of the women in the temple, and this may
      have suggested the saying to John (cp. $7^{37\,f.}$ and Zech. 14^7). Light
      was a symbol used in the O.T. and by the rabbis of the Law and
      Wisdom; in Hellenistic religions of the knowledge of God; and in
      primitive Christianity of the gospel. In making Jesus say *I am the
      light of the world*, John is claiming for Jesus all that Jews and Greeks
      looked for and longed for in the way of salvation. To believe in Jesus,
      and to *follow* him, is to *walk in* (= live) the life which is not ended by
      death. The same thing is said in different words in 8^{51} ('If any one
      keeps my word, he will never see death').

13   Apparently the rabbis extended the rule 'if any one kills a person,
      the murderer shall be put to death on the evidence of witnesses; but
      no person shall be put to death on the testimony of one witness'
      (Num. 35^{30}) to other cases, and made it a general legal principle.

14   Contrast 5^{31}. Jesus claims for himself a unique power to bear witness
      to himself, because he knows his origin and destiny. Other people
      are unreliable, because their self-knowledge is limited; Jesus' self-
      knowledge is complete.

15   They *judge according to the flesh* (= 'by appearances' 7^{24}) and think
      that he is a man from Galilee (7^{52}, etc.), and that he is going to the
      Greeks (7^{35}), or that his end will be suicide (8^{22}).   *I judge no one*: The

16 Yet even if I do judge, my judgment is true, for it is not I
17 alone that judge, but I and he[s] who sent me. In your law it is
18 written that the testimony of two men is true; I bear witness
to myself, and the Father who sent me bears witness to me.'
19 They said to him therefore, 'Where is your Father?' Jesus
answered, 'You know neither me nor my Father; if you knew
20 me, you would know my Father also.' These words he spoke
in the treasury, as he taught in the temple; but no one
arrested him, because his hour had not yet come.
21 Again he said to them, 'I go away, and you will seek me and
22 die in your sin; where I am going, you cannot come.' Then
said the Jews, 'Will he kill himself, since he says, "Where I
23 am going, you cannot come"?' He said to them, 'You are

[s] Other ancient authorities read *the Father*

meaning of this is not immediately apparent, in view of what is said
in 5[22], 9[39], 12[48], and in the following verse here. Possibly the point is
that Jesus does not judge *according to the flesh*, as the Jews do. Or that
his chief purpose is not condemnation, but salvation (cp. 3[17]), and
condemnation or judgement is accidental.

16   Jesus is competent to judge, just as he is to be believed as a witness,
because he is not alone, but the Father is with him, and he is obedient
to him (v. 29).

17   See Deut. 17[6], 19[15]. 'It is unlikely that Jesus himself, speaking as a
Jew to Jews, would have spoken of *your* law' (Barrett, p. 280).

18   Jesus and the Father are the two witnesses.

19   The Jews do not believe that Jesus is the Son of God, the one and
only Revealer of the Father; therefore they do not know the Father.
The only answer Jesus could give to their question would be 'He who
has seen me has seen the Father' (14[9]).

20   *the treasury*: perhaps the court of the women, but it is not certain
what John means. *his hour had not yet come*: cp. 2[4], 7[30], 13[1].

21   Jesus is going to the Father, and the unbeliever cannot follow him
or find mercy from him; cp. 7[33–36].

22   A typical Johannine use of misunderstanding; the Jews ask themselves where a man can go to avoid his opponents, and they can think
only of death by suicide. They are right in thinking of death, but
wrong in thinking of suicide; though note 10[18].

23   Jesus and the unbeliever belong to two distinct worlds. Jesus has

from below, I am from above; you are of this world, I am not
24 of this world. I told you that you would die in your sins, for
you will die in your sins unless you believe that I am he.'
25 They said to him, 'Who are you?' Jesus said to them, 'Even
26 what I have told you from the beginning.[t] I have much to say
about you and much to judge; but he who sent me is true,
and I declare to the world what I have heard from him.'
27 They did not understand that he spoke to them of the Father.
28 So Jesus said, 'When you have lifted up the Son of man, then

[t] Or *Why do I talk to you at all?*

---

come from the world above to reveal the way thither to those who
live below; but if they are to follow him, they must have faith in him.
At this point in the discussion the Jews are addressed as if they would
always remain unbelievers: contrast v. 28.

24   This verse makes it clear that without faith in Jesus as the one sent
by God to bring salvation, there is no possibility of eternal life.

25   The Jews ask the right question, since everything hinges on the
person of Jesus. His answer to it is difficult, and can be taken in
different ways: (a) *Even what I have told you from the beginning* (RSV text,
cp. NEB mg.), but the verb is in the present tense in Greek ($\lambda\alpha\lambda\hat{\omega}$);
(b) 'I am from the beginning what I tell you' (Barrett, p. 283); and (c)
'To think that I am talking with you at all!' (Dodd, *HTFG*, p. 230,
n. 1) or *Why do I talk to you at all?* (RSV mg., cp. NEB text). Whichever
of these is correct, it is clear that the discussion between Jesus and the
Jews has reached an impasse and that this must be so, because unbelief
cannot receive the answer to the question which has been asked,
without ceasing to be unbelief.

26   Jesus will speak about them in judgement, but, as in v. 16 his
judgement is the Fathers' judgement, and it is true, because he is
true. *to the world*: possibly 'in the world' (Barrett, p. 284).

27   For their ignorance of *the Father*, see also v. 19.

28   *lifted up* refers to the crucifixion as the way by which Jesus will
return to the Father; see 3[14] for the previous use of this word, and
12[32, 34]. 3[14 f.] shows that the lifting up of Jesus will bring healing; and
that is the case here too, and in 12[32] ('I, when I am lifted up from the
earth, will draw all men to myself'). Jesus is promising that his death
and exaltation will bring unbelief to an end, even for the Jews. Contrast Barrett (p. 284): 'John cannot mean that they [i.e. the Jews] will
recognize the truth of Jesus' claims after the Crucifixion, since it was

you will know that I am he, and that I do nothing on my own
29 authority but speak thus as the Father taught me. And he
who sent me is with me; he has not left me alone, for I always
30 do what is pleasing to him.' As he spoke thus, many believed
in him.

31   Jesus then said to the Jews who had believed in him, 'If
32 you continue in my word, you are truly my disciples, and you
33 will know the truth, and the truth will make you free.' They
answered him, 'We are descendants of Abraham, and have
never been in bondage to any one. How is it that you say,
"You will be made free"?'

34   Jesus answered them, 'Truly, truly, I say to you, every one
35 who commits sin is a slave to sin. The slave does not con-
36 tinue in the house for ever; the son continues for ever. So if
37 the Son makes you free, you will be free indeed. I know that

---

well known to him that this had not happened. He is addressing his
readers.'

29   The union of Jesus with the Father is a union based on the obedience of Jesus.

30   John frequently says that *many* of the Jews *believed in him*: see 2^{23},
7^{31}, 10^{42}, $12^{11, 42}$. Probably in every case John introduces them as
people with inadequate faith, in order to show by contrast what real
faith is: this is certainly the case here; see what follows.

1 f.   The fiction of believing Jews is now used to explain further what
is meant by faith, and what is offered to the believer, namely, truth
and freedom.

33   The Jews cannot understand that they must receive freedom as
a gift from Jesus, because they suppose that they have it already as
descendants of Abraham. There is a close parallel between this
passage, and the argument in Paul's letter to the Galatians, note
particularly Gal. 5^1 ('For freedom Christ has set us free; stand fast
therefore, and do not submit again to a yoke of slavery').

ff.   Jesus explains in what sense they are slaves, i.e. as sinners; and he
contrasts slaves who may be expelled from a household, with sons
who are not (Barrett recalls Gen. $21^{9 \text{ff.}}$ and Gal. 4^{30}—Ishmael and
Isaac).

37   Jesus returns to the Jews' assertion (v. 33) that they are descendants

you are descendants of Abraham; yet you seek to kill me,
38 because my word finds no place in you. I speak of what I have
seen with my Father, and you do what you have heard from
your father.'

39   They answered him, 'Abraham is our father.' Jesus said to
them, 'If you were Abraham's children, you would do what
40 Abraham did, but now you seek to kill me, a man who has
told you the truth which I heard from God; this is not what
41 Abraham did. You do what your father did.' They said to
him, 'We were not born of fornication; we have one Father,
42 even God.' Jesus said to them, 'If God were your Father,
you would love me, for I proceeded and came forth from
43 God; I came not of my own accord, but he sent me. Why do
you not understand what I say? It is because you cannot bear
44 to hear my word. You are of your father the devil, and your

---

of Abraham, and he admits that this is so, though only in a limited
physical sense: they are not like Abraham (see v. 39), but are seeking
to kill Jesus. His teaching cannot be accepted by them, because they
have no faith to receive it—unlike Abraham.

38   Jesus is speaking about life (8^{12}) and truth (8^{32}) and his Father is
God: the Jews are children of the devil; he is a murderer and a liar
(8^{44}), and they take after him.

39 f.   The Jews misunderstand 'your father' (v. 38) as if it were a reference
to Abraham, and this provides the cue for Jesus' explanation of the
cryptic saying in v. 38. *what Abraham did* = 'he believed the Lord'
(Gen. 15^6).

41   *your father* here = the devil, but this is still left without explanation,
and therefore provides an opportunity for misunderstanding; the
Jews now claim that they are the children of *God*.

42   Jesus is the Son of God; therefore if the Jews were children of God
they would love his Son, their brother.

43   The gulf between Jesus and the Jews is similar to that between
people who do not speak the same language: the cause of it is the
demand which Jesus makes that the Jews should see themselves as
slaves in need of liberation ($8^{31\,\text{ff.}}$); they *cannot bear* to understand themselves in this way.

44   This verse explains the enigmatic statements which have been made

will is to do your father's desires. He was a murderer from the
beginning, and has nothing to do with the truth, because
there is no truth in him. When he lies, he speaks according
45 to his own nature, for he is a liar and the father of lies. But,
46 because I tell the truth, you do not believe me. Which of you
convicts me of sin? If I tell the truth, why do you not believe
47 me? He who is of God hears the words of God; the reason
why you do not hear them is that you are not of God.'

48 The Jews answered him, 'Are we not right in saying that
49 you are a Samaritan and have a demon?' Jesus answered, 'I
have not a demon; but I honour my Father, and you dishonour
50 me. Yet I do not seek my own glory; there is One who seeks
51 it and he will be the judge. Truly, truly, I say to you, if any
52 one keeps my word, he will never see death.' The Jews said
to him, 'Now we know that you have a demon. Abraham
died, as did the prophets; and you say, "If any one keeps my

---

in vv. 31 ff. For the devil as *a murderer from the beginning*, see Gen. 3; and
as *a liar*, note Gen. 3⁴ ('You will not die').

45   They are wholly engulfed in deceit, and therefore incapable of
believing in the truth, i.e. the revelation which is Jesus himself.

5 f.   It is not the sinfulness of Jesus that leads the Jews to seek to kill him,
but their own wickedness. Jesus (and the believer) are of God, and
hear the words of God (vv. 38, 42); the Jews (and all unbelievers)
cannot obey God.

48   The Jews now turn Jesus' statements about them back on him, and
say that he is a *Samaritan* (i.e. of mixed birth: cp. 4¹⁷ f., 8⁴¹) and in the
power of the devil (cp. v. 44).

49   Jesus honours his Father by his obedience to him; the Jews dishonour Jesus, e.g. in their accusation in the previous verse.

50   The honour of Jesus is not self-centred like that of the Jews (5⁴⁴),
but it comes from God; therefore God will judge the Jews.

51   *Truly, truly* introduces a further claim of Jesus (see note on 1⁵¹),
which was already implied in v. 12 ('he who follows me . . . will have
the light of life').

2 f.   This claim is wrongly understood to mean deliverance from the
death of the body, but rightly as an assertion that Jesus is greater than
Abraham and the prophets (cp. 4¹²).

53 word, he will never taste death." Are you greater than our
father Abraham, who died? And the prophets died! Who do
54 you claim to be?' Jesus answered, 'If I glorify myself, my
glory is nothing; it is my Father who glorifies me, of whom
55 you say that he is your God. But you have not known him;
I know him. If I said, I do not know him, I should be a liar
56 like you; but I do know him and I keep his word. Your
father Abraham rejoiced that he was to see my day; he saw it
57 and was glad.' The Jews then said to him, 'You are not yet
58 fifty years old, and have you seen Abraham?'[u] Jesus said to
them, 'Truly, truly, I say to you, before Abraham was, I am.'
59 So they took up stones to throw at him; but Jesus hid himself, and went out of the temple.

9: 2   As he passed by, he saw a man blind from his birth. And

[u] Other ancient authorities read *has Abraham seen you?*

---

54 f.   Jesus' glory depends wholly on the Father, whose agent he is, and
from whom he has received everything. He cannot deny his obedience
to the Father, which is the fact that distinguishes him from them.
56   Apparently Gen. 24[1] ('Now Abraham was old, well advanced in
years'—literally 'He went into the days') was interpreted by some of
the rabbis as meaning that the age to come was revealed to Abraham.
57   The reading in the margin is probably a correction. The Jews think
that Jesus meant that he was a contemporary of Abraham, whereas
in fact v. 56 referred to supernatural foresight granted to Abraham.
58   Jesus existed from eternity (cp. 1[1]); Abraham, like John the Baptist
(1[6, 15]) came into existence in time.
59   Stoning was the punishment for blasphemy (see Lev. 24[16]). Jesus
hides himself, because the time for his death has not yet come (cp. 7[30],
etc.); this concealment of himself is probably meant to be understood
as a 'supernatural disappearance' (Barrett, p. 292), as otherwise John
would have written 'Jesus went out of the temple and hid himself'
(cp. Dodd, *HTFG*, p. 181, n. 1).

9: 1–4 *The gift of faith*

In 8[12] Jesus had said 'I am the light of the world'; he now
repeats this statement (9[5]), and demonstrates it symbolically

his disciples asked him, 'Rabbi, who sinned, this man or his
3 parents, that he was born blind?' Jesus answered, 'It was not

---

by giving sight to a man born blind: just as light means more
than physical illumination in the saying of Jesus, so sight means
more than bodily seeing in the narrative. The discussions which
follow the miracle, between the Pharisees, the blind man, and
his parents, make it clear that seeing is to be understood as a
symbol of faith, and the climax of the whole story comes in
v. 38, 'Lord, I believe'. But there is more to the narrative than
this; light involves judgement, and the gift of faith has the
side-effect of stimulating others to unbelief. There is thus a
second climax in the question of the Pharisees, 'Are we also
blind?' and the answer of Jesus, 'If you were blind, you would
have no guilt; but now that you say, "We see", your guilt
remains' (vv. 40 f.). This use of a miracle-story to convey an
understanding of the nature of faith and unbelief is not peculiar
to this Gospel; compare, for example, the way in which Mark
has placed side by side the healing of the blind man at
Bethsaida and Peter's confession of faith (Mark 8$^{22-30}$), or
Matthew's story of the healing of a blind and dumb man immediately before the Pharisees' charge that Jesus casts out demons
by Beelzebul (Matt. 12$^{22-32}$). The meaning of these passages,
and of the story in John 9, is summed up in the saying of Jesus
'For judgement I came into this world, that those who do
not see may see, and that those who see may become blind'
(v. 39). The background of this chapter is extremely complex,
but some of the elements in it may be analysed as follows:

(a) The miracles of Elisha in 2 Kgs. 5, 6: Naaman's leprosy is
cleansed by washing, but is transferred to Gehazi; the eyes of
his servant are opened, but the Syrians are blinded (Guilding,
pp. 121 ff.).

(b) The prophecies that the blind will see in the last days:
e.g. Isa. 35^5 ('Then the eyes of the blind shall be opened'),
where sight stands for 'knowledge of God and righteousness
of the heart' (Hoskyns, p. 402).

(c) The accounts of the healing of the blind in the Synoptic
Gospels, particularly in Mark 8$^{22\,\text{ff.}}$, 10$^{46\,\text{ff.}}$ (see note on v. 8).

(d) The experience of conversion in the early Church, and
of the persecution of Christian converts by the Jews. John 9 is

that this man sinned, or his parents, but that the works of
4 God might be made manifest in him. We must work the
works of him who sent me, while it is day; night comes, when
5 no one can work. As long as I am in the world, I am the light
6 of the world.' As he said this, he spat on the ground and made

---

probably unique in the four Gospels in that Jesus is 'off-stage'
from v. 8 to v. 34: attention is fixed on the man who was blind
and now sees, and on the attitude of the Jews to him, and to
his parents (note 9²², ³⁴). 'The background of the narrative is
Christianity at the close of the first or the beginning of the
second century, engaged in a fierce battle with Judaism, felt
on both sides to be a battle to the death' (Hoskyns, p. 417).

(e) One of the words used for baptism in the early Church
is 'enlightenment' (Gk. φωτισμός), and a number of commentators have shown the parallels between Chapter 9 and Christian baptism (e.g. O. Cullmann, *Early Christian Worship* (London,
1953), pp. 102 ff.). It is highly likely that part of the background of this chapter is the belief of Christians that by baptism the convert became a new creation (see note on v. 9), and
the fact that as a result of baptism they were excluded from the
Synagogue.

1 f.   There is no break between 7, 8, and 9¹–10²¹; cp. 8¹² with 9⁵, and
9¹⁻⁴¹ with 10²¹. It is pointless to ask how the disciples knew that the man
had been born blind: John is not interested in the story for its own
sake, therefore he does not answer this kind of question; he is interested
in the symbolic significance of the narrative, and *blind from his birth*
links up with what was said about the Jews in the previous chapter,
e.g. 'You are of your father the devil' (8⁴⁴). Thus, the harsh things
which were said in Chapter 8 are somewhat softened in this chapter:
God has power to enlighten unbelief; this was hinted at in 8²⁸. The
disciples raise a question that was debated among the rabbis: If suffering is the punishment of sin, whose sin is punished by congenital
deformity—the sin of the parents or the ante-natal sin of the deformed
person?

3   Jesus directs the disciples from the theoretical problem to the
practical issue, What is to be done about this man's blindness? The
occasion is a providential opportunity for displaying *the works of God*:
cp. the similar idea in 11⁴.

4   *We* has been changed to 'I' in some of the MSS. and Versions, but
the plural is correct, and refers to Jesus and his disciples (cp. 3¹¹,

clay of the spittle and anointed the man's eyes with the clay,
7 saying to him, 'Go, wash in the pool of Siloam' (which means
8 Sent). So he went and washed and came back seeing. The
neighbours and those who had seen him before as a beggar,
9 said, 'Is not this the man who used to sit and beg?' Some said,
'It is he'; others said, 'No, but he is like him.' He said, 'I am
10 the man.' They said to him, 'Then how were your eyes
11 opened?' He answered, 'The man called Jesus made clay

14^{12}). *while it is day* means: (*a*) for Jesus, the time before the crucifixion
(see next verse); (*b*) for the disciples, the time before the judgement.
night comes: 'The night . . . suggests the Passion of the Christ and the
persecution or martyrdom of the Apostles' (Hoskyns, p. 407); and see
note on 3^2.

5   See note on 8^{12}.
6   For the use of spittle in healing, cp. Mark 7^{33}, 8^{23}, and the story of
Vespasian in Tacitus, *Histories*, iv. 81.
7   Cp. 2 Kgs. 5^{10} ('Go and wash in the Jordan seven times'). *the pool
of Siloam (which means Sent)*: the Hebrew word Shiloah is derived from
the verb 'to send', possibly because the pool was filled through a
conduit (2 Kgs. 20^{20}). The words in Gen. 49^{10} (RSV mg., 'until
Shiloh comes') were interpreted messianically; and there was a reference to the pool in Isa. 8^6, which John may have had in mind ('Because this people have refused the waters of Shiloah . . .'). Thus the
etymology of the word, and its use in the O.T., combine to lead John
to say that the name of the pool points to Jesus, the one who was *sent*
into the world by the Father.
8   John had not said before that the man was a *beggar*: he frequently
introduces details at a late point in his narrative, e.g. v. 14 (sabbath)
and see also 5^9, 6^{59}, 8^{20}. The word used here for *beggar* (Gk. προσαίτης)
is comparatively rare (elsewhere in N.T. it is used only of blind
Bartimaeus, Mark 10^{46}).
9   The power of Jesus makes the man different from what he was
before, just as the believer becomes a new man by conversion (cp.
2 Cor. 5^{17}); and the action of Jesus divides the people (cp. 7^{12}, etc.).
I am the man (literally, 'I am'; Gk. ἐγώ εἰμι as in 6^{35}, etc.): the words
probably have no theological connotation in this context.
10 f. At first the man accounts for his changed condition by stating the
facts; later in the chapter he will progress to faith, which is an insight
into the significance of the facts: see vv. 17, 31, 38.

and anointed my eyes and said to me, "Go to Siloam and
12 wash"; so I went and washed and received my sight.' They
said to him, 'Where is he?' He said, 'I do not know.'

13   They brought to the Pharisees the man who had formerly
14 been blind. Now it was a sabbath day when Jesus made the
15 clay and opened his eyes. The Pharisees again asked him
how he had received his sight. And he said to them, 'He put
16 clay on my eyes, and I washed, and I see.' Some of the Pharisees said, 'This man is not from God, for he does not keep
the sabbath.' But others said, 'How can a man who is a sinner
17 do such signs?' There was a division among them. So they
again said to the blind man, 'What do you say about him,
since he has opened your eyes?' He said, 'He is a prophet.'

18   The Jews did not believe that he had been blind and had
received his sight, until they called the parents of the man
19 who had received his sight, and asked them, 'Is this your son,
who you say was born blind? How then does he now see?'
20 His parents answered, 'We know that this is our son, and

---

12   *Where is he? . . . I do not know*: as well as the literal meaning of these words (cp. $5^{12 f.}$), there is, in the light of 7^{34}, 8^{29}, a possible further sense: the man does not yet know that Jesus is 'with the Father', i.e. that he is the agent and Revealer of God.

13 f.   See note on v. 8. It was forbidden to make clay or to anoint eyes on the sabbath. For the significance of Jesus' healings on the sabbath, see note on 5^{17}.

15   See note on vv. 10 f. above.

16   Cp. 7^{43}, 10^{19}: Jesus divides men into those who reject him because they cling to what they have received (in this case, the Law of Moses), and those who are open to new possibilities in faith.

17   *He is a prophet* is an intermediary step towards a more adequate statement of faith (cp. v. 38).

18 f.   The Pharisees attempt to discredit the facts, but the only result of their efforts is to establish them all the more certainly.

20 f.   The parents bear witness to what is within their experience, viz. the identity of the man and the fact that he was born blind: they leave the man himself to testify concerning his cure.

21 that he was born blind; but how he now sees we do not know,
   nor do we know who opened his eyes. Ask him; he is of age,
22 he will speak for himself.' His parents said this because they
   feared the Jews, for the Jews had already agreed that if any
   one should confess him to be Christ, he was to be put out of
23 the synagogue. Therefore his parents said, 'He is of age, ask
   him.'

24   So for the second time they called the man who had been
   blind, and said to him, 'Give God the praise; we know that
25 this man is a sinner.' He answered, 'Whether he is a sinner,
   I do not know; one thing I know, that though I was blind,
26 now I see.' They said to him, 'What did he do to you? How
27 did he open your eyes?' He answered them, 'I have told you
   already, and you would not listen. Why do you want to hear
28 it again? Do you too want to become his disciples?' And they

---

2 f.   John explains the parents' unwillingness to enter further into the
discussions, but his explanation is much coloured by the relationship
between the Church and the Synagogue in the period after *c.* A.D. 85,
when the Jews introduced a form of words into part of their Liturgy,
the Eighteen Benedictions, which made it impossible for Jewish
Christians to attend the Synagogues any longer;[1] similarly, *confess him
to be Christ* is a formulation which was not used until after the resurrection. See also 12[42], 16[2].

24   *Give God the praise*: compare the similar expression in Joshua 7[19]; in
both passages it means 'Speak the truth'. Jesus is *a sinner* in their view
because he has broken the sabbath law: see 9[13–16].

25   The man is certain only of the evidence of his eyes, and he will not
and cannot go back on that.

26   The Jews must attempt to destroy the facts, because the facts might
lead to faith, and to the conclusion that the Law had been superseded
by Christ; they therefore ask the man to repeat what happened, in the
hope that they will find a way of discrediting his statement.

27   The man brings out the irony of the situation: the Jews are forcing
him into the role of an evangelist.

28   See 1[17], for the antithesis, Moses and Jesus.

[1] Benediction 12. For a translation of it, see e.g. C. K. Barrett, *The New
Testament Background: Selected Documents* (London, 1956), pp. 166 f.

reviled him, saying, 'You are his disciple, but we are disciples
29 of Moses. We know that God has spoken to Moses, but as for
30 this man, we do not know where he comes from.' The man
answered, 'Why, this is a marvel! You do not know where he
31 comes from, and yet he opened my eyes. We know that God
does not listen to sinners, but if any one is a worshipper of
32 God and does his will, God listens to him. Never since the
world began has it been heard that any one opened the eyes of
33 a man born blind. If this man were not from God, he could
34 do nothing.' They answered him, 'You were born in utter
sin, and would you teach us?' And they cast him out.

35   Jesus heard that they had cast him out, and having found
36 him he said, 'Do you believe in the Son of man?'*v* He
answered, 'And who is he, sir, that I may believe in him?'
37 Jesus said to him, 'You have seen him, and it is he who
38 speaks to you.' He said, 'Lord, I believe'; and he worshipped

v Other ancient authorities read *the Son of God*

---

29   This verse means: We believe that the Law comes with the authority
of God, but we do not believe this about Jesus.
30 ff.   The man now draws out the significance and implication of the
facts to which he has adhered throughout.
34   The Jews, on the other hand, draw out the implication (as they
believe) of the man's congenital blindness: his birth was the result of
sin (cp. v. 2); therefore he is not a person to whom they need pay
attention.
35   *found him*: cp. 5¹⁴; some of the commentators compare Luke 15⁴,
the shepherd finding the lost sheep (Strachan, p. 220; Barrett, p. 304).
the Son of man (RSV text) is probably correct, and has been changed
to 'the Son of God' (RSV mg.) in some MSS. and Versions; on the
meaning of the former title, see note on 1⁵¹.
36   The man already believes that Jesus is a prophet (9¹⁷) and 'from God'
(9³³); he is therefore willing to learn from Jesus who *the Son of man* is.
37   The man has *seen him*, and been spoken to by him, entirely through
the initiative of Jesus, who first opened his eyes and later 'found him'
(v. 35).
38   'The blind man, who has passed from Judaism to Christianity,
passes out of the story as the typical believer, the worshipper of God in

39 him. Jesus said, 'For judgment I came into this world, that those who do not see may see, and that those who see may
40 become blind.' Some of the Pharisees near him heard this,
41 and they said to him, 'Are we also blind?' Jesus said to them, 'If you were blind, you would have no guilt; but now that you say, "We see," your guilt remains.

10 'TRULY, truly, I say to you, he who does not enter the sheepfold by the door but climbs in by another way, that man
2 is a thief and a robber; but he who enters by the door is the

---

Spirit and in Truth. This is the climax of the narrative and the purpose for which it was told' (Hoskyns, p. 415).

39   Jesus speaks an enigmatic generalizing conclusion to the incident: he has come to bring sight (i.e. understanding, salvation) to the blind (i.e. sinners), and, inevitably, blindness (i.e. unbelief, condemnation) to those who think they see (e.g. the Pharisees).

f.   The enigma of the previous verse is explained in answer to the Pharisees' question: they do not use the light they have (i.e. the Law which points to Jesus, 5[39, 46]); they are not therefore totally blind, and so they are guilty of their unbelief.

0: 1–21 *The shepherd and the sheep*

In order to understand the discourse on the shepherd and the sheep, it is important to remember that it is spoken to the Pharisees (see 9[40] = 'them' (10[6, 7]) = 'the Jews' (10[19])). There is no break between Chapters 9 and 10, but the monologue in Chapter 10 follows on directly from the dialogue in Chapter 9, as in earlier sections of the Gospel (e.g. 3[1–21], 5[10 ff.]). The purpose of the discourse is to contrast the relationship between the Pharisees and the people with the relationship between Jesus and the believers. The Pharisees are those who do not enter by the door; they are thieves and robbers, strangers, hirelings: Jesus is the one who enters by the door, the shepherd, and the door of the sheepfold. The various analogies which are used in this section point to the authority of Jesus, and to the purpose for which he uses it: his authority is like that of the sheep-owner, and it is recognized as such by those who belong to him; the

3 shepherd of the sheep. To him the gatekeeper opens; the
sheep hear his voice, and he calls his own sheep by name and

12. Mosaic in the Basilica of St. Apollinare in Classe, Ravenna; sixth century

purpose for which he uses it is the welfare of the sheep, for
whom he lays down his life.

The background of the discourse is to be found partly in
the Old Testament (e.g. Ezek. 34, 37[16 ff.]) and partly in the
Synoptic tradition (e.g. Mark 6[34], 14[27], Luke 15[3-7]). J. A. T.
Robinson (*Twelve New Testament Studies* (London, 1962), pp.
67 ff.) and C. H. Dodd (*HTFG*, pp. 382 ff.) have suggested that 'we
have in verses 1–5 the wreckage of two parables fused into one,
the fusion having partly destroyed the original form of both'
(Dodd, *HTFG*, p. 383); but, as C. K. Barrett has pointed out,
neither these verses nor the section as a whole is much like the
synoptic parables. There is no story or description of a particular shepherd. . . .' (in *Peake's Commentary on the Bible* (edited by
M. Black) (London, 1962), p. 856). It should also be remembered that the figure of the shepherd is common in hellenistic
writings, where it is used of gods and kings and great men.

1 f.   The discourse begins with the distinction between *a thief and a robber*
on the one hand, and *the shepherd* on the other; and the distinction is
defined in terms of the manner in which each comes to the *sheepfold*—
by the door, or by another way. Allegorical interpretation must not
be applied yet, or confusion will follow. The only point which is being
made here is that the Pharisees have no legitimate authority over
Israel: they seek their own advantage (cp. e.g. Matt. 23, Mark 12[38ff.])
whereas Jesus has the right of entry into the fold.

4 leads them out. When he has brought out all his own, he goes
before them, and the sheep follow him, for they know his
5 voice. A stranger they will not follow, but they will flee from
6 him, for they do not know the voice of strangers.' This figure
Jesus used with them, but they did not understand what he
was saying to them.

7   So Jesus again said to them, 'Truly, truly, I say to you,
8 I am the door of the sheep. All who came before me are
9 thieves and robbers; but the sheep did not heed them. I am
the door; if any one enters by me, he will be saved, and will
0 go in and out and find pasture. The thief comes only to steal
and kill and destroy; I came that they may have life, and have

---

3   *he calls his own sheep by name* apparently need not mean that each
sheep has its own name, but that he calls them 'one by one' (Dodd,
HTFG, p. 384, n. 4). The authority of the shepherd is recognized in
three ways: (*a*) in the analogy, by the gate-keeper and by the sheep;
(*b*) in the Gospel, by the man born blind (9³⁸); and (*c*) in the Church,
by all who believe in Jesus and follow him.

5   Those who have not the authority of Jesus are not followed—e.g.
the man born blind has not agreed with the opinion of the Pharisees
that Jesus is a sinner (9²⁴ ᶠᶠ·); and believers (at the time when John is
writing) have stopped obeying the Law as the rabbis expound it.

6   The word translated *figure* (Gk. παροιμία, see also 16²⁵, ²⁹), probably
means exactly the same as 'parable' (Gk. παραβολή), the word
frequently used by the Synoptists but never by John. *they did not
understand* because *they* (= the Pharisees) did not belong to his sheep
(v. 26).

f.   *I am the door of the sheep* is the third of the 'I am' sayings (see note on
6³⁵), and it refers back to v. 1. The meaning of the saying at this point
in the discourse is that all authority over the flock has been given to
Jesus, and those who do not come in his name and through him, are
illegitimate claimants and pseudo-pastors, unsuccessful in their dealings with *the sheep* (= the elect).

9   He is also *the door* for the sheep to pass through (cp. v. 3); that
is, he is 'the way' of their salvation (14⁶) and the means of their
sustenance.

0   The distinction is now made between the purposes of the two kinds
of entrant into the sheepfold which were mentioned in vv. 1 f.

11 it abundantly. I am the good shepherd. The good shepherd
12 lays down his life for the sheep. He who is a hireling and not a
shepherd, whose own the sheep are not, sees the wolf coming
and leaves the sheep and flees; and the wolf snatches them
13 and scatters them. He flees because he is a hireling and cares
14 nothing for the sheep. I am the good shepherd; I know my
15 own and my own know me, as the Father knows me and I
16 know the Father; and I lay down my life for the sheep. And
I have other sheep, that are not of this fold; I must bring
them also, and they will heed my voice. So there shall be one
17 flock, one shepherd. For this reason the Father loves me,
18 because I lay down my life, that I may take it again. No one
takes it from me, but I lay it down of my own accord. I have
power to lay it down, and I have power to take it again; this
charge I have received from my Father.'

19   There was again a division among the Jews because of
20 these words. Many of them said, 'He has a demon, and he is

---

11   The fourth 'I am' saying (see note on 6[35]) identifies Jesus as 'the
shepherd of the sheep' mentioned in v. 2. In contrast with the thief
he fulfils his purpose of giving them life (v. 10) by surrendering his
own life for them.

12 f.   The *hireling*, that is the man who is hired and paid by the owner of
the sheep, is a new character in the discourse; there is a close parallel
to the thought of these verses in 1 Pet. 5[1-4, 8].

14   See note on v. 11. *I know my own and my own know me* returns to the
idea in vv. 4 f.

15   The communion between Jesus and the believers is analogous to
the communion between Jesus and the Father; in both cases it is a
relationship which belongs to the realm of faith, and issues in
obedience (cp. v. 11).

16   The *other sheep* are the Gentile believers, who are to be united with
the Jewish disciples in one body, the Church (cp. 17[20 ff.]).

17 f.   The believer sees in the death and resurrection of Jesus the willing
obedience of the Son to the Father and the eternal relationship of love
between them, which reaches out to embrace others.

19   See 7[43], 9[16].

20 f.   Cp. 7[20]; the claims of Jesus seem absurd to the unbeliever. On the

1 mad; why listen to him?' Others said, 'These are not the
sayings of one who has a demon. Can a demon open the eyes
of the blind?'

3   It was the feast of the Dedication at Jerusalem; it was
winter, and Jesus was walking in the temple, in the portico of
4 Solomon. So the Jews gathered round him and said to him,
'How long will you keep us in suspense? If you are the Christ,
5 tell us plainly.' Jesus answered them, 'I told you, and you do
not believe. The works that I do in my Father's name, they
6 bear witness to me; but you do not believe, because you do
7 not belong to my sheep. My sheep hear my voice, and I know
8 them, and they follow me; and I give them eternal life, and
they shall never perish, and no one shall snatch them out of

---

other hand, the fact that the blind man was cured argues against the
explanation that Jesus is both bad and mad (cp. $9^{32 \, f.}$).

): 22–42 *The rejection of Jesus*

   This section of the Gospel opens with a reference to time and
place—the feast of Dedication, and the portico of Solomon.
The former creates a problem; it has been argued that Chapter
9 follows on directly from Chapters 7 and 8, and that 10^{1-21}
follows Chapter 9 without a break; similarly $10^{22 \, ff.}$ can be
regarded as the continuation of the previous section (note
$10^{27 \, ff.}$). There is, therefore, no break in time between the references to Tabernacles ($7^{2 \, ff.}$) and Dedication (10^{22}), i.e. between
autumn and winter; it was not John's intention to record the
exact time of the events in his Gospel, but to relate the words
of Jesus to the Jewish festivals in a theological, rather than a
chronological, manner. Some commentators, for example, see
a connection between Dedication (v. 22) and the consecration
of Jesus (v. 36). In the same way, the reference to the portico of
Solomon may be more than an identification of place: Solomon
had built the temple which David his father had planned (e.g.
1 Kgs. $8^{17 \, ff.}$), and Jesus similarly is doing the works of his Father
(v. 37).

29 my hand. My Father, who has given them to me,*w* is greater
than all, and no one is able to snatch them out of the Father's
30 hand. I and the Father are one.'

    w Other ancient authorities read *What my Father has given to me*

The Jews ask Jesus to tell them plainly whether he is the
Messiah (he has claimed as much in the figure or parable in
the previous section). He says that he has told them, both by his
words and by his deeds, but they do not believe because they
are not of the number of the elect, whereas those who are
chosen are in the protection of Jesus, and of the Father. This
leads to the claim of Jesus, 'I and the Father are one', which
provokes a further attempt by the Jews to destroy him, for
blasphemy. Jesus replies that he is not blaspheming; he is the
Son of God, and his deeds show it.

This section ends where the public ministry of Jesus began,
in the place where John the Baptist bore witness to him.

22   The Hebrew name for the festival is *Hanukkah*, and it began on
25th Chisler and continued eight days; it celebrated the re-dedication
of the temple in 164 B.C., three years to the day after its profanation
by Antiochus Epiphanes (see 1 Macc. 4$^{52\,ff.}$).

23   *the portico of Solomon* is mentioned in Acts 3^{11}, 5^{12} as the place where
Christians assembled and Josephus also refers to it; but apart from
these references, nothing further is known about it.

24   *plainly* (Gk. παρρησίᾳ): cp. 16$^{25,\,29}$ where speaking 'plainly' is contrasted with speaking 'in figures'. The Jews are asking Jesus to say
that the shepherd (v. 2) in the figure or parable (v. 6) which he has
recently used means *the Christ*.

25 f.   Jesus has told them that he is the shepherd (vv. 11, 14) and therefore the Christ, but his words fall on deaf (i.e. unbelieving) ears, just
as the deeds which he does in obedience to the Father are not perceived as evidence of his unique status by those who are unbelievers,
and therefore blind.

27 f.   These two verses recapitulate some of the points made in the
previous section; for *My sheep hear my voice*, see v. 3; for *I know them*, see
v. 14; for *they follow me*, see v. 4; for *I give them eternal life*, see vv. 10 f.;
for *no one shall snatch them*, see v. 12. V. 28 is an assurance to the elect
that Christ will keep them from evil for ever (cp. Rom 8$^{35\,ff.}$ 'Who
shall separate us from the love of Christ? . . .').

29 f.   There are five variant readings in the first sentence of this verse;
and it has been argued recently[1] that the original reading was 'My

    [1] J. N. Birdsall, 'John X. 29', *JTS*, NS, xi. 2 (October 1960), pp. 342–4.

32 The Jews took up stones again to stone him. Jesus answered them, 'I have shown you many good works from the Father;
33 for which of these do you stone me?' The Jews answered him, 'We stone you for no good work but for blasphemy; because
34 you, being a man, make yourself God.' Jesus answered them,
35 'Is it not written in your law, "I said, you are gods"? If he called them gods to whom the word of God came (and scrip-
36 ture cannot be broken), do you say of him whom the Father consecrated and sent into the world, "You are blaspheming,"
37 because I said, "I am the Son of God"? If I am not doing the
38 works of my Father, then do not believe me; but if I do them,

---

Father, in regard to what he has given me, is greater than all'. (This is the text of ℵ and W). The gift of the Father is either the sheep (see 17⁶, etc.) or authority to be the Saviour (see 3³⁴ᶠ·, etc.); the two ideas are both referred to in 17², where Jesus says to the Father concerning himself, 'Thou hast given him power over all flesh, to give eternal life to all whom thou hast given him.' The unity of Father and Son is a unity of love and obedience (cp. v. 15) and this unity is the basis of the assurance which the believer has that Christ will keep him for ever in safety; he believes that God was in Christ (cp. 2 Cor. 5¹⁹).

31 The previous reference to an attempt to stone Jesus was at 8⁵⁹, and there too it was provoked by the claim of Jesus to a unique relationship to God, which appeared blasphemous to the Jews. Barrett (p. 318) thinks that John assumed that stoning was 'a matter of lynch law' and says that this 'fits ill with the view that he was himself a Jew who had lived in Palestine before A.D. 70'.

f. These two verses express on the one hand the believers' and on the other hand the unbelievers' attitude to Jesus: the former regard him as the Revealer sent by the Father, to bring life to the world, and wrongly put to death; the latter regard him as a blasphemer, a man who claimed to be God. See also 5¹⁸.

36 The quotation is from Ps. 82⁶, in which the rulers and judges of Israel are addressed as *gods*. The argument is *a fortiori*: if those who received the Law (= *the word of God*) are called *gods*, how much more is it right that the unique agent of God (called 'the Word' in 1¹, ¹⁴) should speak of himself as *the Son of God*?

f. The works of Jesus show that he is the Son and agent of God in the world, and are a way in to faith and knowledge.

even though you do not believe me, believe the works, that
you may know and understand that the Father is in me and
39 I am in the Father.' Again they tried to arrest him, but he
escaped from their hands.

40   He went away again across the Jordan to the place where
41 John at first baptized, and there he remained. And many
came to him; and they said, 'John did no sign, but everything
42 that John said about this man was true.' And many believed
in him there.

11 Now a certain man was ill, Lazarus of Bethany, the village
2 of Mary and her sister Martha. It was Mary who anointed the

---

39   For previous unsuccessful attempts to silence him, see 7^{30}, $8^{20, 59}$, 10^{31}.
40   See 1^{28}.
41 f.   The Baptist's purpose was 'that he [i.e. Jesus] might be revealed to
Israel' (1^{31}). The Evangelist assures his readers that this has been fulfilled, although the Jewish leaders have not received Jesus. In the
place where John was heard bearing witness, many now believe—
though it should be noticed that their faith is still inadequate and
imperfect: see note on 8^{30}.

11: 1–44 *The raising of Lazarus*

The raising of Lazarus is the last miracle of Jesus which John
records. He departs from his usual practice of attaching dialogue to narrative, and instead combines the two elements in
such a way that it is now impossible to separate a basic story
from the Johannine commentary written around it.

There is perhaps a progression in the order of the miracles in
this Gospel, from the first which involves material things
(water and wine), through sickness and lameness, hunger and
blindness, to life for the dead (cp. 1 Cor. 15^{26}, 'The last enemy
to be destroyed is death'). And, as we have seen already on a
number of occasions (e.g. $10^{31, 39}$), the greater the revelation
which Jesus gives, the greater the opposition to him; so the
last miracle finally provokes the Jews to put into effect their
desire to destroy Jesus ($11^{45 \text{ ff.}}$).

Nevertheless, it would be wrong to think of the raising of
Lazarus as simply the climax of the miracles in this Gospel.

The interpretation which John gives directs the reader to a different understanding of the incident; it is not so much the power of Jesus displayed in calling a dead man to life that John puts before us, as the belief which is symbolized by this miracle, namely, that the disciple is united with Christ in such a way that death cannot separate them; or, as John puts it, that the believer 'shall never die'. This interpretation is given in the conversation between Jesus and Martha, and in the saying 'I am the resurrection'. The raising of Lazarus is therefore not to be considered as if it were simply a wonder performed by Jesus, but as a sign which shows that the result of faith is the eternal life of the believer in the present time: he need not wait for it until 'the resurrection at the last day'.

The significance of the sign does not depend on the historicity of the miracle; but it is fair to ask whether the story of the raising of Lazarus is historical. On the one hand, it is possible to point to stories of raising the dead in the Synoptic Gospels (e.g. Mark 5³⁵ ff·, Luke 7¹¹ ff·) and the saying 'The dead are raised up' (Matt. 11⁵ = Luke 7²²); and to argue that John would not have recorded the story if he had not believed that it had happened, because his whole case is that the Word was made flesh and manifested his glory in historical events. On the other hand, it must be said that there is no room (as it were) for the raising of Lazarus in the Synoptic accounts, according to which the Jews take action against Jesus as a result of the cleansing of the temple rather than the restoration of Lazarus; that in Luke (16¹⁹ ff·) there is a parable concerning one Lazarus, who, it is suggested, might rise from the dead, and that John has written this story to show that people will not be convinced 'if some one should rise from the dead'; and that elsewhere in his Gospel John does manipulate history for the purpose of proclamation. Dr. Dodd's conclusion on this point is 'that the story of Lazarus, however deeply stamped with the character of Johannine theological ideas and with the language appropriate to them, is not an original allegorical creation' (*HTFG*, p. 232). Dr. Barrett's is 'that we have no means of investigating the peculiarly Johannine traditions before they were written down in the Gospel' (*Peake's Commentary on the Bible* (edited by M. Black) (London, 1962), p. 858).

ff.   John summarizes the story of the anointing which he will tell in full in 12¹ ff·. See also Luke 10³⁸ ff·.

Lord with ointment and wiped his feet with her hair, whose
3 brother Lazarus was ill. So the sisters sent to him, saying,
4 'Lord, he whom you love is ill.' But when Jesus heard it he
said, 'This illness is not unto death; it is for the glory of God,
so that the Son of God may be glorified by means of it.'

5, 6   Now Jesus loved Martha and her sister and Lazarus. So
when he heard that he was ill, he stayed two days longer in
7 the place where he was. Then after this he said to the dis-
8 ciples, 'Let us go into Judea again.' The disciples said to him,
'Rabbi, the Jews were but now seeking to stone you, and are
9 you going there again?' Jesus answered, 'Are there not

---

4   An example of John's use of ambiguity: Lazarus' illness will lead to
his death, but death will be seen to have no power over him when
Jesus is present; in that sense, *This illness is not unto death*. But John has
another meaning in his mind, as the latter part of the verse shows: the
raising of Lazarus will provoke the Jewish leaders into putting Jesus to
death; and the death of Jesus is the way in which he glorifies God and
is himself glorified—see 17[1], and compare the similar theological
introduction to the story of the blind man in 9[3 ff.].

5   John assures the reader of Jesus' love for the sisters and Lazarus, in
order that it may not be thought that Jesus remained where he was
(v. 6) because he was unconcerned for them. John is thus inviting the
reader to look for a deeper reason for the Lord's delay. (The statement
in this verse that *Jesus loved . . . Lazarus*, cp. vv. 3, 11, 36, is taken by
some scholars as evidence that *the disciple whom Jesus loved* refers to
Lazarus, and that he was the author of this Gospel; e.g. F. V. Filson,
A New Testament History (London, 1965), pp. 372 f.: see Introduction,
p. 12.)

6   For Jesus' initial refusal to do what he is asked to do, and his subsequent compliance, see also 2[3 ff.], 4[47 ff.], 7[1 ff.]. *in the place where he was*: i.e.
'Bethany beyond the Jordan' (1[28], 10[40]).

7   At first, Jesus does not explain to the disciples the purpose of their
journey to Judea, but the reader knows (or soon will) that it is twofold: to raise Lazarus from the dead; and to die and be raised to life
himself.

8   The disciples therefore, accepting the assurance in v. 4 that
Lazarus' illness will not be fatal, express their concern for the safety
of Jesus in Judea. For the previous reference to stoning, see 10[31].

9f.   Another ambiguous saying (cp. v. 4), similar in many respects to

twelve hours in the day? If any one walks in the day, he does
10 not stumble, because he sees the light of this world. But if any
one walks in the night, he stumbles, because the light is not
11 in him.' Thus he spoke, and then he said to them, 'Our
friend Lazarus has fallen asleep, but I go to awake him out of
12 sleep.' The disciples said to him, 'Lord, if he has fallen asleep,
13 he will recover.' Now Jesus had spoken of his death, but they
14 thought that he meant taking rest in sleep. Then Jesus told
15 them plainly, 'Lazarus is dead; and for your sake I am glad
that I was not there, so that you may believe. But let us go to
16 him.' Thomas, called the Twin, said to his fellow disciples,
'Let us also go, that we may die with him.'

17   Now when Jesus came, he found that Lazarus[x] had already

x Greek *he*

9[4 f.] which see: on one level it means simply that he will be safe in the
daytime; but the 'technical' words *hour, day, walk, stumble, night, light,*
suggest another meaning: Jesus' life-time is the *day,* and he is *the light;*
he must obey the Father and go to Judea to work the works of him
who sent him, and the disciples need have no fear for themselves,
because they are with him.

11 ff.   Yet another ambiguous statement (*sleep* = die; *awake* = raise to
life), which the disciples misunderstand, though even their misunderstanding is true, ironically, i.e. in a sense which they do not intend:
he will recover (Gk. σωθήσεται) also means 'he will be saved'.

14   For the contrast between speaking in parables and ambiguities, and
speaking *plainly,* see also notes on 10[24], 16[25, 29].

15   Jesus assumes that if he had been present, Lazarus would not have
died (cp. vv. 21, 32). Lazarus' death and return to life will be the
occasion for faith on the part of the disciples. *But let us go to him*
explains what was meant by 'Let us go into Judea again' in v. 7.

16   Thomas's remark is both a misunderstanding, because it seizes only
on the death of Lazarus (and of Jesus), and an unintentional statement of faith, because the essence of discipleship is dying with Christ
(cp. e.g. Col. 2[20]). *Thomas* (the name means *Twin* in Aramaic), is
mentioned here for the first time in this Gospel: see also 14[5], 20[24 ff.], 21[2].

17   There is some evidence that the Jews believed that the soul finally
left the vicinity of the body three days after death; this verse will,
therefore, heighten the miracle which is to be recorded.

18 been in the tomb four days. Bethany was near Jerusalem,
19 about two miles*y* off, and many of the Jews had come to
Martha and Mary to console them concerning their brother.
20 When Martha heard that Jesus was coming, she went and met
21 him, while Mary sat in the house. Martha said to Jesus, 'Lord,
22 if you had been here, my brother would not have died. And
even now I know that whatever you ask from God, God will
23 give you.' Jesus said to her, 'Your brother will rise again.'
24 Martha said to him, 'I know that he will rise again in the
25 resurrection at the last day.' Jesus said to her, 'I am the
resurrection and the life;*z* he who believes in me, though he
26 die, yet shall he live, and whoever lives and believes in me

y Greek *fifteen stadia*
z Other ancient authorities omit *and the life*

---

18 f.   This *Bethany* is mentioned in John also at 11¹ and 12¹; its proximity
to Jerusalem explains the presence of many of *the Jews*, and the
'danger' to which Jesus is exposing himself (see v. 8).

20   Compare the similar picture of Martha and Mary in Luke 10³⁸ ff..

21 f.   Martha's statement of faith is true, but incomplete: like Jesus in
v. 15, she assumes that Lazarus would not have died in his presence,
because Jesus would have cured him of his illness; and that it is still
possible for Jesus to ask God for a miracle. Full Christian faith, however, goes further than this, and dispenses with cures and miracles
altogether; cp. Rom. 8³⁵ ff..

23   The answer of Jesus is so phrased that it does not distinguish
between a miraculous raising to life now, and the general resurrection
at the end of the world.

24   Martha's faith is now shown more clearly to be inadequate; any
Pharisee could have said this.

25 f.   Jesus' reply (the fifth 'I am' saying: see note on 6³⁵) presents a faith
which is more far-reaching than Martha's, because it claims that death
is already overcome for the believer: the appearance of death remains
(*though he die*), but its reality as extinction is destroyed (*shall never die*);
therefore what Martha looked for at *the resurrection at the last day* (i.e.
the destruction of death) is available in the present to the one who
believes in Jesus; he is *the resurrection*. The words *and the life* are omitted
by some of the Greek, Latin, and Syriac authorities, probably
correctly (cp. 14⁶).

27 shall never die. Do you believe this?' She said to him, 'Yes,
Lord; I believe that you are the Christ, the Son of God, he
who is coming into the world.'

28   When she had said this, she went and called her sister
Mary, saying quietly, 'The Teacher is here and is calling for
29 you.' And when she heard it, she rose quickly and went to
30 him. Now Jesus had not yet come to the village, but was still
31 in the place where Martha had met him. When the Jews who
were with her in the house, consoling her, saw Mary rise
quickly and go out, they followed her, supposing that she was
32 going to the tomb to weep there. Then Mary, when she came
where Jesus was and saw him, fell at his feet, saying to him,
'Lord, if you had been here, my brother would not have died.'
33 When Jesus saw her weeping, and the Jews who came with
her also weeping, he was deeply moved in spirit and troubled;
34 and he said, 'Where have you laid him?' They said to him,
36 'Lord, come and see.' Jesus wept. So the Jews said, 'See how

---

27   It is not altogether clear whether Martha's statement of faith here
is meant to be adequate or inadequate; perhaps the use of the Jewish-
messianic titles *the Christ, the Son of God, he who is coming* here, as in
Chapter 1, indicates incompleteness, and this possibility is confirmed
by Martha's further remark in v. 39 and Jesus' answer to it, and by
the use of the title 'Teacher' in the next verse (see note on 1³⁸).

ff.   The manner in which Martha informs Mary that Jesus has arrived
allows the Jews to misunderstand the situation, and in this way brings
them on the scene expecting something entirely different from what
will, in fact, take place.

32   Cp. the identical words of Martha in v. 21.

3 f.   It is not altogether clear why Jesus is *troubled* (or perhaps the translation should be 'angry'; Barrett, p. 332): one suggestion is that a miracle
is being forced upon him; another, that he is angry because of the
unbelief of Mary and the Jews.

35   Luke 19⁴¹ and Heb. 5⁷ are the only other places in the N.T. which
mention the weeping or tears of Jesus. Again it is not clear whether
John means anger here, or compassion; but see next verse.

36   Words put into the mouth of *the Jews* in this Gospel are often meant

37 he loved him!' But some of them said, 'Could not he who
opened the eyes of the blind man have kept this man from
dying?'

38   Then Jesus, deeply moved again, came to the tomb; it was
39 a cave, and a stone lay upon it. Jesus said, 'Take away the
stone.' Martha, the sister of the dead man, said to him, 'Lord,
by this time there will be an odour, for he has been dead four
40 days.' Jesus said to her, 'Did I not tell you that if you would
41 believe you would see the glory of God?' So they took away
the stone. And Jesus lifted up his eyes and said, 'Father, I
42 thank thee that thou hast heard me. I knew that thou hearest

---

to give an inadequate comment on the situation; if that is the case
here, then the weeping of Jesus in the previous verse will have been
caused by the unbelief of Mary and the Jews, rather than by compassion.

37   Elsewhere, John places two contrasting comments or reactions side
by side, as here—e.g. 7^{12}, $10^{20 f.}$, $11^{45 f.}$, 12^{29}, and cp. $13^{28 f.}$: if, therefore, what is said in v. 36, is meant to be inadequate, perhaps what is
said here is intended to be less so. The reference is to the opening of
the eyes of the blind man in Chapter 9.

38   See note on vv. 33 f. The archaeological evidence of Jewish graves
suggests that this would be a horizontal cave with a stone placed
against the opening (cp. NEB).

39   The command *Take away the stone* contrasts the raising of Lazarus
with the resurrection of Jesus: Jesus, after his resurrection, passes
through the grave-cloths ($20^{5 ff.}$) and through the doors of the building
where the disciples were ($20^{19, 26}$). Lazarus on the other hand is
restored to the life of this world; therefore the stone must be removed
for him to come out of the cave. See also v. 44. Martha still expresses
unbelief: see vv. 21 ff.

40   The sayings of Jesus here recall and combine what he said to the
disciples in v. 4 and to Martha in v. 26.

41   *lifted up his eyes*: cp. 17^1.   *Father*: cp. $17^{1, 11, 25}$.   *I thank thee that thou
hast heard me*: 'The aorist . . . expresses the absolute confidence of Jesus
that his prayer will be granted' (Barrett, p. 336).

42   Jesus prays in the knowledge that he is obedient to the Father, and
that his prayers will therefore be heard by the Father. The purpose of
his prayer is that the onlookers may believe in him as the agent of
God, and not as one who acts on his own authority (cp. $5^{19 ff.}$).

me always, but I have said this on account of the people standing by, that they may believe that thou didst

43 send me.' When he had said this, he cried with a loud voice, 'Lazarus,

44 come out.' The dead man came out, his hands and feet bound with bandages, and his face wrapped with a cloth. Jesus said to them, 'Unbind him, and let him go.'

---

f.   Cp. 10³ ('He calls his own sheep by name, and leads them out'). Lazarus comes from the grave in the same body as that in which he had lived and died, still bandaged and bound according to Jewish burial customs; contrast the resurrection of Jesus (20⁵ ᶠᶠ·) and see note on v. 39.

1: 45–54 *The counsel of Caiaphas*

Jesus has shown himself as the bringer of life, and this revelation is the occasion for faith in some, and hostility in others; the latter report to the Pharisees, and a meeting of the Sanhedrin is called. John's account of what takes place at this meeting is the classic example of his use of irony: the desperation of the chief priests and Pharisees, and their fear for the political future of Judaism, can also be read as an account of what is happening at the time when the Evangelist is writing and of what is still to happen: the Church is to replace the old order of the Law, the nation, and the

13. Lazarus: New College, Oxford; *J. Epstein,* twentieth century

45 Many of the Jews therefore, who had come with Mary and
46 had seen what he did, believed in him; but some of them went
47 to the Pharisees and told them what Jesus had done. So the
    chief priests and the Pharisees gathered the council, and
    said, 'What are we to do? For this man performs many
48 signs. If we let him go on thus, every one will believe in him,
    and the Romans will come and destroy both our holy place*a*
49 and our nation.' But one of them, Caiaphas, who was high

a Greek *our place*

---

temple. The statement of Caiaphas that one should be sacri-
ficed for the welfare of the majority can likewise be read as an
inspired prophecy of the meaning of the death of Jesus, as
John himself points out. The result of this meeting is that the
Sanhedrin is henceforth planning the death of Jesus, while
Jesus himself, aware of what they are doing, withdraws with
his disciples until the hour comes.

45 f. For opposite reactions to the revelation, see note on 11³⁷. The verb
'to see' (Gk. θεᾶσθαι) 'can designate a seeing which penetrates
beneath the surface' (J. Jeremias, *The Central Message of the New Testament* (London, 1965), p. 84). 'The act of seeing and the act of believing
cannot . . . be separated from one another' (F. Mussner, *The Historical
Jesus in the Gospel of St John* (Freiburg, 1967), pp. 19 f.). It is perhaps
significant that the Greek for 'what he did' in v. 45 is in the singular
(Gk. ὃ ἐποίησεν) while in v. 46 it is plural (Gk. ἃ ἐποίησεν): the
believers perceive the unity of Christ's revelation; the unbelievers see
only a multiplicity of disconnected actions (see also note on 14²⁴).

47 *What are we to do?* For a similar statement made by the Pharisees of
their inability to control the situation cp. 12¹⁹ ('You see that you can
do nothing; look, the world has gone after him'). *this man performs
many signs*: the word *signs* here, and in 2¹⁸, 3², 7³¹, 9¹⁶, 10⁴¹, means
'miracles' in the context of the speaker, while it means much more
than this to the Christian reader.

48 See 12³²ᶠ·: it will be by being lifted up in execution that he 'will
draw all men' to believe in him. The Jews are troubled about
political consequences: see also 19¹²·¹⁵; and in fact the temple (= *holy
place*) was destroyed by the Romans in A.D. 70. But to the believer,
the Jews forfeited their status as the people of God when they crucified
Jesus: see 2¹⁹⁻²¹.

49 *Caiaphas* held office *c.* A.D. 18–36, but John is interested only in the

priest that year, said to them, 'You know nothing at all;
50 you do not understand that it is expedient for you that one
man should die for the people, and that the whole nation
51 should not perish.' He did not say this of his own accord, but
being high priest that year he prophesied that Jesus should
52 die for the nation, and not for the nation only, but to gather
53 into one the children of God who are scattered abroad. So
from that day on they took counsel how to put him to death.
54   Jesus therefore no longer went about openly among the
Jews, but went from there to the country near the wilderness,

---

fact that he was *high priest that year* (see also 11⁵¹, 18¹³)—i.e. the year
in which Jesus was crucified.
50   The high priest's statement makes sense as a policy of expediency,
though John intends his readers to see it in another way (vv. 51 f.),
and knows that in fact this policy did not pay off. There is also a sense
in which the death of Jesus is expedient; cp. 16⁷ ('it is to your advantage [the same Greek words as here] that I go away').
51   *of his own accord*: the same preposition (Gk. ἀπό) with a different
pronoun is translated 'on my own authority' in 14¹⁰; Caiaphas is
inspired by God to speak the truth authoritatively, but without
knowing it. In v. 50 'for' (Gk. ὑπέρ) meant 'instead of', here it means
'on behalf of', 'for the sake of'.
52   Cp. 10¹⁶ ('I have other sheep . . .').
53   The Jews seek the death of Jesus, because he gave life to Lazarus;
see also 12¹⁰ ('So the chief priests planned to put Lazarus also to death').
54   *Ephraim* 'is probably to be identified with the modern Et-Taiyibeh,
4 miles NE. of Bethel' (Barrett, p. 340).

11: 55–12: 11 *Before the Passover: The Jews purify themselves, and
Jesus is anointed*

John now describes the various preparations which are being
made for the third and final Passover in this Gospel—the
Passover at which Jesus will die. Jews from outside Jerusalem
go up to the city to purify themselves, and wonder whether Jesus
will come; the Jewish leaders give orders for his arrest; Jesus
himself is anointed and speaks of his burial; and the Jewish
leaders plan to kill Lazarus because through him many are
believing in Jesus. John is here using the final sections of the

to a town called Ephraim; and there he stayed with the disciples.

55   Now the Passover of the Jews was at hand, and many went up from the country to Jerusalem before the Passover, to
56 purify themselves. They were looking for Jesus and saying to one another as they stood in the temple, 'What do you
57 think? That he will not come to the feast?' Now the chief priests and the Pharisees had given orders that if any one knew where he was, he should let them know, so that they might arrest him.

12 S I X days before the Passover, Jesus came to Bethany, where
2   Lazarus was, whom Jesus had raised from the dead. There they made him a supper; Martha served, and Lazarus was
3   one of those at table with him. Mary took a pound of costly

---

first part of his Gospel to set the scene for the events of the second part, the glorifying of the Son of man.

55   For previous references to *Passover* in this Gospel, see 2¹³, 6⁴. For the law about purification, see Num. 9⁶ ᶠᶠ·, and *Pesaḥim* ix. 1, and cp. 18²⁸.
56   The uncertainty of the Jews contrasts with the knowledge and assurance of Jesus, e.g. 12⁷, ²³, ²⁷, ³¹ ᶠᶠ·.
57   A further step following the discussions and plans in vv. 47–53.
12:1 *Six days before the Passover*: i.e. the Saturday before the Friday on which Jesus was crucified, and on the evening of which the Passover was kept, according to this Gospel (see notes on 18²⁸, 19³¹, ⁴²). *Bethany*: see note on 11¹⁸.
2   *Martha served*: Luke has a story involving the two sisters, Martha and Mary, and one important point in it is that 'Martha was distracted with much serving' (Luke 10³⁸ ᶠᶠ·); however, it is not certain whether John used Luke's gospel, or drew on traditions which Luke also used. *Lazarus* is not mentioned by Luke in this context (cp. Luke 16¹⁹ ᶠᶠ·).
3   There are stories of anointing in Matt. 26⁶⁻¹³, Mark 14³⁻⁹, and Luke 7³⁶⁻⁵⁰; John has points of contact with each of them, though here again there may not be sufficient evidence to prove literary dependence of John on other Gospels (so Dodd, *HTFG*, pp. 162 ff.: see also D. Daube, *The New Testament and Rabbinic Judaism* (London, 1956),

ointment of pure nard and anointed the feet of Jesus and
wiped his feet with her hair; and the house was filled with the
4 fragrance of the ointment. But Judas Iscariot, one of his
5 disciples (he who was to betray him), said, 'Why was this
ointment not sold for three hundred denarii[b] and given to the
6 poor?' This he said, not that he cared for the poor but because
he was a thief, and as he had the money box he used to take
7 what was put into it. Jesus said, 'Let her alone, let her keep it

---

b The denarius was worth about seventeen pence

---

pp. 312 ff.). *a pound*: possibly a Roman pound ($=$ *c*. 12 oz.); the
point is the large quantity (cp. 2^6, 19^{39}). *costly ointment of pure nard*:
the word here translated *pure* (Gk. πιστικός) is unknown apart from this
verse, Mark 14^3, and writers dependent on these two passages: its
meaning is uncertain, and other suggestions are 'liquid' or 'from the
pistachio nut'. In Matthew and Mark the woman anoints the head of
Jesus; in Luke and John, the feet. Lightfoot (p. 236) suggests, on the
analogy of 13^{6-10}, that the feet represent the whole body; 'If so, the
reader is invited to see in Mary's action a symbolical embalming of
His body for burial, as though He were already dead'. Lightfoot goes
on to suggest that the wiping of the feet may be intended as a symbol
of the resurrection: others think that John has taken this detail over
from Luke, where however it is her tears that she wipes off, and not the
ointment (Barrett); and others that Mary is repeating, without tears,
the incident which Luke had recorded in Luke 7^{36-50} (Bernard, pp.
409 ff.: see also W. Temple, *Readings in St. John's Gospel* (London,
1939), p. 189). *the house was filled with the fragrance of the ointment*:
Hoskyns, following some of the patristic commentators, sees this as in
some sense equivalent to Mark 14^9 ('wherever the gospel is preached
in the whole world, what she has done will be told in memory of her').

4 f.   For previous mention of *Judas Iscariot* in John, see 6^{71}. John's
account is very similar at this point to Mark $14^{4 f.}$.

6   Only in this Gospel is Judas said to have been a thief. Cp. 13^{29}.

7   *let her keep it for the day of my burial*: these words present a problem,
and Barrett concludes his discussion of it as follows: 'It must however
be admitted that no explanation of this difficult verse is entirely satisfactory' (p. 346). The meaning may be that Mary kept the ointment
for the burial of Jesus, which she now anticipates by pouring it on the
feet of Jesus (just as, by wiping it off, she anticipates the resurrection
also: see note on v. 3).

8 for the day of my burial. The poor you always have with you, but you do not always have me.'

9 When the great crowd of the Jews learned that he was there, they came, not only on account of Jesus but also to see
10 Lazarus, whom he had raised from the dead. So the chief
11 priests planned to put Lazarus also to death, because on account of him many of the Jews were going away and believing in Jesus.

---

8   This verse is omitted by two of the textual authorities, and may have been copied into John from Matt. 26[11] (so Dodd, Barrett).

9 ff.   For the relations between signs and faith, see 2[11], 4[48], 6[26], 10[37 f.]: John means that their faith was imperfect; the crowd were treating Lazarus as a spectacle, and placing him alongside Jesus. The chief priests meet this situation by planning to kill Lazarus.

12: 12–19 *The entry into Jerusalem*

John, like the Synoptists (Matt. 21[1ff.], Mark 11[1ff.], Luke 19[29 ff.]), tells the story of the entry of Jesus into Jerusalem riding on an ass; but he tells it in his own way. In John, the crowd goes to meet Jesus with palm branches, and greets him as 'King of Israel'; only then does Jesus find the ass and ride on it in fulfilment of the prophecy; whereas in the Synoptics, the finding of the ass comes before the greetings of the crowd. Moreover, John adds explanatory notes, in which he tells us that the disciples did not understand the significance of what was happening until after the death and resurrection of Jesus, and that the reason why the crowd acted as they did was because they had heard of the raising of Lazarus. The point which John is making by telling the story in this way is that the crowd acts without understanding what it is doing: Jesus corrects the error in their minds by fulfilling the prophecy of Zechariah; and that this was understood by the disciples at a later date, and in the light of Jesus' death and resurrection. The error of the crowd hinges on the sense in which he is 'King of Israel'—on which John will have more to say in the passion narrative, but notice specially 18[36] ('My kingship is not of this world'—i.e. his authority is not given to him by the world, but by God). There is, therefore, an ironical misunderstanding on

12   The next day a great crowd who had come to the feast
13 heard that Jesus was coming to Jerusalem. So they took
branches of palm trees and went out to meet him, crying,
'Hosanna! Blessed is he who comes in the name of the Lord,
14 even the King of Israel!' And Jesus found a young ass and sat
upon it; as it is written,

15   'Fear not, daughter of Zion;
     behold, your king is coming,
     sitting on an ass's colt!'

16 His disciples did not understand this at first; but when Jesus

---

the part of the Pharisees when they say 'The world has gone
after him'.

12   *The next day*: i.e. Sunday; see note on 12¹. *a great crowd who had come to the feast*: see 11⁵⁵ f. and perhaps 12⁹ (see note on v. 18 below).

13   'To carry palms was a mark of triumphant homage to a victor or a king (cf. Rev. 7⁹)', Lightfoot, p. 250. *Hosanna!* means 'Save now' (Ps. 118²⁵); but it became a liturgical expression of joy. *Blessed is he who comes in the name of the Lord* is a quotation from Ps. 118²⁶: originally it meant 'Blessed in the name of the Lord is he who comes', and it was used to greet pilgrims arriving at the temple. In the Gospels, however, and most clearly in John (who adds *even the King of Israel*), *he who comes in the name of the Lord* refers to Jesus, coming with God's authority. The crowd thinks of Jesus as *King* in the same sense as those in 6¹⁵ who wished to take Jesus 'by force to make him king': i.e. they think of him as a political and revolutionary leader (cp. also 1⁴⁹).

f.   The quotation is from Zech. 9⁹, but it is not given in the form of either the Hebrew or the LXX text. Zechariah goes on to say 'he shall command peace to the nations', and this may be how John understood the incident: Jesus offers a different conception of himself from that which the crowd has; he is not Messiah in their sense.

16   Understanding Jesus (which is inseparable from faith) comes only after his death and resurrection (= *when Jesus was glorified*) and the coming of the Spirit (cp. 14²⁶ 'the Holy Spirit . . . will teach you all things, and bring to your remembrance all that I have said to you'). That is to say, under the inspiration of the Spirit the disciples perceive the fulfilment of prophecy, and the real significance of the acclamation of the crowd. Cp. 2¹⁷, ²², and see F. Mussner, *The Historical Jesus in the Gospel of St John* (Freiburg, 1967), pp. 42 ff.

was glorified, then they remembered that this had been
17 written of him and had been done to him. The crowd that
had been with him when he called Lazarus out of the tomb
18 and raised him from the dead bore witness. The reason why
the crowd went to meet him was that they heard he had done
19 this sign. The Pharisees then said to one another, 'You see
that you can do nothing; look, the world has gone after him.'

---

17   For this reference to *The crowd*, cp. 11[19].
18   The *crowd* in this verse however, seems to be different from that in
the previous verse, but the same as that in v. 12 and possibly in v. 9.
19   The words of the Pharisees are meant to be taken in a number of
ways: (*a*) as a statement of their failure, so far, to check the movement towards faith in Jesus (cp. vv. 10 f.); (*b*) as an unwitting
prophecy of *the* conversion of *the world* (cp. vv. 20 ff. in which Greeks
ask to see Jesus); and (*c*) as again an unintentional, true statement of
the present situation—'the crowd' are here spoken of as *the world* in
the sense of darkness and ignorance which it frequently has in this
Gospel (cp. 1[10]).

12: 20–36a *The Son of man and the Gentiles*

The Fourth Evangelist is as clear as the Synoptists and Paul
(Rom. 15[8]) that the ministry of Jesus before the passion was to
the Jews primarily, and that Gentiles were involved only after
the resurrection (see, e.g., J. Jeremias, *Jesus' Promise to the
Nations* (London, 1958)). Although it must have been apparent
to John at the time when he was writing his Gospel that
Gentiles were outnumbering Jews in the Church, and although he may have had these Gentile Christians in mind as
the future readers of his book, nevertheless he does not bring
them on to the stage until this late point in his narrative (but
see notes on 4[46 ff.]), and it is significant that their request, 'We
wish to see Jesus', is not answered: no meeting is arranged,
because they can only see him in and through the ministry of
the disciples, and this ministry cannot begin until Jesus has
been glorified.

The request of the Greeks is a sign that 'the hour' has come:
Jesus can 'bear fruit' in the Gentile mission only through dying,
and this law of gain through loss holds good for the disciples as
well as for himself.

20   Now among those who went up to worship at the feast
21 were some Greeks. So these came to Philip, who was from
Bethsaida in Galilee, and said to him, 'Sir, we wish to see
22 Jesus.' Philip went and told Andrew; Andrew went with
23 Philip and they told Jesus. And Jesus answered them, 'The
24 hour has come for the Son of man to be glorified. Truly,

There follows a passage which may be regarded as the
Johannine equivalent of the Synoptic account of the prayer of
Jesus in Gethsemane. The purpose of the Synoptists and of
John is the same here: to show the obedience of Jesus to the
Father, unto death. But John goes further than the Synoptists
in making clear to the reader what is to be the result of the death
of Jesus: the world is to be judged; Satan is to be cast out; all
men will be drawn to Jesus. The crowd expresses amazement
at this prediction of Christ's death, but the only answer that
they are offered is an invitation to believe.

20   Here (as in 7³⁵) *Greeks* mean Gentiles. In Mark, the cleansing of
the temple follows on soon after the entry into Jerusalem (Mark
11¹⁻¹⁹), and some commentators think that the significance of the
cleansing of the temple in Mark lies in the fact that it was the court
of the Gentiles that Jesus cleared of animals, etc.: it was to be 'a house
of prayer for all the nations' (e.g. R. H. Lightfoot, *The Gospel Message
of St. Mark* (Oxford, 1950), ch. v). It may be that John is comment-
ing on the Marcan material at this point.

f.   *Philip* and *Andrew* are the only two of the twelve who have Greek
names; this may be the reason why John selects them to be the inter-
mediaries between the Greeks and Jesus. *we wish to see Jesus*: although
nothing further is said about the *Greeks*, or about their desire to meet
Jesus, in a sense the answer to their request is to be found in 20²⁹
('Blessed are those who have not seen and yet believe').

23   *The hour has come*: contrast 2⁴ 'My hour has not yet come' and 7³⁰,
8²⁰; and see below 12²⁷, 13¹, 17¹, where *the hour* is said to be present.
The evangelization of the Gentiles belongs to the time after the death
and resurrection of Jesus; therefore the arrival of the Greeks shows
that the time for Jesus to die has drawn near. *the Son of man* (see note
on 1⁵¹) was used by the Synoptists in their accounts of the predictions
of the passion and resurrection, e.g. Mark 8³¹: possibly this is why John
uses it here (cp. also 3¹⁴). *to be glorified*: that is, to return to the glory
which he had with the Father, through being lifted up on the cross.

24   *Truly, truly*: see note on 1⁵¹. The same lesson of life through death

truly, I say to you, unless a grain of wheat falls into the earth and dies, it remains alone; but if it dies, it bears much

25 fruit. He who loves his life loses it, and he who hates his life

26 in this world will keep it for eternal life. If any one serves me, he must follow me; and where I am, there shall my servant be also; if any one serves me, the Father will honour him.

27   'Now is my soul troubled. And what shall I say? "Father, save me from this hour"? No, for this purpose I have come

28 to this hour. Father, glorify thy name.' Then a voice came from heaven, 'I have glorified it, and I will glorify it again.'

---

is taught by means of the same metaphor in 1 Cor. 15^{36}. The metaphor of fruitfulness is used again in 15$^{1\,ff.}$.

25   There are a number of sayings similar to this in the Synoptic Gospels, notice particularly Mark 8^{35} (and see Dodd, *HTFG*, pp. 338 ff.): they refer to the suffering of disciples. John is adapting such a saying, but using it primarily of the suffering of the Son of man, and secondarily (as the next verse shows) of his followers. *hate* = regard as of secondary importance (cp. Luke 14^{26}).

26   Cp. Mark 8^{34}: the use of the verb to *serve* in this saying is Johannine (cp. 12^2, 'Martha served'). *follow*: see note on 1^{37}. *where I am*: the meaning may be 'in life or death, humiliation and glory' (Barrett, p. 353) or perhaps 'with the Father' (Lightfoot, p. 252), which is what the references which Barrett gives suggest—viz. 14^3, 17^{24}; this is also suggested by the last part of the saying, *the Father will honour him*, i.e. with his presence.

27   *Now is my soul troubled*: cp. Mark's account of Jesus in Gethsemane, and particularly Mark 14^{34} with its allusion to Ps. 42^5. *And what shall I say? Father, save me from this hour?*: cp. Mark 14^{36} ('Abba, Father, ... remove this cup from me ...'). *No, for this purpose I have come to this hour*: John shows both the reality of the suffering of Jesus, and the willingness of Jesus to undergo it.

28   *Father, glorify thy name*: In Matthew's Gospel, Jesus prays in Gethsemane 'thy will be done' (Matt. 26^{42}); and in the Lord's prayer, the hallowing of God's name and the doing of his will are synonymous expressions (Matt. 6$^{9\,f.}$). *glorify thy name* thus means both 'Do thy will', and 'Reveal thyself as glorious in doing it'. *a voice came from heaven*: cp. the voice at the Baptism of Jesus (Mark 1^{11} and parallels) and at the Transfiguration (Mark 9^7 and parallels) in the Synoptic Gospels: John has no such voice in his account of the Baptism (1$^{32\,f.}$) and he does not

29 The crowd standing by heard it and said that it had thun-
30 dered. Others said, 'An angel has spoken to him.' Jesus
   answered, 'This voice has come for your sake, not for mine.
31 Now is the judgment of this world, now shall the ruler of this
32 world be cast out; and I, when I am lifted up from the earth,
33 will draw all men to myself.' He said this to show by what
34 death he was to die. The crowd answered him, 'We have

---

include the Transfiguration in his Gospel. *I have glorified it*: the works of Jesus, because they have been done in obedience to the Father, have shown forth the glory of God (cp. 2¹¹, 11⁴⁰); *and I will glorify it again*: that is, in the coming death and resurrection of Jesus (cp. 17¹ ᶠᶠ.). This saying, therefore, links together the two halves of the Gospel, Chapters 1–12 and Chapters 13–21.

29   See note on 11³⁷ for twofold comments from the crowd, both in-adequate, one of them (*An angel has spoken to him*) less so than the other. Cp. Luke 22⁴³ for mention of an angel in the Gethsemane story, though notice that some of the textual authorities omit this verse in Luke.

30   Cp. 11⁴², where Jesus prays 'on account of the people standing by' (the same Greek preposition (διά) is used in both passages). He him-self needs no assurance from God, just as he does not need to make petitions to God in the way that men do; his union with God is of a different kind from theirs. The *voice* has come in order that the believers may know that the Father is at work in the Son, but the crowd has not heard it, because they are not believers.

31   *Now is the judgment of this world*: cp. 9³⁹ ('For judgment I came into this world'); Jesus has divided men by his words and deeds; *now*, in the crucifixion, he will do that supremely. *now shall the ruler of this world be cast out*: *the ruler of this world* = Satan, here and in 14³⁰, 16¹¹; similar expressions can be quoted from other Christian writings (e.g. 2 Cor. 4⁴ 'the god of this world'), but not from Jewish. He will be *cast out* of heaven by the death and exaltation of Jesus, who will take Satan's place, but use it for a different purpose: Satan accused men before God (Rev. 12¹⁰); Jesus will be their advocate (1 John 2¹).

f.   For the intentional ambiguity of the verb *lift up*, see 3¹⁴, 8²⁸, and v. 34 below: it refers both to the manner of his death (see v. 33) and the result of it, i.e. his exaltation to the Father. *will draw all men to myself* means 'will give faith and salvation to all men'; see 6⁴⁴ for the connec-tion between 'drawing' and 'believing' or 'coming'.

34   John says *the law* when he means the Old Testament (cp. 10³⁴); various passages have been suggested, e.g. Ps. 110⁴, Isa. 9⁶, Dan. 7¹³ ᶠ·;

heard from the law that the Christ remains for ever. How can you say that the Son of man must be lifted up? Who is this
35 Son of man?' Jesus said to them, 'The light is with you for a little longer. Walk while you have the light, lest the darkness overtake you; he who walks in the darkness does not know
36 where he goes. While you have the light, believe in the light, that you may become sons of light.'

When Jesus had said this, he departed and hid himself
37 from them. Though he had done so many signs before them,
38 yet they did not believe in him; it was that the word spoken by the prophet Isaiah might be fulfilled:

---

but it may be that John means no more than that it was the Jewish belief that the Messiah would live for ever. Jesus has spoken of the glorifying of the Son of man (v. 23) and of his being 'lifted up from the earth' (v. 32): the crowd understands *lifted up* as a reference to death, not resurrection; hence the question, How is it that the *Son of man* must die? There is, however, in the crowd's question here, an echo of the statement in 3¹⁴ ('so must the Son of man be lifted up').

35 f.   Jesus' answer is that he is the revelation (= *the light*) but that he will soon be with them no more: they have now a final opportunity for believing, and thus for understanding, and for becoming *sons of light*—i.e. those who are saved.

12: 36b–50 *Epilogue to the Signs*

The last two paragraphs of Chapter 12 form an epilogue to the first half of the Gospel. In the former paragraph, John explains the unbelief of the Jews, both theologically (as the fulfilment of scripture) and morally (as the result of fear and vanity). In the latter, Jesus makes a final statement concerning faith and unbelief, which sums up the main points of the Gospel.

36 b   For previous accounts of the withdrawal of Jesus from the crowd, see 8⁵⁹, 10³⁹ ᶠ·, 11⁵⁴.

37   John looks back over what he has written in Chapters 2–12, and sums up the contents of the first half of his book as *so many signs*, the purpose of which was to awaken faith. The disciples believed (2¹¹), but the Jews did not (cp. 20³⁰ ᶠ·).

38   The unbelief of the Jews is seen as the fulfilment of the prophecy of

'Lord, who has believed our report,
    and to whom has the arm of the Lord been revealed?'

39 Therefore they could not believe. For Isaiah again said,

40 'He has blinded their eyes and hardened their heart,
    lest they should see with their eyes and perceive with
        their heart,
    and turn for me to heal them.'

41 Isaiah said this because he saw his glory and spoke of him.

42 Nevertheless many even of the authorities believed in him,
    but for fear of the Pharisees they did not confess it, lest they

43 should be put out of the synagogue: for they loved the praise
    of men more than the praise of God.

Isaiah (53[1], the 'suffering servant' passage). 'Isaiah' had not found faith among the Jews, and his words were prophecies of Jesus (= *the arm of the Lord*) and his teaching (= *our report*).

39   *Therefore they could not believe*: i.e. the prophecy had to be fulfilled, and the unbelief of the Jews was inevitable. This kind of predestinarian language is not confined to John among N.T. authors. Cp. also e.g. 1 Pet. 2[8]; and it is to be expected in writers who were more convinced of the power and control of God over the world, than of the freedom of the individual. *For Isaiah again said*: introduces the quotation in the next verse (Isa. 6[10]), a passage which all four of the evangelists have used (see Matt. 13[14 f.], Mark 4[12], Acts 28[25 ff.]).

40   John seems to be quoting freely, perhaps from memory: the point of this quotation is the same as that in v. 38—the unbelief of the Jews is within the purpose and control of God.

41   *he saw his glory*: the reference is to Isa. 6[1] ('I saw the Lord sitting upon a throne, high and lifted up'). There is a number of passages in the N.T. in which Christ is identified with a figure in the Old Testament—e.g. 1 Cor. 10[4].

2 f.   For imperfect faith in Jesus see note on 8[30], and notice other places where two reactions, one less inadequate than the other, are stated side by side, e.g. 11[36 f.], 12[29]. *lest they should be put out of the synagogue*: see note on 9[22].

43   *praise* in both parts of this sentence translates the Greek word, δόξα, which is usually rendered 'glory', as in 5[44] ('How can you believe, who receive glory from one another and do not seek the glory that comes from the only God?'). The same point is made frequently in the

44   And Jesus cried out and said, 'He who believes in me,
45 believes not in me but in him who sent me. And he who sees
46 me sees him who sent me. I have come as light into the world,
47 that whoever believes in me may not remain in darkness. If
      any one hears my sayings and does not keep them, I do not
      judge him; for I did not come to judge the world but to save
48 the world. He who rejects me and does not receive my sayings
      has a judge; the word that I have spoken will be his judge on
49 the last day. For I have not spoken on my own authority; the
      Father who sent me has himself given me commandment
50 what to say and what to speak. And I know that his command-
      ment is eternal life. What I say, therefore, I say as the Father
      has bidden me.'

---

teaching of Jesus in the Synoptic Gospels, e.g. Matt. 6^{1-21}: faith in
God and vain-glory are mutually exclusive. The name 'Judah' (=
Jew) means 'praised' (see Gen. 29^{35}, 49^8): Paul has this meaning of the
name in mind when he says of the true Jew, 'His praise is not from men
but from God' (Rom. 2^{29}).

44   *cried out* (Gr. ἔκραξεν): the verb is used four times in John (1^{15},
$7^{28,\ 37}$, and here): in each case it introduces a proclamation which
declares who Jesus is. He is the agent of God, who does nothing on
his own authority, but acts entirely in obedience to God. Therefore
faith in him is faith in the Father whom he obeys and by whom he was
authenticated.

45   To *see* (Gk. θεωρεῖν) Jesus means 'to believe in him' (cp. next verse).

46   Jesus is the bringer of salvation (= *light*) into the realm of unbelief
and disobedience (= *the world, darkness*), in order that men may
believe in him and be saved (= *not remain in darkness*).

47   Cp. 3^{17}: the primary purpose of the coming of Jesus was the salvation, not the condemnation, of the world.

48   *the word that I have spoken will be his judge on the last day*: cp. the Jewish
idea that the Law will judge the disobedient.

49   The word of Jesus is the word of the Father; it has therefore the
authority of God.

50   The coming of Jesus, and his word, have only one purpose—to
give life.

3 Now before the feast of the Passover, when Jesus knew that
   his hour had come to depart out of this world to the Father,
   having loved his own who were in the world, he loved them

In the earlier part of the Gospel, John's method was first to
describe an action of Jesus, and then to introduce a discussion
or discourse which explained the meaning of the action. In the
second part, which begins at this point, John reverses the order:
the discussion and discourses take place first, at the supper, and
the action follows on later—viz. the arrest, the trials, the crucifixion, and the resurrection. Nevertheless, John does not completely abandon his usual method of expounding a sign by
means of a discourse following it, in the second part of his
Gospel; he introduces the discourses and discussions at the
supper by means of another sign, the foot-washing.

The washing of the disciples' feet is a sign which John understands in more than one way, and he makes it clear to his
readers that this is so. First, he makes Jesus say that what he
has done is an example for his disciples to follow; they are to be
servants of one another, just as Jesus has acted as servant to
them (vv. 12–17). But secondly, washing suggests something
other than simply the work of a servant: washing means cleansing, and it reminds the Christian of his baptism; and to be
baptized is to enter into the benefits of Christ's death and
resurrection. So the washing stands for the whole mission of
Jesus, and just as the purpose of his mission is to associate
people with himself in a fellowship, so Jesus says that if he does
not wash them, they will not be partners with him (vv. 6–10).
However (and this is a third element in the understanding of
this sign), neither the washing, nor the death and resurrection
of which it is a symbol, can be effective without faith and love
on the part of the disciple; so John reminds us that Judas was
present and was washed, but was not clean (vv. 10[b], 11).

It should perhaps be added that these three elements in the
understanding of this sign are connected with one another, and
are not alternative interpretations of it, or separable from one
another. The purpose of the mission of Jesus is to create a
fellowship of love among men which exists because of the love

2 to the end. And during supper, when the devil had already
  put it into the heart of Judas Iscariot, Simon's son, to betray

---

of Jesus for them (v. 1); the cleansing of which he speaks is
cleansing from everything that contradicts love; the only kind
of impurity which is recognized by this fellowship is selfishness,
represented here by Judas (cp. 12⁶). The foot-washing is not
first a symbol of the passion, and secondly an example for the
disciple: the purpose of the passion and the substance of
discipleship are identical (cp. v. 34).

1   *before the feast of the Passover*: cp. 11⁵⁵, 12¹. According to the Synoptists, the last supper was the Passover meal (Mark 14¹²ᶠᶠ· and parallels):
according to John, on the other hand, the Passover was to be eaten on
the next day (18²⁸, 19¹⁴), Friday evening. John's reference to *Passover*
here, while it contradicts the Synoptic identification of the supper
with the feast, does associate the death of Jesus, which on his dating
takes place at the time when the Passover-lambs were killed, with the
supper, and thus with the foot-washing.   *when Jesus knew that his hour
had come*: see, above, notes on 12²³, ²⁷.   *to depart out of this world to the
Father*: John uses this way of speaking of the death of Jesus in the
following chapters (e.g. 13³, ³³, 14²ᶠᶠ·, ¹², ²⁸, 16⁵ᶠᶠ·, 17, 28, 17¹¹ᶠᶠ·): he
means by it that the departure of Jesus does not involve a real separation from the disciples, because it is a departure *out of this world* (and
the disciples 'are not of the world', 17¹⁶), and *to the Father* (whence he
will send them the Paraclete, 16⁷).   *having loved his own who were in the
world*: John recognizes a sense in which Jesus and his disciples (= *his
own*, cp. 1¹¹, 10³ᶠ·, 15¹⁹) will be separated (cp. 17¹¹ ,'I am no more in
the world, but they are in the world'); however, this separation is more
apparent than real, because it is overcome by the love of Jesus.   *he
loved them to the end*: i.e. (*a*) completely; (*b*) to the end of his life; and (*c*)
to the end of the world.

2   *during supper*: there has not been any previous mention of the supper
in this Gospel (contrast the Synoptics), but the Christian reader will
be familiar with the occasion (cp. 1 Cor. 11²³ᶠᶠ·). Foot-washing would
normally be done before the meal began, not during it: John is not
concerned to say whether it had been done once already, or if not,
why not; this is a symbolic occasion, and John is not attempting to
write a 'naturalistic' account of it. John further emphasizes the close
connection between the supper, the foot-washing, and the death of
Jesus, by saying that 'the devil had already made up his mind that
Judas should betray him' (so Barrett translates this verse; pp. 365 f.):
Luke also connects the betrayal with the devil (Luke 22³). Apart from

3 him, Jesus, knowing that the Father had given all things into
  his hands, and that he had come from God and was going to
4 God, rose from supper, laid aside his garments, and girded
5 himself with a towel. Then he poured water into a basin, and
  began to wash the disciples' feet, and to wipe them with the
6 towel with which he was girded. He came to Simon Peter;
7 and Peter said to him, 'Lord, do you wash my feet?' Jesus
  answered him, 'What I am doing you do not know now, but
8 afterward you will understand.' Peter said to him, 'You shall
  never wash my feet.' Jesus answered him, 'If I do not wash

---

the statement that Judas was a thief (12⁶), the Evangelists provide no
further explanation for his action, and this again is because it was not
their intention to inform their readers of these things, even if they
themselves knew them.

3   *knowing that the Father had given all things into his hands*: see 3³⁵ for
similar words; the meaning is that Jesus knew that the Father had
laid upon him the work of salvation. *that he had come from God*: i.e. that
he came as the emissary of the Father, with the Father's authority
(cp. 7²⁹). *and was going to God*: see note on v. 1.

4   *rose from supper*: see note on v. 2. *laid aside his garments*: the verb
which is used here (Gk. τιθέναι) is also used of Jesus laying down his
life (e.g. 10¹⁷), and the commentators suggest that John has the
parallel in mind; see also note on 'taken his garments' in v. 12.
girded himself with a towel: there is some evidence to connect the word
used here for *towel*, with slaves: for the idea of the death of Jesus as the
act of a slave, cp. e.g. Mark 10⁴⁵ ('the Son of man also came not to
be served but to serve, and to give his life as a ransom for many') and
Phil. 2⁷ᶠ· ('taking the form of a servant . . . became obedient unto
death').

5   Washing another's feet was a menial task, such as one would
certainly not expect a teacher to do for his pupils; see vv. 6, 8, 14.

6   The order of words in Greek emphasizes the pronouns *you* and *my*;
with Peter's false humility here, compare his false heroism in v. 37.

7   Peter understands neither the foot-washing nor Christ's work of
which it is a symbol; he cannot understand either until the latter is
complete, and the Spirit has come to interpret these things (14²⁶).

8   *You shall never wash my feet*: cp. Peter's rebuke of Jesus, when Jesus
foretells his passion and resurrection, 'God forbid, Lord! This shall
never happen to you' (Matt. 16²²). *If I do not wash you, you have no part*

9 you, you have no part in me.' Simon Peter said to him, 'Lord,
10 not my feet only but also my hands and my head!' Jesus said
   to him, 'He who has bathed does not need to wash, except
   for his feet,*c* but he is clean all over; and you are clean, but
11 not all of you.' For he knew who was to betray him; that was
   why he said, 'You are not all clean.'

12   When he had washed their feet, and taken his garments,
   and resumed his place, he said to them, 'Do you know what
13 I have done to you? You call me Teacher and Lord; and you

---

c Other ancient authorities omit *except for his feet*

---

in me: this saying makes it clear that the foot-washing is a symbol: to
'have a part' in Jesus means to 'abide' in him (see the figure of the
vine and the branches (15^{1-11}) and note $15^{2 f.}$, where abiding is conditional upon being cleansed). The same idea is found in the First
Letter of John, 'The blood of Jesus his Son cleanses us from all sin'
(1 John 1^7).

9   Peter's further misunderstanding also indicates to the reader that
the foot-washing is symbolic, and not effective by itself.

10   The shorter text, omitting *except for his feet* (RSV mg.) is preferred
by NEB, Barrett (p. 368), Hoskyns (pp. 514 f.), Lightfoot (p. 273),
Strachan (p. 266): in that case, to *bathe* and to *wash* are used synony-
mously, and the additional words, *except for his feet* were added at an
early date (they are found in the majority of MSS, etc.), possibly to
introduce the idea of absolution for post-baptismal sin. *you are clean,
but not all of you* again points to the symbolic nature of the incident (see
notes on vv. 8 f.): the foot-washing has not made them clean, but the
mission of Jesus as a whole has done so, and the foot-washing is the
sign of it; this mission must be received by faith, and Judas Iscariot
is not a man of faith (cp. 6^{64}).

11   For Jesus' fore-knowledge of Judas' betrayal, see 6^{64}, and cp. also
the Synoptists, e.g. Mark $14^{18 ff.}$, and for Jesus' supernatural knowledge in general, see note on 1^{42}.

12   *taken his garments*: the same verb (Gk. $\lambda\alpha\mu\beta\acute{\alpha}\nu\epsilon\iota\nu$) is used at 10^{17} of
Jesus taking his life again at the resurrection; see also note on v. 4
above. *Do you know* here means 'Do you understand the significance of?'

13   Jesus is never in fact addressed as *Teacher* (Gk. $\delta\iota\delta\acute{\alpha}\sigma\kappa\alpha\lambda\epsilon$) in this
Gospel as he frequently is in the Synoptics: he is, however, addressed
as 'Rabbi' at $1^{38, 49}$, 3^2, 4^{31}, 6^{25}, 9^2, 11^8 (as also in the Synoptics) and
as 'Rabboni' at 20^{16}; and the Evangelist gives 'Teacher' as the
meaning of both 'Rabbi' and 'Rabboni' (1^{38}, 20^{16}; cp. also 3^2 and 11^{28}).

14 are right, for so I am. If I then, your Lord and Teacher,
have washed your feet, you also ought to wash one another's
15 feet. For I have given you an example, that you also should
16 do as I have done to you. Truly, truly, I say to you, a servant
is not greater than his master; nor is he who is sent greater
17 than he who sent him. If you know these things, blessed are
18 you if you do them. I am not speaking of you all; I know whom
I have chosen; it is that the scripture may be fulfilled, "He
19 who ate my bread has lifted his heel against me." I tell you

d Or *slave*

Lord (Gk. Κύριε) as a mode of address is frequent both in John and the
Synoptics, though it may mean little more than 'Sir'; see note on 20².
4 f.   What is meant by *to wash one another's feet*? Clearly it includes
any kind of service, indeed all that is involved in the commandment
'love one another' (v. 34); but in view of the fact that the foot-washing
stands for the whole mission and work of Jesus, the question may be
asked whether John means something more than this; does he perhaps
mean that the believer participates in Christ's work of salvation, and
that he is in a sense his brother's saviour (cp. 13²⁰, 14¹², 20²¹, ²³)?
16   There is a similar saying in Matt. 10²⁴. *master* here is the word
(Gk. κύριος) which is translated *Lord* in vv. 13 f. above. *he who is sent*
(Gk. ἀπόστολος, 'apostle'): this is the only occasion on which John uses
the word in the Gospel.
17   'Religious knowledge, if it is to remain and to increase, must also
express itself in action' (Lightfoot, p. 273); cp. 1 John 3¹⁸.
18   Judas has not yet gone out (see v. 30), and *I am not speaking of you all*
refers to the fact that he is still present. The connection is not altogether
clear, but the idea may be that Judas will exclude himself from the
blessing mentioned in the previous verse, by betraying Jesus. *I know
whom I have chosen*: in 6⁷⁰ it was said that Jesus chose the twelve including Judas, knowing him to be a 'devil'. The reason for the choice of
Judas is now given: *it is that the scripture may be fulfilled*; cp. Mark 14²¹
('the Son of man goes as is written of him, but woe to that man by
whom the Son of man is betrayed!'). *the scripture* is Ps. 41⁹: it is
possible that Mark referred to the same passage in Mark 14¹⁸ ('One
of you will betray me, one who is eating with me'). *lifted his heel
against me*: it is not certain what this means, either in the Psalm or in
the Gospel: for the latter, NEB suggests 'turned against me'; other
suggestions are 'scorn', 'kick'.
19   Cp. 14²⁹. In the perspective of the Gospel narrative, the words of

this now, before it takes place, that when it does take place
20 you may believe that I am he. Truly, truly, I say to you, he
who receives any one whom I send receives me; and he who
receives me receives him who sent me.'

21   When Jesus had thus spoken, he was troubled in spirit, and
testified, 'Truly, truly, I say to you, one of you will betray

---

Jesus precede the events which they describe in order that faith may
come later; historically it was in many cases the other way round: the
faith of the disciples in Jesus as the Christ determined the way in
which they described the events of his life, and many of his words were
composed as prophecies after the event. See Introduction, p. 26.

20   There are similar sayings in the Synoptic Gospels, e.g. Matt. 10⁴⁰.
John is returning to the thought of the sender and the one who is sent
(v. 16), and he means that though the one who is sent is not to think
of himself as greater than the one who sent him, nevertheless *he who
receives* one sent by Jesus, receives both Jesus and the Father *who sent
him*; see also 20²¹ for the same idea. It is possible that John is also
referring to the saying in v. 14: one of the ways in which the disciples
can 'wash one another's feet' is by being sent to others, to represent
Christ to them.

13: 21-30 *Jesus and Judas*

The presence of the betrayer in the company at the supper
has already been mentioned twice (13¹⁰ ᶠᶠ·, ¹⁸): now it is to be
dealt with more fully. John describes the emotion of Jesus as
he declares that one of those present will betray him. Peter
asks the beloved disciple who it is, and he in turn asks Jesus,
who gives him a sign: it is the one to whom he will give something dipped in one of the dishes of the meal. He gives it to
Judas, and commands Judas to do what he is about to do. Judas
obeys, and goes out into the night.

The paragraph raises many questions. First, concerning the
relationship of this account of the prediction of the betrayer, to
those in the Synoptic Gospels (Matt. 26²¹⁻²⁵, Mark 14¹⁸⁻²¹,
Luke 22²¹⁻²³): the closest parallels are with Mark and Luke,
but there is not enough common material to prove the dependence of John on one or both of them (Dodd, *HTFG*, pp. 52–54).
Secondly, John introduces here, without any explanation 'one
of the disciples whom Jesus loved'. Does he mean one of the

22 me.' The disciples looked at one another, uncertain of whom
23 he spoke. One of his disciples, whom Jesus loved, was lying
24 close to the breast of Jesus; so Simon Peter beckoned to him
25 and said, 'Tell us who it is of whom he speaks.' So lying thus,
close to the breast of Jesus, he said to him, 'Lord, who is it?'

---

twelve? Can we find out anything further about this disciple?
For what little can be said in answer to these questions, see
Introduction, pp. 11ff. Thirdly, the story itself (as John tells it) is
difficult to understand. Does he mean that the sign was given
to the beloved disciple alone, or to all the disciples? The former
is more likely in view of the misunderstanding of all those at
the table (vv. 28 f.). But in that case, why did not the beloved
disciple understand? (and, it might be added, why did he not
act?). Fourthly, there is a number of details in this paragraph
which would fit in with the Synoptists' statement that the meal
was the Passover (e.g. reclining at table, v. 25; dipping in a
dish, v. 26; almsgiving, v. 29; an evening meal, v. 30); but
John himself did not think so—see note on 13¹.

John's real interests do not lie in answering these questions.
His purpose is to show his readers that Jesus knew which of the
twelve would betray him, and that the betrayer was unable to
act until Jesus commanded him to do so. He also explains that
the betrayal of Jesus was not simply an individual human lapse,
but the work of Satan, who used Judas as the instrument of his
purpose. He introduces the beloved disciple in relationship
with Simon Peter, and shows the former's greater nearness to
Jesus, as he will do again ($18^{15\,f.\,(?)}$, $19^{25\,ff.}$, 20^{1-10}, $21^{7,\,20-24}$).
This paragraph reveals the nature of the Evangelist's intention:
his primary purpose is theological, not historical.

21   *troubled in spirit*: cp. similar expressions at 11^{33}, 12^{27}. There may be
an echo here of Ps. 42^6 ('My soul is cast down within me': so Dodd,
HTFG, pp. 35 f., 53). The cause of the agitation may be, as at 11^{33}, 'the
presence of absolute unbelief in the midst of His disciples' (Hoskyns,
p. 518): see 6^{64}. *Truly, truly, I say to you, one of you will betray me*: the
wording here is identical with Matt. 26^{21} and Mark 14^{18}, apart from
the Johannine double amen (= *truly*: see note on 1^{51}).

22   In Matthew and Mark the disciples ask Jesus 'Is it I?' In John,
a similar question is asked by the beloved disciple at the instigation

26 Jesus answered, 'It is he to whom I shall give this morsel
   when I have dipped it.' So when he had dipped the morsel, he
27 gave it to Judas, the son of Simon Iscariot. Then after the
   morsel, Satan entered into him. Jesus said to him, 'What you
28 are going to do, do quickly.' Now no one at the table knew

---

of Peter (vv. 24 f.). Therefore, the uncertainty of the disciples in this
Gospel is indicated by their *looking at one another*, instead of by their
questioning Jesus directly.

23 f.   If John did not mean that Lazarus was the beloved disciple (see
note on 11⁵), this is the first reference to this figure (see also on 19²⁶ ᶠ·,
20², 21⁷, ²⁰, and Introduction, pp. 11ff.). *lying close to the breast of Jesus*:
i.e. on his right, because one reclined on one's left side; but apparently
the chief seat was not on the right, but on the left of the host (Barrett,
p. 372). The commentators refer here to 1¹⁸ ('the only Son, who is in
the bosom of the Father') and draw attention to 13²⁰, where it is said
that the relationship between Jesus and the Father is the same as that
between the disciples and Jesus: this may suggest that the beloved
disciple is an 'ideal' figure (but cp. Barrett, p. 373).

25   *Lord, who is it?* Contrast Matthew and Mark, 'Is it I, (Lord)?'
which would be inappropriate in the mouth of the beloved disciple.

26   The device of the sign makes it possible for Jesus to indicate the
betrayer to the beloved disciple, while leaving the others in ignorance
(see vv. 28 f.).   *morsel*: the authorities seem to be divided as to whether
this necessarily means a piece of bread (e.g. W. F. Arndt and F. W.
Gingrich, *A Greek–English Lexicon of the New Testament* (Cambridge,
1957), sub ψωμίον) or not (Barrett, p. 373). Dipping bitter herbs in
a special sauce was a feature of the Passover meal.

27   Satan uses Judas as his agent for the betrayal only when Jesus has
designated Judas as the betrayer; and both Judas and Satan are
unable to act until Jesus gives the command—cp. 'He has no power
over me' (14³⁰) and the account of the arrest in 18¹⁻¹²; and for a
similar belief in Satan's inability to act without divine permission,
see e.g. Job 1¹², 2⁶.

28 f.   See note on 11³⁷ for twofold reactions in this Gospel: here, however,
it is the disciples, not the Jews, who are in ignorance. The reference to
Judas and the *money box* recalls 12⁶, where it was said that Judas was
a thief. Possibly John's irony is to be seen here: far from buying what
is needed for the feast, or from giving alms to the poor, Judas' intention is to sell the Lord for his own profit (though it must be said that
John does not record this transaction; contrast Mark 14¹⁰ ᶠ· and
parallels). Furthermore, the unintended result of his action is that he

₉ why he said this to him. Some thought that, because Judas had the money box, Jesus was telling him, 'Buy what we need for the feast'; or, that he should give something to the
₀ poor. So, after receiving the morsel, he immediately went out; and it was night.

₁   When he had gone out, Jesus said, 'Now is the Son of man
₂ glorified, and in him God is glorified; if God is glorified in him, God will also glorify him in himself, and glorify him at
₃ once. Little children, yet a little while I am with you. You will seek me; and as I said to the Jews so now I say to you,

---

does procure the true Lamb of God *for the feast*, and thereby gives salvation *to the poor*.

₀   In obedience to the word of Jesus, and in fulfilment of the sign which he has given (v. 26), Judas goes out both from the room and from the company of Jesus and his disciples (cp. 1 John 2¹⁹ [of the false teachers] 'they went out from us') into the *night*, both literally and in the metaphorical sense in which this word is frequently used by John (see note on 3²).

31–38 *The departure of Jesus*

The withdrawal of Judas to betray Jesus is the cue for Jesus to declare in anticipation that the Son of man is now glorified— that is to say, the events which will issue in his being lifted up from the earth have already begun; and because he and the Father are one, the glorifying of the Son is also the glorifying of the Father, and will be immediately endorsed and ratified by the Father's glorification of the Son in resurrection and exaltation. All this must inevitably involve the separation of Jesus from his disciples in the visible sense. Looked at in this way, the disciples could no more follow Jesus than the unbelieving Jews could do so: the disciples remain in the world, whereas Jesus is going to the Father. It is important therefore that they should know how they are to conduct themselves in this time of separation; so Jesus gives them the commandment to love one another, which is new, not because it has not been given to men before this, but because of the qualification which Jesus adds, 'even as I have loved you'. This mutual love will distinguish them from others, and bring faith to everybody. Peter

34 "Where I am going you cannot come." A new commandment I give to you, that you love one another; even as I have
35 loved you, that you also love one another. By this all men will know that you are my disciples, if you have love for one another.'

---

asks where Jesus is going, and the answer of Jesus declares both Peter's present weakness and his future strength: Peter disputes the former, and protests his present strength, but Jesus tells Peter that Peter will disown him three times before the night is out.

31   Cp. 12²³ ('The hour has come for the Son of man to be glorified'). *glorified* here refers both to the crucifixion and to the exaltation of Jesus, but with special emphasis on the former. *God is glorified* in the death of Jesus, because in it God's grace and love are revealed.

32   *if God is glorified in him* should be probably omitted with the majority of the textual authorities. *God will also glorify him* (i.e. Jesus) *in himself* (i.e. the Father): the reference here is the exaltation of Jesus to the glory which he had 'before the world was made' (17⁵). *glorify him at once*: even the three days interval between Good Friday and Easter Day disappear in John's thought: the crucifixion is itself the exaltation.

33   *Little children*: only here in John, frequently in 1 John (cp. note on 14¹⁸). *a little while* is a favourite expression in this Gospel: see also 7³³, 12³⁵, 14¹⁹, 16¹⁶⁻¹⁹. It refers here to the few hours which are left of the life of Jesus in the flesh. *You will seek me*: cp. 7³⁴, 8²¹, where these words are said to the Jews; it is not clear whether the meaning is the same in this context, or whether the words refer to the search for the body of Jesus on Easter Day, e.g. 20¹⁵. *as I said to the Jews*: i.e. in 7³⁴, 8²¹. *Where I am going you cannot come*: there will be a real separation, but, as John will show in the discourse as it proceeds, it will be overcome through the action of Jesus in sending the Spirit, and through the faith of the disciples.

34   The commandment 'You shall love your neighbour as yourself' is found in Lev. 19¹⁸, and frequently quoted in the N.T. John says, instead of 'neighbour', *one another* (here and at 15¹², ¹⁷); and it is possible to detect an element of narrowness and exclusiveness here, though this is denied by Hoskyns (p. 530) and Barrett (p. 377). See also Introduction, p. 27. On the sense in which this commandment is *new*, see 1 John 2⁷ᶠᶠ.

35   Mutual love is the essence of discipleship, and the only manifestation of it.

6   Simon Peter said to him, 'Lord, where are you going?'
Jesus answered, 'Where I am going you cannot follow me
7 now; but you shall follow afterward.' Peter said to him,
'Lord, why cannot I follow you now? I will lay down my life
8 for you.' Jesus answered, 'Will you lay down your life for me?
Truly, truly, I say to you, the cock will not crow, till you have
denied me three times.

4 'LET not your hearts be troubled; believe*e* in God, believe

e Or *you believe*

---

6   Peter's question is almost the same as that of the Jews in 7³⁵: cp.
v. 33, where Jesus addressed them as he had addressed the Jews.
Because Peter is still as ignorant of Jesus' meaning as they were, it is
not surprising that Jesus says to him, *you cannot follow me now. you shall
follow afterward* refers both to Peter's discipleship and to his martyrdom
(see note on 21¹⁸ ᶠ·).

f.   Peter's denial (18¹⁵ ᶠᶠ·, 25 ᶠᶠ·), which Jesus predicts, explains why it is
that Peter cannot follow Jesus now: he cannot bear witness to Jesus
without the help of the Paraclete (cp. 15²⁶ ᶠ·, 'he shall bear witness to
me, and you also are witnesses').   *I will lay down my life for you* is
ironical in view of the denials: Jesus will lay down his life for Peter,
and thus enable Peter to lay down his life in martyrdom, so that Peter
will indeed eventually 'follow afterward'.

: 1–31 *Jesus reassures the disciples*

Jesus had told the disciples that he would soon be separated
from them, and that Peter, their leader and spokesman, would
deny him three times before the morning. The distress which
(we are to imagine) these words caused in the minds of the
disciples, is the background against which the present chapter
is to be understood; because all through it, in varying ways,
Jesus is reassuring the disciples.

They must believe in Jesus, just as they must believe in God,
and then it will follow that the departure of Jesus will be seen
to be for their own good. Moreover, since they know Jesus,
they know 'the way' to the Father, because this is what he is:
he is all that men need for salvation, because he is, by his

2   also in me. In my Father's house are many rooms; if it were
    not so, would I have told you that I go to prepare a place for
    you? And when I go and prepare a place for you, I will come

---

obedience, the one in whom the Father is at work for the
salvation of the world.

Again, because they believe in Jesus, and because Jesus is
going to the Father, they will be able to do greater things than
Jesus did; they will bear fruit in the conversion of the world
and prepare men for the many rooms in the Father's house.

Jesus is going to the Father, and this means that he will be
available to answer the prayers of the disciples, which they will
pray in his name, and above all to send them the Paraclete who
will be with them for ever.

It is thus becoming clear that the departure of Jesus is
entirely for the good of the disciples, and not at all to their
disadvantage: to believe in Jesus is to accept that he will only
do them good. But now, a further point is made: in a sense,
Jesus is not going from them at all; he is coming to them—
certainly not in a way that the world could understand, but
only in a way that is understood by faith. They will see him,
and they will live by his life; they themselves will be the man-
sions in which the Father and the Son dwell.

Finally, they need not worry if they do not understand Jesus
yet, or if they forget what he has said, because the Paraclete
will teach them and remind them. They can, therefore, rest in
the peace which Jesus gives them without distress or fear. His
going is a going to the Father: it opens out a new and greater
situation for the disciples; ultimately it is not a going at all, but
a coming. This is how faith understands it, because faith sees
more than what appears to be the case: it will appear as though
Jesus is destroyed by the evil powers; in fact, the evil powers
have no claim against him, but he is simply obeying the Father
for the sake of the world. If they see it in this way, they will
accompany him out of this world and into the Father's
presence.

1   *Let not your hearts be troubled*: this is the link between Chapter 13 and
    Chapter 14; in the former, Jesus warned the disciples of the treachery
    of Judas and the denials of Peter; in this chapter, he will reassure them
    that all shall be well. *believe in God, believe also in me*: *believe* (Gk.

again and will take you to myself, that where I am you may be
4, 5 also. And you know the way where I am going.'*ᶠ* Thomas said
to him, 'Lord, we do not know where you are going; how
6 can we know the way?' Jesus said to him, 'I am the way, and
the truth, and the life; no one comes to the Father, but by
7 me. If you had known me, you would have known my Father
also; henceforth you know him and have seen him.'

f Other ancient authorities read *where I am going you know, and the way you
know*

πιστεύετε) in both places may be either indicative or imperative, and
the commentators do not agree which is which. What is clear is that
Jesus is saying that the assurance offered to the disciples in this chapter
can only be accepted by faith in God, and in Jesus who is his agent
(see also note on v. 10).

2   *In my Father's house are many rooms*: i.e. there is plenty of room in
heaven, whither Jesus is going. To believe in God (v. 1) involves
believing that he wills the salvation of men, who are to occupy the
many rooms; and to believe in Jesus means (in this context) to believe
that his departure to the Father is for the salvation of men, which is
here spoken of as preparing a place for them in heaven. The punctuation of the latter half of this verse in RSV creates the problem, when
before this did Jesus say that he was going to prepare a place for them?
Since he has not said so, it may be better to punctuate 'if it were not
so I should have told you; for I am going there on purpose to prepare
a place for you' (NEB text).

3   John deliberately does not make it clear, at this point in the discourse, when Jesus will return to take the disciples to himself: the time
of the re-union is left uncertain on purpose, in order that, though
misunderstanding, the truth may eventually emerge as the discourse
progresses.

4   The shorter text (RSV text) is probably right, and the longer
reading (RSV mg.) is a simplification of it. The *way* is (*a*) outwardly,
death; (*b*) inwardly, obedience to the Father; therefore (*c*) the glorification of Jesus. Again, this is said in such a way as to provoke misunderstanding, and so provide an occasion for further explanation.

Thomas is also mentioned in this gospel at 11¹⁶, 20²⁴ ᶠᶠ·, 21². His statement here is true in two senses: (*a*) in the literal sense: if the destination
is unknown, the route is *eo ipso* unknown; (*b*) in the context of the
departure of Jesus: if they do not know that he is going to the Father,
they cannot understand the reality of what is about to happen.

8   Philip said to him, 'Lord, show us the Father, and we shall
9 be satisfied.' Jesus said to him, 'Have I been with you so long,
   and yet you do not know me, Philip? He who has seen me has
10 seen the Father; how can you say, "Show us the Father"? Do
   you not believe that I am in the Father and the Father in me?
   The words that I say to you I do not speak on my own
   authority; but the Father who dwells in me does his works.

---

6   The sixth 'I am' saying (see note on 6³⁵). The language of movement
   (*go, come, way*, etc.) is being used metaphorically and not so as to give
   a literal description of what is about to happen: thus, whereas it cannot be said literally that a person is a *way* (= road), it can be said that
   somebody is the means whereby one person comes to another; and this
   is what is meant by *I am the way*. The addition of *and the truth, and the
   life*, explains this: Jesus is the means by which men come to the
   Father (= believe in God and enter into communion with him),
   because he is the Mediator, who imparts *truth* (= knowledge of God)
   and *life* (= participation in the life of God).

7   The text is uncertain, and it may be that what John wrote was
   a promise rather than a rebuke: 'If you know me you will know my
   Father too' (NEB mg.). The second half of the verse assures them that
   this will happen *henceforth*, i.e. as a result of the coming death of Jesus.
   To *know*, to *see*, to *come to* (v. 6) and to *believe in* (v. 1) are all virtually
   synonymous.

8   *Philip* is mentioned also at 1⁴³ ᶠᶠ·, 6⁵ ᶠᶠ·, 12²¹ ᶠᶠ·. What he says here
   shows that he has not yet understood the relationship between Jesus
   and the Father, links up with the previous saying of Jesus, and provides
   the 'feed' for what follows.

9   Jesus is the Son who is wholly obedient to the Father (cp. 5¹⁹, etc.);
   therefore to *know* him (as the Son) and to *see* him (as the agent of God)
   is to see and know the Father also as the one who is being obeyed by
   the Son.

10   The language of position (*in*), like the language of movement (see
   note on v. 6), is metaphorical, because it is not possible in a literal
   sense for A to be in B, and B to be in A. Jesus is *in the Father*, in the
   sense that he is inspired and directed by the Father, and lives through
   him: the Father is *in* Jesus, in the sense that he is at work in him. This
   mutual indwelling of Father and Son is not apparent except to faith;
   hence, *Do you not believe . . . ?* This saying, therefore, throws more light
   on the meaning of v. 1 ('believe in God, believe also in me'). We see
   now that the disciples are not asked to believe two doctrines, one

11 Believe me that I am in the Father and the Father in me; or else believe me for the sake of the works themselves.

12 'Truly, truly, I say to you, he who believes in me will also do the works that I do; and greater works than these will he

13 do, because I go to the Father. Whatever you ask in my name,

14 I will do it, that the Father may be glorified in the Son; if you ask*g* anything in my name, I will do it.

16 'If you love me, you will keep my commandments. And I will pray the Father, and he will give you another Counsellor,

g Other ancient authorities add *me*

---

about God and another about Jesus, but one, about the Son in the Father and the Father in the Son. Notice the parallel between *words* and *works* in this verse, and see the next verse.

11   Again there is the insistence on faith: *Believe me* (cp. vv. 1, 6, 7, 10). And again (as in v. 10) there is the parallel between the words and the *works* (i.e. the signs): the Father is the source of both.

12   *Truly, truly* (see note on 1⁵¹) introduces further reassurance for the disciples as they face the imminent departure of Jesus. He has spoken of believing in him, and of his *works* (v. 11); now he says that he who believes in him will do the same *works*, and *greater works*. That is to say, the Father will dwell in the believer (see below v. 23), and work in him as he has done in Jesus (v. 10); and the works of the believer will be *greater* than the works of Jesus, because of the death of Jesus (= *I go to the Father*), which liberates the gospel for proclamation to the Greeks (see 12²⁰ᶠᶠ·, and notice specially 12²⁴).

13   It is not altogether clear what is the connection between this verse and what has gone before. Possibly the line of thought is that the 'greater works' of the believer are the works of the Father done in response to the prayer of the believer, just as at the raising of Lazarus Jesus thanked the Father for hearing him (11⁴¹ ᶠ·). *in my name* apparently means 'with the invocation of my name' (Barrett, p. 384). *I will do it*: the activity of the Son is identical with the activity of the Father, and each is glorified by the other, see 13³¹ ᶠ·.

14   *me* (RSV mg.) is probably correct (Hoskyns, p. 539).

15   The connection between *love* and obedience is often emphasized in the Johannine writings (e.g. 14²¹, ²³ ᶠ·, 15¹⁰, ¹⁴; 1 John 5³). John may have made the point here in order to explain what is involved in asking 'in my name' (vv. 13 f.): the name may not be used without love and obedience.

16   Jesus will pray the Father (cp. 1 John 2¹, 'we have an advocate [Gk.

17 to be with you for ever, even the Spirit of truth, whom the world cannot receive, because it neither sees him nor knows him; you know him, for he dwells with you, and will be in you.

18, 19 'I will not leave you desolate; I will come to you. Yet a little while, and the world will see me no more, but you will

20 see me; because I live, you will live also. In that day you will

---

παράκλητον, Paraclete] with the Father, Jesus Christ the righteous'), and the Father will give them another Paraclete (= *Counsellor*). This is the first reference to the Paraclete in the Gospel: see also 14²⁶, 15²⁶, 16⁷ ᶠᶠ·. Whatever the exact meaning of the title ('Counsellor', RSV; 'Advocate', NEB), it is clear from this verse that the Spirit is to continue the work of Jesus among the disciples *for ever*.

17   *the Spirit of truth* (see also 15²⁶, 16¹³): the Spirit continues the work of Jesus by making the truth about it known to the disciples; he is 'the Spirit who communicates truth' (Barrett, p. 386), and Jesus is the truth (v. 6). *the world* cannot, by definition, receive the teaching of the Spirit, because *the world*, in this context, means those who are not believers (= *neither sees him nor knows him*). The disciples, on the other hand, have the Spirit *with* them in the fellowship, and *in* them as individuals (RSV is probably following the inferior text in its translation *will be*; NEB prefers the alternative reading, 'is'. John is writing from the point of view of those who live after the coming of the Spirit).

18   *desolate* (Gk. ὀρφανούς, literally 'orphans', 'deprived'): to believe in Jesus (v. 1) rules out in advance the possibility that he would leave them unprotected. *I will come to you*: as in v. 3 John still uses an ambiguous expression, which he will soon define more clearly (see vv. 21, 23): he is deliberately using traditional Christian apocalyptic language (e.g. Mark 13²⁶), but using it in a new and different sense.

19   *Yet a little while* (see 7³³, 12³⁵, 13³³, 16¹⁶ ᶠᶠ·): i.e. after a few more hours. *the world* will not *see* Jesus, because he will have died, and *the world* will not believe in him, because it cannot (cp. v. 17). The disciples, on the other hand, will *see* Jesus through believing in him, and they will *live* with his eternal life which he is giving them through his death and resurrection (cp. 10¹¹).

20   *In that day*: i.e. in the new situation which will follow the death and resurrection of Jesus. The faith of the disciples (= *you will know*) is again (cp. v. 10) described in terms of position, and the meaning of it is that the disciples will believe that Jesus is the agent of the Father for salvation, and that they are saved by him.

know that I am in my Father, and you in me, and I in you.

21 He who has my commandments and keeps them, he it is who loves me; and he who loves me will be loved by my Father,

22 and I will love him and manifest myself to him.' Judas (not Iscariot) said to him, 'Lord, how is it that you will manifest

23 yourself to us, and not to the world?' Jesus answered him, 'If a man loves me, he will keep my word, and my Father will love him, and we will come to him and make our home with

24 him. He who does not love me does not keep my words; and the word which you hear is not mine but the Father's who sent me.

---

21   See note on v. 15. The love of the believer for Jesus unites him to Jesus, and brings him within the love of the Father for the Son. This is the situation in which Jesus will come to them (v. 18): he will *manifest* himself to the disciples in the life of the community, as their Lord. But again (cp. vv. 3, 18) this is expressed in a way which can be misunderstood, and is misunderstood by Judas in the next verse.

22   *Judas (not Iscariot)*: there is a second *Judas* ('the son of James') in the lists of the twelve in Luke 6^{16} and Acts 1^{13}, but not in the Matthean or Marcan lists. *Judas* misunderstands the manner of Jesus' manifestation (v. 21), and cannot see how it is possible unless it is an open revelation of himself to the world, such as Jews and earlier Christians had expected. (It is possibly significant that in Greek there is very little difference between the word Jew ('Ιουδαῖος) and the name *Judas* ('Ιούδας). He speaks for the Jewish point of view. See also note on 19^{11}.)

23   The first part of this verse repeats what was said of the believer in v. 21, the second part answers Judas' question—*we will come to him and make our home* (Gk. μονήν: the same word is translated 'rooms' in v. 2) *with him*. We can now see that the language of movement (vv. 2 ff.) was metaphorical and not literal, and that the 'departure' of Jesus is, in fact, his 'coming', with the Father, to abide in the believer—i.e. into fellowship with him.

24   The unbeliever (= *He who does not love me*: cp. 'the world' in vv. 17, 22) does not obey Jesus, and therefore (since Jesus is the agent of the Father) does not obey God. There will and can therefore be no 'coming' of the Father and the Son to the world. This answers the second part of Judas' question in v. 22 ('. . . and not to the world'). Notice also the same change from plural (*words*) to singular (*word*), as in 11$^{45 f.}$ (see note).

25   'These things I have spoken to you, while I am still with
26   you. But the Counsellor, the Holy Spirit, whom the Father
     will send in my name, he will teach you all things, and bring
27   to your remembrance all that I have said to you. Peace I leave
     with you; my peace I give to you; not as the world gives do I
     give to you. Let not your hearts be troubled, neither let them
28   be afraid. You heard me say to you, "I go away, and I will
     come to you." If you loved me, you would have rejoiced,
     because I go to the Father; for the Father is greater than I.
29   And now I have told you before it takes place, so that when it
30   does take place, you may believe. I will no longer talk much

---

25 f.   The work of the Paraclete (= *the Counsellor*: see note on v. 16) will
         be to bring to mind the teaching of Jesus. As John's Gospel as a whole
         shows, this is not simply to remind them of what Jesus had said by
         recalling his *ipsissima verba*, but to interpret the meaning of his words
         and deeds for the life of the Church. *whom the Father will send in my
         name*: perhaps 'as my representative' (cp. v. 16 'another Counsellor').
27   The discourse started with the words 'Let not your hearts be
         troubled' (v. 1); now it returns to that theme. Distress is the very
         opposite to what they should be feeling. Jesus is giving them *peace*—
         i.e. the prosperity which follows from the divine favour: Jesus says *my
         peace*, both because it has been brought to them by Jesus and his death,
         and because it is his gift and not a reward which they have earned
         (cp. Rom. 6^{23}). *not as the world gives do I give to you*: the world *gives* in
         payment for services rendered, or as a bribe for future favours; Jesus'
         gift is entirely motivated by love.
28   The discourse is summed up in the two sayings *I go away* and *I will
         come to you*; and it is now clear that both sayings refer to the same event
         (the death and glorification of Jesus), and the new situation which
         this event will create for the disciples. The believer (i.e. he who loves
         Jesus) rejoices over this event: Jesus' going to the Father brings him
         all the benefits of the new life as a disciple. Moreover, because *the
         Father is greater than I* the believer will do 'greater works' than Jesus
         (v. 12).
29   This verse repeats 13^{19}, with slight variation: see note there.
30   The time for talking will soon be over, because Satan (= *the ruler of
         this world*: cp. 12^{31}, 16^{11}) is coming in the person of Judas Iscariot
         (13^{27}), and this will mark the change-over from speech to action (cp.
         v. 29). *He has no power over me*: literally 'has nothing in me', and so

with you, for the ruler of this world is coming. He has no
31 power over me; but I do as the Father has commanded me,
so that the world may know that I love the Father. Rise, let
us go hence.

1,2 'I AM the true vine, and my Father is the vinedresser. Every
branch of mine that bears no fruit, he takes away, and every

'has no claim against me'. Satan's power over men depends on their
sin, which puts them into his hands. Jesus is without sin, and so
immune from the power of Satan. (For a different punctuation of this
verse, see note on v. 31.)

31   Jesus' obedience to the Father's commandments includes laying
down his life, and the purpose of this is that the world may believe
(= know) that Jesus is the one who is obedient to (= love) the Father.
Rise, let us go hence: almost exactly the same words occur in Mark 14[42],
where Jesus invites the disciples to go with him to the betrayer. Some
think that originally the Johannine discourse ended here, and that
hence meant from the supper to the garden which is mentioned in 18[1]
(Barrett, p. 392); some think that John means that they went out of the
room at this point, and that the discourses in vv. 15–17 were said on the
way to the garden (Westcott, ii, p. 187); and others take the command
in a metaphorical sense—e.g. C. H. Dodd, 'The Ruler of this world is
coming. He has no claim upon me; but to show the world that I love the
Father, and do exactly as He commands—up, let us march to meet
him!' (*IFG*, p. 409; cp. Lightfoot, p. 278); and Hoskyns, 'Arise, let us
remove from death unto life, and from corruption unto incorruption'
(p. 548). A decision on the interpretation of these words must depend
on (*a*) whether it is thought that there have been dislocations in or
additions to the text, and on (*b*) whether it is thought that John is using
Mark.

5: 1–17 *The meaning of abiding*

In the previous discourse Jesus explained his departure from
the disciples as a return to them in a new way, and he promised
them that when this happened they would know that he was
in the Father, and they in him, and he in them (14[20]). This
promise is now repeated by means of the metaphor of the vine
and the branches: Jesus will be the source of their life as
believers, and of the good works which they will do.

The previous discourse was, as we saw, controlled by the

branch that does bear fruit he prunes, that it may bear more
3 fruit. You are already made clean by the word which I have

---

command which came at the beginning of it: 'Believe in God,
believe also in me' (14¹). Now, however, the command to
believe is expressed by means of a metaphor from the language
of space and movement, namely 'abide in'; and it may be
significant that the only comparable passage earlier in the
book where John has used this expression is 6⁵⁶, 'He who eats
my flesh and drinks my blood abides in me, and I in him' (see
Lightfoot, p. 282). The idea of abiding in Christ may therefore
be connected with the Eucharist; and many of the commentators have suggested that the discourse on the vine is placed at
the supper so as to be in some sense an equivalent of the Synoptic institution narrative (e.g. Hoskyns, pp. 555 f.; Barrett,
p. 393).

This section of the words of Jesus at the supper explains what
it means to be a believer. It is to bear fruit in good works; to
pray, knowing that prayer will be answered; to glorify the
Father; and to keep the commandments of Jesus by loving the
brethren. The subject of the section is therefore the essence of
Church membership.

1   *I am the true vine*: this is the seventh and last 'I am' saying (see note
on 6³⁵). In the O.T. the vine is often used as a metaphor for Israel, e.g.
Ps. 80⁸ ('Thou didst bring a vine out of Egypt') and Jer. 2²¹ ('I planted
you a choice vine', which the LXX translates 'true vine', as here).
John's point is that Jesus, not the Jewish people, is the *true vine. my
Father is the vinedresser*: the dependence of Jesus on the Father, and his
'subordination' to him, are stressed throughout this Gospel; see e.g.
14²⁸ ('the Father is greater than I').
2   That the *branches* are the disciples will be explained in v. 5. To *bear
fruit* is frequently used in the Synoptic Gospels for to do good works,
e.g. Matt. 3⁸. The unfruitful branches are almost certainly faithless
and apostate disciples, of whom Judas Iscariot is typical. There is a
play on words in the Greek here: *he takes away* (Gk. αἴρει) is similar
in sound to *he prunes* (Gk. καθαίρει, literally 'he cleanses'). How the
disciple is pruned or cleansed is explained in the next verse.
3   In 13¹⁰ Jesus declared some of the disciples 'clean', and we saw that
the meaning was that they were purified by the whole mission of Jesus,
summed up in his death (cp. 1 John 1⁷, 'the blood of Jesus his Son

4 spoken to you. Abide in me, and I in you. As the branch
cannot bear fruit by itself, unless it abides in the vine, neither
5 can you, unless you abide in me. I am the vine, you are the
branches. He who abides in me, and I in him, he it is that
6 bears much fruit, for apart from me you can do nothing. If a
man does not abide in me, he is cast forth as a branch and
withers; and the branches are gathered, thrown into the fire
7 and burned. If you abide in me, and my words abide in you,
8 ask whatever you will, and it shall be done for you. By this
my Father is glorified, that you bear much fruit, and so

---

cleanses us from all sin'). Here, the cleansing of the disciples is attributed to *the word which I have spoken to you*, that is the communication of
Jesus to the disciples through his coming into the world.

4 The word *abide* will be used eleven times in this section, and it
provides the theme. The disciples are to remain in union with Jesus,
although they will see him no longer in a physical, or worldly, way
(14^{19}); and Jesus, for his part, promises to continue to maintain his
union with them (cp. 14^{18}, 'I will come to you'). This union is essential
in order that they may be fruitful, i.e. in order that they may live that
life of good works which God expects of them (see v. 2). In the Second
Letter of John, the apostate is described as 'Anyone who goes ahead
and does not abide in the doctrine of Christ', and the believer is
referred to as 'he who abides in the doctrine' (2 John 9).

5 For repetition of 'I am' sayings, cp. 8^{12}, 9^5, $10^{7, 9}$, and $10^{11, 14}$.

6 Cp. Matt. 3^{10} ('Every tree therefore that does not bear good fruit is
cut down and thrown into the fire'). Possibly John means by *cast forth
. . . and withers*, the fate of the faithless disciple in this world, and by
thrown into the fire and burned his fate in the world to come.

7 See note on $14^{12 \, ff.}$ for the connection between being a disciple and
prayer. Here, as there, they are assured that their union with Jesus will
be such that their petitions will be answered.

8 As in $14^{12 \, ff.}$ the thought of the union between Jesus and the disciples
in the coming age (there referred to as believing in him, here as
abiding in him) is followed by a reference to the glorifying of the
Father. The 'greater works' (= *much fruit*) of the disciples of Jesus
bring glory to the Father who sent him (cp. Matt. 5^{16}, 'Let your light
so shine before men, that they may see your good works and give glory
to your Father who is in heaven').

9 prove to be my disciples. As the Father has loved me, so
10 have I loved you; abide in my love. If you keep my commandments, you will abide in my love, just as I have kept my
11 Father's commandments and abide in his love. These things
I have spoken to you, that my joy may be in you, and that
your joy may be full.

12 'This is my commandment, that you love one another as I
13 have loved you. Greater love has no man than this, that a
14 man lay down his life for his friends. You are my friends if
15 you do what I command you. No longer do I call you servants,[h] for the servant[i] does not know what his master is

         [h] Or *slaves*   [i] Or *slave*

---

9   'The Father loves the Son' (3[35]), and the Son loves the disciples (see 13[1]): this is the ground of Christian faith and discipleship; and the disciples are to *abide in* this *love* of the Son for them by obedience to him; see next verse.

10   For love and obedience see note on 14[15]: the disciple is united with Jesus by love and obedience, just as Jesus is united with the Father by love and obedience.

11   The explanation which Jesus has given of his departure and its consequences should lead the disciple to share in the joy of salvation —the joy which is first that of Jesus, and then given to the disciples.

12   The 'commandments' were mentioned in v. 10, and before that in 13[34] (which is repeated here) and in 14[15]: see note on 13[34].

13   It is possible to ask the question whether John's conception of love is as far-reaching as Paul's: see Rom. 5[6 ff.] for the love which goes beyond dying for one's friends to dying for one's enemies; and see Introduction, p. 27.

14   The same idea is expressed in this verse as in v. 10; and note the same tendency as in the previous verses to limit the love of Jesus, on this occasion by the addition of the conditional clause, *if you do what I command you.*

15   The contrast is between *slaves* who have no knowledge of their master, and *friends* who know him; cp. a somewhat similar distinction between slaves and sons in 8[35], and in Paul (Gal. 4[1 ff.]). It is also very likely that this is at least part of the meaning of the parable of the Prodigal Son (Luke 15[11 ff.]—note Luke 15[29], 'You know how I have slaved for you all these years' (NEB)). Jesus has brought the disciples into the status of friends, by revealing to them God's love for them.

doing; but I have called you friends, for all that I have
16 heard from my Father I have made known to you. You did
not choose me, but I chose you and appointed you that you
should go and bear fruit and that your fruit should abide; so
that whatever you ask the Father in my name, he may give it
17 to you. This I command you, to love one another.
18 'If the world hates you, know that it has hated me before it
19 hated you. If you were of the world, the world would love its

---

16   The disciples are the elect, those whom Jesus has chosen: their
salvation is by God's grace, not by their works. *bear fruit*: see vv. 2,
4, 5, 8. *that your fruit should abide*: the good works of the disciples
remain for ever, and they will be rewarded for them by God (cp. 1 Cor.
15⁵⁸, 1 Thess. 2¹⁹ f., Rev. 14¹³). Possibly the translation of the last part
of this verse should be, 'and that whatever you ask . . .', i.e. this clause
is parallel to the previous clause, and not dependent upon it (Barrett,
p. 399). For prayer and its effectiveness: see also 14¹³ f., 15⁷.
17   This verse repeats v. 12, and rounds off this section of the discourse.

5: 18–27 *The Church and the world*

  John's mind worked in contrasts, and the connection between this section and the previous section is an example of
his linking by opposites. He has said that the disciples are to
love one another, as Jesus loved them: the antithesis of love is
hate. He has been talking about the life of the disciples, that is,
the Church (a word he does not use in the Gospel): the opposite
to the Church, in John's way of thinking, is the world. The
disciples are the friends of Jesus who love him: the world
hates him. The disciples know him and his Father: the world
does not.
  Thus, the main part of this section has been produced by
working out the antitheses of what was said before, in the light
of the experience of persecution and hatred which the Church
has undergone. Towards the end of the section, John returns
to the thought of the coming of the Paraclete, because his work
will be to continue the opposition between Jesus and the
world, in the life of the Church; that is an idea which John will
develop further in the next chapter, especially in 16⁸⁻¹¹.

own; but because you are not of the world, but I chose you
20 out of the world, therefore the world hates you. Remember
the word that I said to you, "A servant[i] is not greater than his
master." If they persecuted me, they will persecute you; if
21 they kept my word, they will keep yours also. But all this
they will do to you on my account, because they do not know
22 him who sent me. If I had not come and spoken to them, they

i Or *slave*

---

18   Persecution of believers, first by Jews and then by Gentiles, was the
constant experience of the Church from the earliest times: see for
example 1 Thess. 2[13 ff.] (1 Thess. is probably the earliest surviving
Christian writing) and Acts *passim*. The impression one gets from the
Synoptic Gospels is that Jesus was hated more by the Jewish leaders
(the Pharisees and the scribes) than by the common people either in
Galilee or Jerusalem. John is, however, concentrating upon the outcome of Jesus' mission, the crucifixion; and he sees this as the typical
reaction of *the world* to Jesus. This is what he is referring to when he
says that *the world . . . hated me before it hated you.*

19   *If you were of the world*: the disciples 'are not of the world' (17[14]);
they belong to the Father and the Son; they are the elect, chosen by
Jesus (v. 16), given to him by the Father (17[6]). This action of God
upon the disciples separates them from the world, and provokes the
world to hate them.

20   For the saying about a *servant* and his *master*, see 13[16]. The point of
that saying (which the disciples are to ponder in time of persecution
in order that their faith may be strengthened: cp. 16[1]) is that if the
master was subjected to humiliation by the world (= crucifixion), his
servant cannot expect any better treatment; but on the other hand, if
there were those who believed through the coming of Jesus (e.g. the
disciples themselves), there will also be those who will believe in him
'through their word' (17[20]).

21   The words *all this* seem to refer only to the persecution of the
disciples, and not to the faithful hearing of them mentioned in the
latter part of the previous verse. The world will hate and persecute
the disciples, because it hates their Lord, and does not believe that he
was sent by God.

22   Cp. for the same idea 9[39 ff.] (where 'guilt' (RSV) translates the

would not have sin; but now they have no excuse for their
24 sin. He who hates me hates my Father also. If I had not done
among them the works which no one else did, they would not
have sin; but now they have seen and hated both me and my
25 Father. It is to fulfil the word that is written in their law,
26 "They hated me without a cause." But when the Counsellor
comes, whom I shall send to you from the Father, even the
Spirit of truth, who proceeds from the Father, he will bear
27 witness to me; and you also are witnesses, because you have
been with me from the beginning.

Greek word ἁμαρτία $=$ *sin* here); and note 16⁹, where *sin* is defined as
not believing in Jesus. Sin, in the sense of rejecting Jesus as the agent
of God, was not possible apart from the coming of Jesus. This rejection
has been deliberate, and is therefore inexcusable (cp. 9⁴¹). John does
not harmonize this view of sin with that in 12³⁹ ('they could believe').

23   Cp. 5²³ ('He who does not honour the Son does not honour the
Father who sent him'). Jesus and the Father cannot be separated
(cp. 10³⁰).

24   Cp. 9³² ('Never since the world began has it been heard that anyone
opened the eyes of a man born blind'). The miracles ($=$ *the works*) of
Jesus have left men with no excuse for not believing in him. To reject
him in the face of these deeds is to reject the Father also (see previous
verse).

25   The quotation is from Ps. 35¹⁹ or 69⁴, which is referred to as *their law*
as in 10³⁴ ('your law'). The quotation shows that the fault lies with
those who have hated Jesus, not with Jesus himself; and the fact that
it is in *their law* shows that they are self-condemned (cp. 5⁴⁵, 'it is
Moses who accuses you').

26   For the Paraclete ($=$ *Counsellor*) see note on 14¹⁶. *whom I shall send*:
cp. 14²⁶ ('whom the Father will send in my name'); John does not
intend there to be any distinction between these two statements.
the Spirit of truth: see note on 14¹⁷.   *he will bear witness to me*: i.e. he will
teach the disciples, and bring to their remembrance what Jesus said
to them (14²⁶), and thus make them into witnesses (see next verse, and
cp. Luke 24⁴⁸ ᶠ·).

27   The disciples are witnesses because of the coming of the Spirit which
Jesus has promised, and because of their faithfulness to Jesus *from the
beginning* (i.e. throughout his ministry, cp. 16⁴).

16 'I HAVE said all this to you to keep you from falling away.
 2 They will put you out of the synagogues; indeed, the hour is
   coming when whoever kills you will think he is offering
 3 service to God. And they will do this because they have not
 4 known the Father, nor me. But I have said these things to

16: 1-15 *The Paraclete, the Church, and the world*

The discourse which started in 13³¹ now begins to draw to
its close. The disciples have been silent since the question of
Judas in 14²², but they will begin to ask questions in the following section (16¹⁶ ᶠᶠ·). Jesus explains why he has spoken to them
now, and why he has not spoken to them in this way before;
but even now he cannot tell them all that he has to say. (Note
the repeated 'I have said all this', etc., in 16¹, ⁴ᵃ, ᵇ, ⁶, ¹².) He
has forewarned them of persecution, in order that they may be
forearmed and stand firm when it comes upon them. He did
not say these things before, because he was present; but now
he is going. Yet, as we know (though the disciples at the time
did not), his going is to be to their advantage because it means
the coming of the Paraclete for his work of witnessing to Jesus
and carrying on the opposition between Jesus and the world.
Moreover it does not matter that the disciples are not yet
ready to learn more from Jesus, because the Spirit will teach
them.

1   *to keep you from falling away*: literally, 'in order that you may not be
     offended' (Gk. ἵνα μὴ σκανδαλισθῆτε): cp. 6⁶¹, the only other occasion on
     which the word is used in this Gospel; in both places, it refers to
     apostasy. For the idea of this verse, cp. 13¹⁹, 14²⁹, 16⁴.

2   *they will put you out of the synagogues*: so far as we can tell, this did not
     happen until nearly the end of the first century, *c.* A.D. 85; see note on
     9²², and cp. 12⁴². For the killing of Christians as a religious act on the
     part of the Jews, cp. Phil. 3⁶ ('as to zeal a persecutor of the church');
     but note the irony here, as in 11⁵⁰ ᶠᶠ· (Barrett, p. 404): those who kill
     the Christians think of it as worship (Gk. λατρεία) offered to God,
     and the martyr does indeed 'glorify God' by his death (21¹⁹). The
     phrase *the hour is coming* is used also of the death of Jesus (e.g. 16³²):
     the disciples will share in the death of their Lord (see note on 11¹⁶,
     'Let us also go, that we may die with him').

3   See 15²¹.

4   See note on v. 1.   *their hour*: does John mean 'the time when these

you, that when their hour comes you may remember that I told you of them.

'I did not say these things to you from the beginning,
5 because I was with you. But now I am going to him who sent
6 me; yet none of you asks me, "Where are you going?" But because I have said these things to you, sorrow has filled your
7 hearts. Nevertheless I tell you the truth: it is to your advantage that I go away, for if I do not go away, the Counselor
8 will not come to you; but if I go, I will send him to you. And

---

things will happen' (cp. NEB), or 'the hour of your persecutors'? The similar expression in Luke 22⁵³, where Jesus says to those who have come to arrest him, 'This is your hour' suggests the latter (Barrett, p. 404). *from the beginning* here, as in 15²⁷, means from the beginning of the ministry. *because I was with you* and could therefore, like the good shepherd (10¹⁰ᶠᶠ·), protect them from attack (cp. 17¹²).

f.   *I am going to him who sent me*: cp. 13³, ³³. *yet none of you asks me, Where are you going?* Contrast 13³⁶, where Peter asks 'Lord, where are you going?' and 14⁵. In so far as they do not remember where Jesus is going, they will be sorrowful; in so far as they do remember it, they will rejoice (14²⁸).

7   The departure of Jesus is for the good of the disciples, because Jesus is about to die for them. This advantage is expressed here in terms of the coming of the Paraclete to the disciples, and this waits upon the departure of Jesus. John does not explain why Jesus had to go, in order to send the Spirit; he accepts it as a fact that the one could not happen without the other happening first (cp. 7³⁹, 'as yet the Spirit had not been given, because Jesus was not yet glorified'). One explanation might be that the understanding and faith of the disciples needed the events of the death and resurrection of Jesus, before it was possible for them to live the life of Spirit-filled men; that is to say, the 'impossibility' of the coming of the Paraclete before the death of Jesus lay in the minds of the disciples. John, however, expresses this in mythological terms—going, sending, and coming. *it is to your advantage* (Gk. συμφέρει ὑμῖν): these words occur also in the (ironical) statement of Caiaphas, 'it is expedient for you' (11⁵⁰: cp. 18¹⁴). Jesus is telling them *the truth*, and he knows it; Caiaphas is also telling them the truth, but without knowing it.

f.   The meaning of these verses is not at all clear, and the difficulty lies partly in the understanding of the Greek verb (ἐλέγχειν, RSV *convince*). John has used this word twice before in the Gospel, in 3²⁰ (where

when he comes, he will convince the world of sin and of
9 righteousness and of judgment: of sin, because they do not
10 believe in me; of righteousness, because I go to the Father,
11 and you will see me no more; of judgment, because the ruler
of this world is judged.

12 'I have yet many things to say to you, but you cannot bear
13 them now. When the Spirit of truth comes, he will guide you

---

RSV translates it as 'expose'), and in 8⁴⁶ ('convict'). NEB paraphrases
freely, and employs four English words to bring out the various mean-
ings of the one Greek word: 'confute', 'show', 'convict', 'convince'.
The fundamental sense of ἐλέγχειν is 'to bring to light', and if we
take this meaning here, the passage can be understood as follows:
When the Paraclete comes to the disciples, and makes them the
witnesses of Jesus (15²⁶ ᶠ·), three things will become clear: (a) the sin of
the world; (b) the righteousness of Jesus and of those who believe in
him; and (c) the condemnation of Satan. First, the sin of the world.
This will become clear, because the continuing existence of the disciples after the death of Jesus, and their loyalty to him, will show up
the unbelief of those who crucified him; the fact of the Church will
be a standing witness against unbelief in Jesus. Secondly, righteousness. The Church will preach the exaltation of Jesus to the Father, and
live by faith in him as present but unseen. Thus the Holy Spirit will
declare the righteousness both of Jesus and of the faithful. Thirdly,
judgement. The exaltation of Jesus involves the casting out of Satan
from his position of power (see Rev. 12⁷ᶠᶠ·) and the condemnation of
the world which crucified Christ. The Spirit, bearing witness to Jesus in
the life of the Church, will be a continual reminder of God's judgement on the world and on its ruler.

12 The teaching which John has put into the mouth of Jesus in these
discourses reflects the post-Easter faith of the disciples; in fact, as the
Synoptic Gospels show, Jesus probably said little about the coming of
the Spirit and the life of the Church. This historical fact is recognized
by John, in this verse, but the reason which is provided for it is not
historical: it was not because the disciples could not receive his teaching, but because Jesus himself expected the end of the world to come
soon, that he said little about the future.

13 The Paraclete (= *the Spirit of truth*; cp. 14¹⁶ ᶠ· and 15²⁶) will teach
them and lead them. He does not act independently, but just as Jesus
says what he has seen with his Father (8³⁸), and is dependent upon
him, so the Spirit will make known what God has done in Jesus. *and
he will declare to you the things that are to come*: that is, the meaning of the

into all the truth; for he will not speak on his own authority,
but whatever he hears he will speak, and he will declare to
14 you the things that are to come. He will glorify me, for he
15 will take what is mine and declare it to you. All that the Father
has is mine; therefore I said that he will take what is mine
and declare it to you.

16 'A little while, and you will see me no more; again a little
17 while, and you will see me.' Some of his disciples said to one

---

death and resurrection of Jesus as the gift of righteousness to the faithful, and as the condemnation of the world (cp. vv. 8 ff., and see note
on 18⁴).

14   The Spirit *will glorify* Jesus by showing the disciples that the death
of Jesus is his exaltation to the Father. For *glorify* meaning 'to show
the glory of', see 13³¹ f., 17¹, ⁴.

15   The Son is the fully authorized plenipotentiary of the Father (3³⁵),
therefore 'what is mine' (v. 14) means that Jesus is the agent of God
for salvation. This is what the Spirit will declare to the disciples.

6: 16–33 *The end of the discourse at the supper*

The last discourse ends as it began in dialogue with the disciples. Jesus sums up all that he has told them in the pregnant
saying 'A little while, and you will see me no more; again a
little while, and you will see me' (v. 16). The reader knows, by
now, what this means: the death and resurrection of Jesus, his
exaltation to the Father, the coming of the Paraclete, and the
new order in which the faithful will be united with the Father
and the Son. But, for dramatic effect, John represents the
disciples as still in the dark, asking questions of one another
about the 'little while' and the departure of Jesus to the Father.
So Jesus begins again: the disciples will be thrown into despair
by the coming events, but the world will rejoice because it will
think that it has destroyed Jesus. The sorrow of the disciples
will be short-lived and will be replaced by joy—like the sorrow
and joy of a woman at childbirth. The sorrow corresponds to
'you will see me no more', the joy to 'you will see me'. As
before in these discourses, John describes the coming situation
as a time when prayer will be effective. Jesus has been talking

another, 'What is this that he says to us, "A little while, and
you will not see me, and again a little while, and you will see
18 me"; and, "because I go to the Father"?' They said, 'What
does he mean by "a little while"? We do not know what he
19 means.' Jesus knew that they wanted to ask him; so he said to
them, 'Is this what you are asking yourselves, what I meant
by saying, "A little while, and you will not see me, and again
20 a little while, and you will see me"? Truly, truly, I say to you,

---

to them in parabolic language of going and coming, of praying
the Father and sending the Spirit, but the time will come
when this parabolic speech will give way to the reality to which
it refers. The disciples, however, mistake Jesus again: they
think that the parables are the realities, and they confess their
faith in Jesus in inadequate terms. Jesus says that they will fail
when the hour comes, as indeed they must, without the help of
the Spirit and the understanding which he will bring. But Jesus
himself will not fail: he is united with the Father by obedience
and love. And he has given them words, on which they can
ponder later, and so come to faith, understanding, and joy.
They will remain in the world, and they will be persecuted by
the world; but he has been victorious over the world, and they
will share his victory.

16   Cp. 14[19] of which this verse is an expansion. The first *little while* is
the time between Thursday night and Friday; the second between
Friday and Sunday. (Some commentators, however, understand the
first as Thursday to Sunday (the ascension; see 20[17]), and the second
as the time until the second coming; but this does not seem to be in
line with the whole argument of these chapters, and particularly
14[18 ff.])

17 ff.   John reintroduces the disciples, in order to elucidate the meaning of
the saying in v. 16. Notice that John adds to their questions, *Because I
go to the Father*; if they had understood that, they would have understood the rest also (cp. vv. 5 ff.).

20   *weep*: the word is used in this Gospel 'only in connection with death
(11[31, 33]; 20[11, 13, 15])' (Barrett, p. 410). *your sorrow will be turned into
joy*: the narratives of Mary Magdalene and the disciples in Chapter
20 illustrate this saying; and notice particularly 20[18] ('I have seen the
Lord') and 20[25] ('We have seen the Lord'); cp. 16[16] ('You will see me').

you will weep and lament, but the world will rejoice; you will
21 be sorrowful, but your sorrow will turn into joy. When a
woman is in travail she has sorrow, because her hour has
come; but when she is delivered of the child, she no longer
remembers the anguish, for joy that a child[j] is born into the
22 world. So you have sorrow now, but I will see you again and
your hearts will rejoice, and no one will take your joy from
23 you. In that day you will ask nothing of me. Truly, truly,
I say to you, if you ask anything of the Father, he will give it
24 to you in my name. Hitherto you have asked nothing in my
name; ask, and you will receive, that your joy may be full.
25   'I have said this to you in figures; the hour is coming when

----

j Greek *a human being*

----

21   The Jews referred to the woes of the last days as the birth-pangs of
the Messiah, and this usage was employed by Christian writers, e.g.
Mark 13[8] ('the beginning of the sufferings'—literally 'of the birth-
pains'). John says that the *anguish* of the disciples at the time of the
crucifixion will be followed by the *joy* of the age to come at the resurrection of Jesus.
22   *I will see you again and your hearts will rejoice*: cp. Isa. 66[14] ('You shall
see, and your heart shall rejoice'). *no one will take your joy from you*: their
joy depends on nothing in the world, but on Jesus, his presence and
his victory: therefore their joy, like their faith, can withstand persecution (vv. 1 ff.).
23 f.   *In that day*: see on 14[20]; as there, the reference is to the resurrection
of Jesus. *you will ask nothing of me*: either, You will ask me no questions
(because 'you will know', 14[20]); or, You will ask the Father, not me.
For the efficacy of prayer 'in the name' of Jesus, see 14[13 f.], 15[16]. Their
joy will not be that of self-sufficiency, but will consist in their complete
dependence on God, expressed in petition.   *that your joy may be full*:
cp. 15[11].
25   *I have said this to you in figures*: the same word, 'figure' (Gk. παροιμία),
was used in 10[6] with reference to the analogy of the shepherd and the
door; here it may refer to all that Jesus has said in explanation of his
death and resurrection and their consequences.   *the hour* in the Gospel
has usually meant the death of Jesus, e.g. 12[23]: if that is the case here,
then John means that the reality, which the discourse has explained

I shall no longer speak to you in figures but tell you plainly of
26 the Father. In that day you will ask in my name; and I do not
27 say to you that I shall pray the Father for you; for the Father
himself loves you, because you have loved me and have
28 believed that I came from the Father. I came from the Father
and have come into the world; again, I am leaving the world
and going to the Father.'

29 His disciples said, 'Ah, now you are speaking plainly, not
30 in any figure! Now we know that you know all things, and

---

in *figures*, is Jesus' laying down his life and taking it again; when he
does this, he will tell them *plainly* (Gk. παρρησία; cp. 10²⁴) *of the Father*,
and of the Father's love for them (cp. 3¹⁶ and below v. 27).

26 f.   *In that day you will ask in my name*: cp. v. 23. Jesus and the Father are
one (10³⁰), therefore Jesus will not *pray the Father for* the disciples; the
Father, Jesus and the disciples will be united by mutual love. *you have
loved me and have believed . . .*: to love Jesus and to believe in Jesus are
almost synonymous in John; cp. 14¹² ('he who believes in me') with
14¹⁵ ('if you love me').

28   This verse sums up the discourse, picking up a verse at the beginning of Chapter 13 ('he had come from God and was going to God',
13³). Nevertheless, as the discourse has been at pains to show, this
language of movement in space is not adequate to express the reality:
Jesus never left the Father, he has always been in the Father, and the
Father in him (14¹¹); and he is not about to leave the world and go to
the Father, because he is coming to them in the world in a new and
better way (14¹⁸ ff.).

29   The disciples think that the figurative language in v. 28 is the plain
speaking which Jesus had promised in v. 25; but, as usual in this
Gospel, they are wrong: v. 25 referred to *the hour*, i.e. the events of the
death and resurrection, but these have not yet taken place.

30   The disciples confess their faith in Jesus in gnostic terminology—*you
know all things*. Similar language is used in the First Letter of John (e.g.
1 John 2²⁰ (RSV mg.)), and it seems to be the way in which the false
teachers who are mentioned in the Letter themselves spoke. Possibly,
John uses it here in the Gospel to show its inadequacy (see vv. 31 ff.).
and need none to question you: i.e. Jesus can answer a man's question
without its being put to him. Barrett (p. 415) refers back to v. 19 above,
where Jesus knows what is in the minds of the disciples. Cp. also 1⁴⁸ ff.,
2²⁵: belief in Jesus' supernatural powers is not enough. *by this we*

need none to question you; by this we believe that you came
32 from God.' Jesus answered them, 'Do you now believe? The
hour is coming, indeed it has come, when you will be scattered, every man to his home, and will leave me alone; yet I
33 am not alone, for the Father is with me. I have said this to
you, that in me you may have peace. In the world you have
tribulation; but be of good cheer, I have overcome the
world.'

---

believe that you came from God: cp. the similar passage in 1⁵⁰ ('Because I
said to you, I saw you under the fig tree, do you believe?') and see the
note there.

1 f.   Their belief is inadequate, and their confidence misplaced; *The hour*
will show that: what Jesus said to Peter in 13³⁶ ᶠᶠ⁻ still stands, and
applies to all of them. *scattered* may be an allusion to Zechariah 13⁷
('Strike the shepherd, that the sheep may be scattered'; this prophecy
is also quoted in Mark 14²⁷). *the Father is with me*: cp. 14¹⁰ ᶠ⁻. John
brings out the theological point, that Jesus' death is the will both of
the Father and of the Son; therefore they are not separated from one
another. Mark, in quoting Ps. 22¹ (Mark 15³⁴), brought out other
theological points—e.g. fulfilment of scripture, the cost of redemption,
the genuineness of the humanity of Jesus. Some commentators think
that John is deliberately correcting Mark here; others, that he is
interpreting him (Hoskyns, p. 582).

33   *I have said this to you* probably refers to all that Jesus has said in
Chapters 13–16; cp. the same expression in 16¹, ⁴, ²⁵. *that in me you may
have peace*: the reason for the discourse was in order that, after the
death and resurrection and the coming of the Paraclete, the disciples
might understand what had happened in the light of what Jesus had
said before (cp. 13¹⁹, 14²⁹). This understanding is faith in Jesus as the
agent of God, and one of the results of faith is *peace* (cp. Rom. 5¹); see
also 14²⁷. Note the antithetic parallelism: *in me . . . peace/in the world . . .
tribulation*.   *I have overcome the world*: this saying (with its emphasis on *I*
in Greek) brings together the 'me' and 'the world' in the previous
parallel sayings, and resolves the tension between them.   It looks upon
the events as past, and the victory of Jesus as achieved. Cp. the sayings
about *the ruler of this world* in 12³¹, 14³⁰, 16¹¹, and the closer parallels in
1 John 5⁴ ᶠ⁻ which show that *I have overcome the world* is an expression of
faith: the believer enters into Christ's victory, and knows Christ's
protection from the evil powers.

17 WHEN Jesus had spoken these words, he lifted up his eyes to heaven and said, 'Father, the hour has come; glorify thy

---

17: 1–26 *The prayer of Jesus*

In the Synoptic Gospels, Jesus goes from the supper to Gethsemane where he prays: in John, the discourse at the supper is followed by a prayer, but the prayer is made in the room where the supper was held, and it is only after this that Jesus goes out across the Kidron (18¹). The prayer in the Synoptic Gospels is recorded in order to show the readers the inner truth of the coming passion and resurrection: Jesus speaks of his sorrow, and asks that the cup (that is, the suffering) may be removed, 'yet not what I will, but what thou wilt' (Mark 14³⁶)—that is to say, the readers are shown that the crucifixion is accepted by Jesus in obedience to the Father, but at great cost to himself. The prayer of Jesus in John is also recorded in order to show the readers the truth about the crucifixion and resurrection, but here there is no mention of the sorrow of Jesus; in fact, no distress is mentioned at all. Nor could it be, after the assurance of joy and victory which (according to this Gospel) Jesus had given to the disciples in 16³³.

The prayer is thoroughly Johannine, and contains many of John's characteristic words: 'the hour', 'glorify', 'eternal life', 'the work', 'the world', 'send', 'know', etc. Like the discourses in the earlier part of the Gospel, the prayer is a Johannine composition; but like them again, it may be based on the tradition of the sayings of Jesus; it has been suggested that John is using here themes from the Lord's Prayer (cp. C. F. Evans, *The Lord's Prayer* (London, 1963), pp. 75 ff.; and see below, notes on vv. 1, 6, 11, 12, 15, 17).

The prayer moves outwards from its starting-point, which is the arrival of the hour when the Father glorifies the Son, and the Son glorifies the Father (vv. 1–5), through petitions for the disciples (vv. 6–19), to prayer for those who will become disciples in the future (vv. 20–24); but then in the last two verses (vv. 25 f.), it moves back to the obedience of the Son to the Father, and the inclusion of the believers in their mutual love and in-dwelling.

2 Son that the Son may glorify thee, since thou hast given him
  power over all flesh, to give eternal life to all whom thou hast
3 given him. And this is eternal life, that they know thee the
  only true God, and Jesus Christ whom thou hast sent.
4 I glorified thee on earth, having accomplished the work
5 which thou gavest me to do; and now, Father, glorify thou
  me in thy own presence with the glory which I had with
  thee before the world was made.

---

1   *When Jesus had spoken these words*: the discourses in Chapters 13–16
     are linked to the prayer in Chapter 17 by these words. *he lifted up his
     eyes to heaven*: cp. 6⁵, 11⁴¹ and see next note. *Father*: cp. the Synoptic
     Gospels, *Abba* (e.g. Mark 14³⁶), and see J. Jeremias, *The Prayers of Jesus*
     (London, 1967), pp. 11 ff. Note also the Lord's Prayer, 'Our Father,
     who art in heaven' (Matt. 6⁹). *the hour has come*: cp. 12²³, 13¹: it is the
     hour for the Son 'to depart out of this world to the Father', and the
     hour 'for the Son of man to be glorified'. *glorify thy Son*: in 12²³ ff. it
     was made clear that the glorifying of the Son of man involved his
     death; therefore the prayer here is equivalent to the Marcan 'yet not
     what I will, but what thou wilt' (Mark 14³⁶), and to the Matthean
     'Thy will be done' (Matt. 26⁴²; cp. the Lord's Prayer, Matt. 6¹⁰). *that
     the Son may glorify thee*: Jesus reveals the glory of the Father by being
     glorified by the Father; i.e. Jesus shows the love of the Father by
     means of his death, which he undergoes in obedience to the Father.
     He therefore prays to the Father to accept his obedience and to declare
     his acceptance of it in order that the Father's love may be known.

2   Jesus' petition in the previous verse is grounded in the will of God,
     who has appointed him Saviour of the world (4⁴²); and his work as
     Saviour is to give *eternal life* to the elect, who are the gift of the Father
     to the Son (cp. 6³⁷ ff.).

3   *eternal life* (mentioned in the previous verse) is now explained and
     defined as knowledge of God (that is, faith and obedience and love),
     and of Jesus Christ his agent who has made him known (cp. v. 26).

4 f. These two verses look back on the ministry, and forward to the
     passion and resurrection, cp. 12²⁸ ('I have glorified it [sc. my name],
     and I will glorify it again'). Jesus revealed the glory of the Father in
     the work of the ministry, by his obedience to God; *now*, in the coming
     passion and resurrection, he asks to be restored to the position of glory
     which he had with the Father 'in the beginning' (1¹).

6   'I have manifested thy name to the men whom thou gavest
me out of the world; thine they were, and thou gavest them
7   to me, and they have kept thy word. Now they know that
8   everything that thou hast given me is from thee; for I have
given them the words which thou gavest me, and they have
received them and know in truth that I came from thee; and
9   they have believed that thou didst send me. I am praying for
them; I am not praying for the world but for those whom thou
10   hast given me, for they are thine; all mine are thine, and
11   thine are mine, and I am glorified in them. And now I am no

---

6   *I have manifested thy name*: cp. the first petition of the Lord's Prayer
'Hallowed be thy name' (Matt. 6⁹), which means 'Reveal yourself
in order that men may worship you'. John, as is his custom, interprets
this: Jesus has revealed God to the disciples (= *the men whom thou gavest
me out of the world*; cp. v. 2). *and they have kept thy word*: i.e. accepted
God's revelation in Jesus, with faith and obedience (cp. 15¹⁰).

7 f.   The disciples believe that Jesus has received his status and authority from the Father. Note the synonymous expressions: to receive
the words of Jesus; to know in truth; and to believe.

9 f.   Jesus is praying for the disciples: the Father has given them to him
(see vv. 2, 6) without ceasing to possess them himself—there is no
separation between the Father and the Son. *I am not praying for the
world*: although these words suggest a certain narrowness and exclusiveness, as though Jesus were concerned only with believers and not
with everybody, John's idea may be that Jesus saves the world through
the mission of the disciples, and not, as it were, directly, by manifesting
himself to the world (cp. 7⁴, 14²²). The prayer will move outwards to
others who are not present, beyond the circle of the disciples, in vv.
20 ff., and see also vv. 15 ff. *I am glorified in them*: as the Father is
glorified in the Son (13³¹), so the Son is glorified in the disciples—
i.e. their mission will make him known, as his mission has made
the Father known (cp. 20²¹).

11   *I am no more in the world*: i.e. in the way in which he was *in the world*
during the days of his flesh; in another sense, as has been explained in
14¹⁸ ᶠᶠ·, he is still with the disciples, who themselves *are in the world*. *Holy
Father, keep them in thy name*: cp. again the Lord's Prayer, 'Our Father
. . . hallowed [from the same root as the word *Holy* here] be thy name'
(Matt. 6⁹). 'The name of God . . . is his revealed character' (Barrett,
p. 424), and the point may be that the name of God is 'love' (see note

more in the world, but they are in the world, and I am
coming to thee. Holy Father, keep them in thy name, which
thou hast given me, that they may be one, even as we are one.

12 While I was with them, I kept them in thy name, which
thou hast given me; I have guarded them, and none of them
is lost but the son of perdition, that the scripture might be

13 fulfilled. But now I am coming to thee; and these things I

---

on v. 26, and cp. 1 John 4$^{8, 16}$). *which thou hast given me: which* (Gk. ϕ)
refers to the *name*, not to *them*; God has entrusted Jesus with the work
of manifesting his character to men (cp. v. 6). *that they may be one, even
as we are one*: if by the *name* he means love, then to *keep them in* the *name*
means to keep them united in love for one another; and this love is
the love of the Father for the Son and of the Son for the Father; so
the unity of the Church is grounded upon, and manifests, the unity
of the Godhead.

12   During the ministry Jesus kept the disciples from evil, and in God's
possession and love. *which thou hast given me* refers to *the name*, as in the
previous verse. Cp. again the Lord's prayer '. . . lead us not into
temptation, But deliver us from the evil one' (Matt. 6^{13} RSV mg.)
and notice that (as in v. 6) John re-interprets the prayer by trans-
forming a petition for the future into a statement about the past. *and
none of them is lost, but the son of perdition*: see note on 18$^{8\,f.}$. *the son of
perdition* means the one who is destined for damnation, and refers to
Judas Iscariot. But notice that exactly the same expression is used in
2 Thess. 2^3 with reference to antichrist who must come before the day
of the Lord. In this Gospel, Satan has used Judas as his instrument
(13$^{2, 27}$): Judas therefore is antichrist, and the day of the Lord is the
glorifying ($=$ crucifixion and resurrection) of Jesus (cp. 14^{20} 'In
that day'). *that the scripture might be fulfilled*: see note on 13^{18} where
Ps. 41^9 was quoted concerning Judas Iscariot.

13   *But now I am coming to thee* contrasts the new situation with the
ministry which was described in the previous verse: the new situation
is to be a time of *joy* for the disciples, not a time of sorrow; but it
can only be so if the disciples understand it in the way in which Jesus
has explained it to them in the previous discourses. It may be, however,
that *these things I speak in the world* refers to the prayer in Chapter 17,
and not to the previous discourses (cp. 11^{42}, where Jesus prays 'on
account of the people standing by'): if this is so, John's point here is
that Jesus is not praying because he needs to pray, but in order to
reveal the truth to the disciples. For *joy* see also 14^{28}, 15^{11}, 16$^{20-24}$.

speak in the world, that they may have my joy fulfilled in
14 themselves. I have given them thy word; and the world has
hated them because they are not of the world, even as I am
15 not of the world. I do not pray that thou shouldst take them
out of the world, but that thou shouldst keep them from the
16 evil one.*k* They are not of the world, even as I am not of the
17, 18 world. Sanctify them in the truth; thy word is truth. As thou
didst send me into the world, so I have sent them into the
19 world. And for their sake I consecrate myself, that they also
may be consecrated in truth.

k Or *from evil*

---

14   *I have given them thy word*: i.e. the truth that he is the agent of the
Father. *the world has hated them*: see 15¹⁸⁻²⁷. *not of the world*: i.e. they
belong to God.

15   The disciples are to remain in the world, in order to bear fruit
through their witness to Jesus. This verse mitigates the apparent
exclusiveness of v. 9 ('I am not praying for the world'). *keep them from
the evil one*: cp. the Lord's Prayer 'deliver us from the evil one', Matt.
6¹³ (RSV mg.).

16   John repeats what he had said in v. 14, because it is the ground of
the petition in v. 15; Jesus asks God to protect those who belong to
him from the power of Satan.

17   *Sanctify them*: there is another verbal link here between the prayer of
Jesus and the Lord's Prayer: *sanctify* (Gk. ἁγιάζειν) is the word which
is translated 'hallowed' in Matt. 6⁹, but the meaning is different; here
it means 'consecrate', as in 10³⁶ and v. 19 below. *Sanctify them in the truth*
therefore means consecrate them for their mission to the world with
the revelation that Jesus has given to them (= *the truth*, cp. 14⁶).

18   The mission of the disciples is recorded in 20²¹, but the prayer refers
to it in the past tense, possibly in view of what has been said in 13²⁰
and 15¹⁶.

19   The Father sends the Son, and the Son obeys the Father; his
obedience includes, and reaches its climax in, his death, which he
accepts willingly. This is the Son's consecration of himself *for their sake*
(the Greek word is ἁγιάζειν, as in 10³⁶ and v. 17 above). The result of
what the Son does is the mission of the disciples to the world: they are
consecrated for their mission by *the truth* which Jesus has delivered to
them through his mission.

20 'I do not pray for these only, but also for those who
21 believe in me through their word, that they may all be one;
even as thou, Father, art in me, and I in thee, that they also
may be in us, so that the world may believe that thou hast
22 sent me. The glory which thou hast given me I have given to
23 them, that they may be one even as we are one, I in them and
thou in me, that they may become perfectly one, so that the
world may know that thou hast sent me and hast loved them
24 even as thou hast loved me. Father, I desire that they also,
whom thou hast given me, may be with me where I am, to
behold my glory which thou hast given me in thy love for me
25 before the foundation of the world. O righteous Father, the

---

20   The mission of the original disciples (v. 18) will bear fruit in
others who will believe on account of their preaching, and Jesus includes them in his prayer.

21   The content of Jesus' prayer for the faithful of the future is *that they
may all be one*, and that as a result of this *the world may believe*. The unity
for which he prays is the unity which is made possible by love, and
that means the love and in-dwelling of the Father in the Son, and of
the Son in the Father. The unity of the believer will manifest the
divine unity to the world, in order that the world may recognize Jesus
as the agent of God.

2 f. *The glory* here is the Father's acceptance of the Son (cp. v. 5): Jesus
has *given* this to the faithful, and this it is which unites them with one
another. This is expressed in terms of in-dwelling: Jesus in the faithful,
and the Father in Jesus. The result will be the faith (note *know* here =
'believe' in v. 21) of the world; it will see that the unity of the believers
is based on the mission of Jesus and the love of God for the believers
and for Jesus which he manifested.

24   *Father*, see note on v. 1. *they also, whom*: some of the texts have the
neuter singular here, 'that also, which'—i.e. the disciples are thought
of as a single entity, namely, the gift of the Father to the Son (cp. 6³⁷,
'All that the Father gives me'). *may be with me where I am*: either may
follow him through death to glory (cp. 13³⁶), or may enter by faith
into the situation which is about to come to pass (cp. 14¹⁸⁻²⁴). Faith in
Jesus is defined as beholding his *glory*, and that means here his position
and status as the agent of God, which the Father has given to him: it
is an eternal status, and it comes from the love of the Father (5²⁰).

25   *O righteous Father*: for *Father*, see note on v. 1; for *righteous*, cp. 16¹⁰.

world has not known thee, but I have known thee; and these
26 know that thou hast sent me. I made known to them thy
name, and I will make it known, that the love with which
thou hast loved me may be in them, and I in them.'

18 WHEN Jesus had spoken these words, he went forth with his
disciples across the Kidron valley, where there was a garden,
2 which he and his disciples entered. Now Judas, who betrayed

---

The righteousness of the Father is seen in the separation which he has
made between the world and the disciples (= *these*): the former has
not acknowledged God; the latter have done so in response to the
mission of Jesus.

26   *I made known to them thy name*: i.e. in the ministry (cp. v. 6).   *and I
will make it known*: i.e. in the passion and resurrection (cp. 12²⁸).   *that
the love with which thou hast loved me may be in them, and I in them*: notice
the parallelism of *name* and *love* (see note on v. 11). The love of the
Father for the Son is known by faith in Jesus. Faith is, in fact, believing
that Jesus is the one whom the Father loves. But it is the nature of love
to bestow itself on others, and this is what Jesus has done in his dealings with the disciples. He dwells in them, and the Father's love for
him dwells in them also.

18: 1–11 *The arrest*

There is a change in the Gospel at this point. Whereas in the
previous chapters, and particularly in 13–17, John has mainly
portrayed Jesus as a speaker, now, on the other hand, his
words become less frequent, and the interest of the Evangelist
is in events; in what Jesus did, and in what people did to him.
A comparison of the speeches of Jesus in the Fourth Gospel with
his words in the Synoptic Gospels shows that John has written
the speeches in his own style. When we come to the events of
the passion and resurrection, we shall not be surprised if we
find that these also have been rewritten by John, in such a way
as to express his theological ideas. The account of the arrest of
Jesus is a clear illustration of this.

The ideas which John brings out here are that Jesus knew
what was to happen, and that it could only happen when he
commanded that it should; that Jesus laid down his life for the

14. Jerusalem, from Mount Scopus looking across the Kidron Valley

15. The Kidron Valley

him, also knew the place; for Jesus often met there with his
3 disciples. So Judas, procuring a band of soldiers and some
officers from the chief priests and the Pharisees, went there
4 with lanterns and torches and weapons. Then Jesus, knowing
all that was to befall him, came forward and said to them,
5 'Whom do you seek?' They answered him, 'Jesus of Nazareth.'

---

disciples, and that in this way they were set free; and that Jesus
was obeying the commandment of the Father.

The Synoptic Gospels contain an account of the arrest,
which is similar to John's in many respects (Mark 14$^{43-52}$ and
parallels), and some scholars think that John knew one or
more of these accounts, while others think that John is using
independent traditions (for the latter view, see e.g. Dodd,
HTFG, pp. 65–81). The use of independent traditions would
account for some of the details in this account of the arrest
which are not given in the Synoptic Gospels (e.g. the Kidron
Valley; Peter, as the disciple who drew the sword; Malchus):
on the theory that John had only the Synoptic materials, these
details have to be explained in other ways (see notes below).

1   *he went forth*: it is not clear whether this means from the supper-
room (13^2), or from the City, or both. *the Kidron valley* is not mentioned in the Synoptic Gospels: Mark and Matthew call the place
Gethsemane, whereas John (like Luke) does not. The valley is east of
Jerusalem, and the brook Kidron is mentioned in the O.T. (e.g.
2 Sam. 15^{23}) and by Josephus. The occurrence of the place-name is
scarcely evidence that the Evangelist was using a source. *a garden*:
only John so describes the place, and this is all he says about it; he
uses the word again in 19^{41}. The traditional name, 'The Garden of
Gethsemane', is an example of harmonization, combining the Marcan–
Matthean with the Johannine descriptions.

2   This verse explains to the reader how Judas was able to find Jesus.
3   Apart from the previous verse, Judas was last mentioned by name
in 13$^{21-30}$ (note particularly 13^{30}, 'he immediately went out; and it
was night'). Hoskyns suggests that this reference to Judas' departure
into the night helps to explain the presence of Roman soldiers (*a band*
= a cohort, 600 men) at the arrest, a detail which is recorded only
in this Gospel: 'In the Johannine account the forces of darkness,
the Roman and Jewish authorities, and the apostate disciple are

Jesus said to them, 'I am he.' Judas, who betrayed him,
6 was standing with them. When he said to them, 'I am he,'
7 they drew back and fell to the ground. Again he asked them,
'Whom do you seek?' And they said, 'Jesus of Nazareth.'
8 Jesus answered, 'I told you that I am he; so, if you seek me,
9 let these men go.' This was to fulfil the word which he had
10 spoken, 'Of those whom thou gavest me I lost not one.' Then

---

arrayed against the Christ from the beginning' (p. 605; but see also
Guilding, pp. 167 f.). *with lanterns and torches and weapons*: only John
mentions the lights—'an unconscious comment on i. 5' (Hoskyns,
p. 605).

4 *knowing all that was to befall him*: i.e. the arrest, death, and resurrection, as the will of God for him. The same expression is used in
16¹³ (the Spirit 'will declare to you the things that are to come').
came forward (Gk. ἐξῆλθεν): better, 'went out' [sc. of the garden].
It is important to John to emphasize that Jesus took the initiative
(cp. 10¹⁸).

5 *Jesus of Nazareth*: the home of Jesus in Nazareth in Galilee is always
mentioned with contempt in this Gospel; see 1⁴⁵ᶠ·, 19¹⁹, and cp.
7²⁷, ⁴¹, ⁵². *I am he* (Gk. Ἐγώ εἰμι): Judas does not kiss Jesus (as in Mark
and Matt.), but Jesus identifies himself, and though these words are
used by the beggar in 9⁹ without any deep meaning, John may have
intended his readers to recall, at this point, their use in the formulae
in 6³⁵, etc.

f. The forces of darkness are powerless, and are driven back by the
self-revelation of Jesus. This is repeated in v. 7, for emphasis.

8 f. Jesus offers himself to them, in order that his disciples may not be
harmed (cp. 10¹¹), and thus fulfils his own words. The reference is to
17¹², though notice that there it was 'the name' that was given to
Jesus; for the disciples as the gift of the Father to the Son, see 6³⁷,
17⁶, ²⁴. Cp. also 18³².

10 The Synoptists do not say which disciple attempted to defend
Jesus. John says it was Peter (here and at 18²⁶). For Peter's 'misunderstanding', see also 13³⁶ᶠᶠ·, and cp. 18³⁶ ('if my kingship were of this
world, my servants would fight'). *right ear*: so also Luke 22⁵⁰ (contrast
Matt. 26⁵¹ and Mark 14⁴⁷). *Malchus*: the name is probably from the
Hebrew root meaning 'King'. Only John gives the name, and it is
difficult to know how he came by it, whether from tradition, or (as in
the case of names in the apocryphal Gospels) through the tendency
of story-tellers to add proper names, or, as it has also been suggested,

Simon Peter, having a sword, drew it and struck the high priest's slave and cut off his right ear. The slave's name was 11 Malchus. Jesus said to Peter, 'Put your sword into its sheath; shall I not drink the cup which the Father has given me?'

---

from Zech. 11[6] ('I will cause men to fall . . . each into the hand of his king'); so Guilding, pp. 232 f.

11 For the saying about the *sword*, cp. Matt. 26[52]; and for *the cup*, cp. Mark 14[36] and parallels, where Jesus prays 'Remove this cup from me': in John, on the other hand, he affirms his determination to do what the Father has commanded him to do.

18: 12–27 *Jesus before the chief priests and Peter's denial*

At this point John's narrative presents certain difficulties. He says that Jesus was taken first to Annas the father-in-law of Caiaphas the high priest, and that Peter and another disciple followed Jesus. Peter enters the courtyard with the aid of the other disciple, and there he makes his first denial. The scene changes to the inside of the high priest's house, where Jesus is questioned, then bound and sent to Caiaphas. After this, John records the other two denials by Peter. There is no further account of a trial before Caiaphas (see v. 28). It is not at all clear why Jesus is taken to Annas rather than to Caiaphas, or why he is taken on to Caiaphas after Annas, or whether the high priest mentioned in vv. 19 ff. is Annas. There have been both ancient and modern attempts to overcome these difficulties, either by rearranging the material, or by a theory of later insertions. Others suggest that John harmonized Marcan–Matthean with Lucan material, or that he rewrote Mark, expanding the two Jewish trials mentioned there (Mark 14[53 ff.], 15[1 ff.]), or that he was confused about the chief priests.

But, in spite of these difficulties, John's intention is fairly clear. He reminds the reader of the counsel of Caiaphas, in order that the meaning of the death of Jesus may be recalled; and he contrasts the faithless behaviour of Peter with the outspokenness of Jesus before the high priest. This section should be read in the light of the words of Jesus to Peter 'Where I am going you cannot follow me now; but you shall follow afterward' (13[36]); Peter cannot follow Jesus, until Jesus has died for him.

12   So the band of soldiers and their captain and the officers of
13 the Jews seized Jesus and bound him. First they led him to
    Annas; for he was the father-in-law of Caiaphas, who was
14 high priest that year. It was Caiaphas who had given counsel
    to the Jews that it was expedient that one man should die for
    the people.

15   Simon Peter followed Jesus, and so did another disciple.
    As this disciple was known to the high priest, he entered the
16 court of the high priest along with Jesus, while Peter stood
    outside at the door. So the other disciple, who was known to
    the high priest, went out and spoke to the maid who kept the
17 door, and brought Peter in. The maid who kept the door said

---

12   See note on v. 3.

13   *Annas* was high priest from A.D. 6 until he was deposed in A.D. 15,
      but it is thought that he continued to be influential after his deposition.
      There is no other evidence that he was *the father-in-law of Caiaphas.
      who was high priest that year*: see $11^{49, 51}$; Dodd thinks that John wrongly
      supposed that high priests held office for one year, like the priests in
      the Greek cities, and that such an error was excusable, in view of the
      rapid changes in the office under the Romans (*HTFG*, p. 94, n. 3).

14   See $11^{49\,ff.}$.

15   *Simon Peter followed Jesus*: cp. 13^{36} quoted above (p. 182). *another
      disciple*: the only indication that John means by this 'the disciple whom
      Jesus loved' is that elsewhere the latter is usually mentioned along with
      Peter ($13^{23\,f.}$, $20^{2\,ff.}$, 21^{7}, $20^{ff.}$; the exception is 19^{26}), and that is so here;
      see note on vv. 16 f. *the court* (Gk. αὐλή): the word can mean courtyard
      (it is used in $10^{1, 16}$ for 'sheepfold'), court of the temple, or palace; any
      of these meanings is possible here.

16 f. Peter is able to enter because of the word of the other disciple. This
      explains how he came to be there, and why the first question was
      asked by *the maid who kept the door*. Notice that *Are not you also* implies[1]
      that *the maid* knew that *the other disciple* was *one of this man's disciples*; if,
      therefore, John means that this is 'the disciple whom Jesus loved' he
      shows again the superiority of this disciple to Peter, as in the other
      passages where they appear together; see note on v. 15. *I am not*:
      contrast the 'I am he' of Jesus in vv. 5, 6, 8.

      [1] Though it should be noted that in Mark 14^{67} the maid likewise says
    'You also were with the Nazarene, Jesus.'

to Peter, 'Are not you also one of this man's disciples?' He
18 said, 'I am not.' Now the servants[l] and officers had made a
charcoal fire, because it was cold, and they were standing and
warming themselves; Peter also was with them, standing and
warming himself.

19   The high priest then questioned Jesus about his disciples
20 and his teaching. Jesus answered him, 'I have spoken openly
to the world; I have always taught in synagogues and in the
temple, where all Jews come together; I have said nothing
21 secretly. Why do you ask me? Ask those who have heard me,
22 what I said to them; they know what I said.' When he had
said this, one of the officers standing by struck Jesus with his
23 hand, saying, 'Is that how you answer the high priest?' Jesus
answered him, 'If I have spoken wrongly, bear witness to the
wrong; but if I have spoken rightly, why do you strike me?'
24 Annas then sent him bound to Caiaphas the high priest.

25   Now Simon Peter was standing and warming himself.
They said to him, 'Are not you also one of his disciples?' He
26 denied it and said, 'I am not.' One of the servants[l] of the high

l Or *slaves*

---

18   This verse prepares the scene for the further denials; see vv. 25 ff.
19   In view of what Peter has said in v. 17 there is a certain irony in the
mention of *his disciples* here.
20 f.   For teaching in a synagogue, see note on 6⁵⁹; and in the temple, see
2¹³ ᶠᶠ·, 7¹⁴, ²⁸, 10²² ᶠ·. Jesus says that he has *spoken openly to the world*, but
the reader knows that *the world* has not been able to receive his word.
Notice how *the world* and the *Jews* are equated here and cp. 1¹⁰ ᶠ·.
22   *struck . . . with his hand* (Gk. ἔδωκεν ῥάπισμα): the rare word ῥάπισμα
is possibly an allusion to Isa. 50⁶ (LXX); see also 19³, where it is used
again.
23   The questions of Jesus are left unanswered, and no evidence is
brought concerning his disciples or his teaching, because the Jews have
already decided to put Jesus to death (cp. 11⁵³).
25   See v. 18. *I am not*: see note on vv. 16 f.
26   See v. 10.

priest, a kinsman of the man whose ear Peter had cut off,
7 asked, 'Did I not see you in the garden with him?' Peter
again denied it; and at once the cock crowed.

8   Then they led Jesus from the house of Caiaphas to the
praetorium. It was early. They themselves did not enter the

---

7   See 13³⁸.

: 28–19: 16 *The trial before Pilate*

If the trial before the chief priests was described briefly in
this Gospel (perhaps because so much had been said earlier in
the Gospel about the Jews' rejection of Jesus' claims), the trial
before the Roman governor is far more detailed and elaborate.
John uses what has been called 'the device of two stages' (Dodd,
HTFG, p. 96), i.e. the outside of the praetorium and the
inside. The Jews remain outside, and John explains why they
do so—in order that they may preserve their purity and so
be able to eat the Passover lamb; Pilate and Jesus enter the
building; and the scenes take place outside and inside alter-
nately, with Pilate passing in and out. When Pilate is with the
Jews, he is subjected to their pressure to condemn Jesus to
death; when he is with Jesus, he is exposed to the supernatural
claims which Jesus makes. From a dramatic point of view,
Pilate is the chief character in these scenes, and the action
revolves around him.

He goes out to the Jews and asks them what the accusation
against Jesus is, but their answer does not specify any charge
other than that Jesus is an evildoer. Pilate, who is represented
throughout as unwilling to act in the case, tells the Jews to try
it themselves. They say that they have no power of execution,
and John comments that this happened in accordance with
the prediction of Jesus, that he would die by lifting up (i.e.
by the Roman method of execution, not by stoning, which was
the Jewish).

Pilate goes into the building for his first interview with Jesus,
and asks him whether he is the King of the Jews. Jesus defines
in what sense he is not a king, and in what sense he is. Pilate
then goes out to the Jews, and makes the first of his three
declarations of the innocence of Jesus. Still unwilling to do

what the Jews want, he suggests that he make use of the custom of releasing a prisoner at Passover. But this fails, because the Jews ask for another man, a robber. Pilate has Jesus scourged, and the soldiers dress him up in mockery of the claim to kingship. Pilate makes his second declaration of Jesus' innocence and presents Jesus to them. The Jewish leaders shout for crucifixion: Pilate declares Jesus' innocence for the third time, but offers him to the Jews; and the Jews then make a more specific charge: 'he has made himself the Son of God' (19^7). A further scene follows in which Pilate and Jesus are inside the building; Pilate speaks of his authority, but Jesus says that Pilate's authority is from God. In the final section, Pilate is won over by the Jews: they say that Jesus sets himself up as king against Caesar; Pilate asks 'Shall I crucify your King?' and they reply, 'We have no king but Caesar' (19^{15}). In saying this, they have confessed their apostasy, and Pilate's role in the story is complete: he hands Jesus over to them.

While the dramatic quality of this part of the Gospel is recognized and admitted on all sides, scholars do not agree on the process by which it came to be written; and whereas some of them think that John was using, and possibly elaborating on, an earlier narrative of the trial, which was independent of the Synoptic accounts (e.g. Dodd, *HTFG*, pp. 96–120), others attribute a greater element to the creative skill of the writer, and find no need to think that he had any other source than Mark (e.g. Barrett, p. 443). That some parts of this account of the trial of Jesus are the work of the Evangelist, can scarcely be denied: it is difficult to think that he had access to reports of conversations which apparently took place in private; and the language in which they are conducted is Johannine (e.g. 'of this world', 'the Jews' (18^{36}), 'the truth' (18^{37}), 'from above' (19^{11})). If this be admitted, the question then is, how much of the account is Johannine, and how much must be attributed to an earlier source? If we bear in mind the techniques which John has used earlier in his Gospel, and the extent to which he has remoulded traditional material, it becomes less and less necessary to claim that for this part of the Gospel he had access to any narratives, other than those in the Synoptic Gospels.

28   *from the house of Caiaphas*: see v. 24.   *to the praetorium*: i.e. to the Governor's residence, and this, in Jerusalem, was apparently the old palace of Herod the Great. This raises difficulties about the suggested

praetorium, so that they might not be defiled, but might eat
29 the passover. So Pilate went out to them and said, 'What
30 accusation do you bring against this man?' They answered
him, 'If this man were not an evildoer, we would not have
31 handed him over.' Pilate said to them, 'Take him yourselves
and judge him by your own law.' The Jews said to him, 'It is
32 not lawful for us to put any man to death.' This was to fulfil
the word which Jesus had spoken to show by what death he
was to die.

33   Pilate entered the praetorium again and called Jesus, and

---

identification of 'the pavement' (see note on 19¹³, and Dodd, *HTFG*,
pp. 108 f.). *It was early*: i.e. the fourth watch of the night, 3–6 a.m.
John's statement that the Jews remained outside to avoid defilement
before Passover (cp. 11⁵⁵) explains the subsequent movement between
the 'two stages' (see above), but raises historical problems: (*a*)
according to the Synoptists, the Passover had been eaten on the
previous evening; (*b*) apparently this kind of uncleanness could be
adequately removed by a bath in the evening. This verse is therefore
questionable from a historical point of view, and may show that John
was more interested in drama and irony (the Jews maintaining purity
while contriving the execution of Jesus and intent on keeping the old
Passover although the new was there), than in recording what happened.
29   Pilate asks them to state the charge against Jesus, and John will show
the difficulty which the Jews find in doing this (cp. v. 30, 19⁷˒ ¹²).
30   The Jews' answer is an ill-tempered appeal to the obvious, which
reveals the insecurity of their position.
31   Compare the refusal of Gallio to judge Paul (Acts 18¹²ᶠᶠ·). *It is not lawful
for us to put any man to death*: it is not known for certain whether the
Sanhedrin had power to execute at this time. Here again, as in v. 28,
John may have been more interested in dramatic irony and theology,
than in historical accuracy.
32   For the fulfilment of a prophecy of Jesus cp. 18⁹. The *word* in this
case is the saying in 12³², and note the Evangelist's comment on it
in 12³³.
33   Pilate's question comes abruptly, without any preparation for it in
the previous encounter with the Jews: this is so in Mark 15² also. *the
King of the Jews*: cp. 1⁴⁹ ('the King of Israel', where the speaker is
himself a Jew). There is some evidence that the Jews preferred to

34 said to him, 'Are you the King of the Jews?' Jesus answered,
'Do you say this of your own accord, or did others say it to
35 you about me?' Pilate answered, 'Am I a Jew? Your own
nation and the chief priests have handed you over to me;
36 what have you done?' Jesus answered, 'My kingship is not of
this world; if my kingship were of this world, my servants
would fight, that I might not be handed over to the Jews; but
37 my kingship is not from the world.' Pilate said to him, 'So
you are a king?' Jesus answered, 'You say that I am a king. For
this I was born, and for this I have come into the world, to
bear witness to the truth. Every one who is of the truth hears
38 my voice.' Pilate said to him, 'What is truth?'

---

speak of themselves as Israelites, rather than as Jews; but John does
not follow this practice consistently—see, e.g. v. 36. See also notes on
6¹⁵ and 12¹⁵ for *King*.

34   It may be that John has three possibilities in mind, and that he puts
two of them into the mouth of Jesus: (*a*) that Pilate has perceived the
royalty of Jesus *of his own accord* (cp. 1⁴⁹); (*b*) that he had been informed
of the charge by the Jews; (*c*) that Pilate, like Caiaphas, was not
speaking *of his own accord*, but by divine inspiration (cp. 11⁵¹). If this is
so, then John himself believes (*c*), since he is clearly using Pilate as an
unconscious witness to the truth about Jesus; see v. 38, 19⁴, ⁶, ¹⁴, ¹⁹ff..
See also note on next verse.

35   Pilate's answer denies the first possibility in v. 34. He is not a Jew,
therefore he has not recognized Jesus as king of the Jews 'of [his] own
accord'. He neither confirms nor denies the second; he simply says
that the Jews have handed him over, and asks Jesus what he has done.
He could not admit the third, because he was prophesying unwittingly.

36   The kingship of Jesus is given to him by God (= *not from the world*),
and is therefore not to be defended by force (contrast 18¹⁰f.).

37   In order that the Christian belief about the kingship of Jesus may
be still more clearly defined, Pilate is made to repeat the question, and
Jesus answers that *king* is Pilate's word; he himself prefers to speak of
bearing witness to *the truth*—that is, of revealing God to those who are
chosen by God to receive his message (cp. 10²⁷, 'My sheep hear my
voice').

38   *What is truth?* Pilate is not one of those who hear Jesus' voice, and
is not 'of the truth' (i.e. not of God, but of the world): his conduct of
the affair will illustrate this.   *I find no crime in him*: this answers the first

After he had said this, he went out to the Jews again, and
39 told them, 'I find no crime in him. But you have a custom
that I should release one man for you at the Passover; will
40 you have me release for you the King of the Jews?' They
cried out again, 'Not this man, but Barabbas!' Now Barabbas was a robber.

1, 2 THEN Pilate took Jesus and scourged him. And the soldiers
plaited a crown of thorns, and put it on his head, and arrayed
3 him in a purple robe; they came up to him, saying, 'Hail,
4 King of the Jews!' and struck him with their hands. Pilate
went out again, and said to them, 'Behold, I am bringing

---

charge which the Jews brought (v. 30), and it is so important from
John's point of view that he makes Pilate say it twice more (19⁴, ⁶);
see note on v. 34

39 'There is no extra-biblical evidence for this custom' (Barrett, p. 448).
Notice that Pilate uses the title *the King of the Jews*: his intention is to
mock, but in effect he is acting as a witness to the truth.

40 *Now Barabbas was a robber* (Gk. λῃστής): 'It is the term regularly
used by Josephus for the malcontents who took to the hills during
times of trouble in Judaea, in protest against the existing administra-
tion, whether of Herod the Great or of Roman governors' (Dodd,
HTFG, p. 100); cp. also 10¹, ⁸.

9: 1 Scourging was the normal preliminary to crucifixion (cp. Mark
15¹⁵), and it was also used to extract evidence from a prisoner (Dodd,
HTFG, pp. 102 f.): neither consideration explains the reference to
it at this point in John. In Luke 23¹⁶ Pilate suggests scourging as a less
severe punishment, and some think that is John's point also, but he
does not say so. It may be simply that he is following the order of
events in Mark: Barrabas, scourging, mocking by the soldiers; or that
he is preparing for the next scene, in which Jesus will be presented to
the Jews. There is a possible echo of Isa. 50⁶ (LXX) here, as in 18²²,
and v. 3 below.

2 The *crown* and the *purple robe* are symbols of royalty.

3 *struck him with their hands* (Gk. ἐδίδοσαν αὐτῷ ῥαπίσματα): cp. Isa.
50⁶ (LXX), and see notes on 18²² and 19¹.

4 Pilate goes out before Jesus to prepare for the dramatic announce-
ment in the next verse, and to make his second declaration of the
innocence of Jesus (cp. 18³⁸, and below, v. 6).

16. Ecce Homo: Coventry Cathedral; *J. Epstein*, twentieth century

him out to you, that you may know that I find no crime in
5 him.' So Jesus came out, wearing the crown of thorns and the
6 purple robe. Pilate said to them, 'Here is the man!' When the
chief priests and the officers saw him, they cried out,
'Crucify him, crucify him!' Pilate said to them, 'Take him
7 yourselves and crucify him, for I find no crime in him.' The
Jews answered him, 'We have a law, and by that law he
ought to die, because he has made himself the Son of God.'
9 When Pilate heard these words, he was the more afraid; he
entered the praetorium again and said to Jesus, 'Where are

---

5 *Here is the man!*: Jesus is dressed like a king, but declared by Pilate
to be a man; John and his readers believe him to be the Son of God,
and the heavenly man of the last days (= 'the Son of man'). Pilate's
word will be taken up by the Jews and contradicted in v. 7.

6 This is the first explicit reference to crucifixion in John, but see
18³¹ᶠ·. Pilate's offer, *Take him yourselves and crucify him*, is not meant
seriously; John has already said that the Jews had no power to put
a man to death (18³¹), and in any case they would not do it in this
way. This is Pilate's third and final declaration of Jesus' innocence
(cp. 18³⁸, and v. 4 above).

7 The *law* here is Lev. 24¹⁶ ('He who blasphemes the name of the
Lord shall be put to death; all the congregation shall stone him'). The
argument is that to claim to be the *Son of God* is to claim equality with
God, and that this is blasphemy against 'the name of the Lord'
(cp. 5¹⁸, 10³³).

8 Fear has not been mentioned before this point. John says that Pilate
was *the more afraid* (or 'very much afraid') to mark the change from
the original charge (18³⁰) to what the Jews have said in v. 7; and to
prepare for the final scene (vv. 12–16), in which the Jews will play on
Pilate's fear.

9 *Where are you from?* Cp. Pilate's inquiry in Luke 23⁶ ('whether the
man was a Galilean'). The question in John is deliberately ambiguous;
the same play on the two senses of 'where I come from' was employed
in Chapters 7, 8 (e.g. 7²⁸, ⁴¹ᶠ·, 8¹⁴). *But Jesus gave no answer*: cp. the
'answer' to the question in 8²⁵ (and see note there); also the silence of
Jesus before the Sanhedrin and before Pilate in Mark 14⁶¹, 15⁵ (and
parallels); and the prophecy in Isa. 53⁷ ('he opened not his mouth').
Also notice that the silence provokes the next question (Barrett,
p. 451).

10 you from?' But Jesus gave no answer. Pilate therefore said
    to him, 'You will not speak to me? Do you not know that I
11 have power to release you, and power to crucify you?' Jesus
    answered him, 'You would have no power over me unless it
    had been given you from above; therefore he who delivered
    me to you has the greater sin.'
12   Upon this Pilate sought to release him, but the Jews cried
    out, 'If you release this man, you are not Caesar's friend; every
    one who makes himself a king sets himself against Caesar.'
13 When Pilate heard these words, he brought Jesus out and sat
    down on the judgment seat at a place called The Pavement,

---

10   *to me* is emphatic, and is explained by the reminder that Pilate has
     the power of life and death over Jesus.
11   Jesus denies Pilate's claim in the previous verse: the power of Pilate
     over Jesus is from God (= *from above*; cp. 3³); see 10¹⁸, and compare
     Rom. 13¹⁻⁷. *he who delivered me* (Gk. ὁ παραδούς μέ) probably means
     Judas, thought of as the representative of the Jews (see note on the
     name 'Judas' at 14²²). *has the greater sin* (NEB 'deeper guilt'): John
     lays the guilt of the crucifixion on Judas and the Jews, and regards
     Pilate as the unconscious agent of God.
12   It is not clear why John says *Upon this* (Gk. ἐκ τούτου), which can
     mean 'from that moment' (NEB) or 'for that reason'—probably the
     latter: the problem is, why did Pilate seek to release Jesus now?
     Whatever the answer, the statement that Pilate intended to do this
     gives the Jews their cue for their last, successful, move against Pilate.
     He was, in fact, recalled by the Emperor on charges brought by the
     Jews (Josephus, *Ant.* xviii. iv. 2 (89); Dodd, *HTFG*, p. 120, n. 1).
13   *he brought Jesus out and sat down on the judgment seat*: the second verb
     could be transitive, i.e. Pilate 'made him [sc. Jesus] sit in the judge-
     ment seat'—continuing the mocking of vv. 2–5, and preparing for the
     announcement in the next verse, 'Here is your King!' The arguments
     for and against this interpretation are set out in Barrett, pp. 452 f.;
     cp. Dodd, *HTFG*, p. 119, n. 1. *The Pavement* (Gk. Λιθόστρωτον): the
     excavation of large blocks of stone near the Antonia cannot be
     identified as *The Pavement* without hesitation: it would involve the
     theory that Pilate stayed in the Antonia, which is not otherwise
     certain; see note on 18²⁸, and cp. Dodd, *HTFG*, pp. 108 f. *Gabbatha*:
     neither the meaning of the word, nor what it refers to, is known with
     certainty.

14 and in Hebrew, Gabbatha. Now it was the day of Preparation
   of the Passover; it was about the sixth hour. He said to the
15 Jews, 'Here is your King!' They cried out, 'Away with him,
   away with him, crucify him!' Pilate said to them, 'Shall I
   crucify your King?' The chief priests answered, 'We have no
16 king but Caesar.' Then he handed him over to them to be
   crucified.

17   So they took Jesus, and he went out, bearing his own cross,
   to the place called the place of a skull, which is called in

---

14   *the day of Preparation of the Passover*: the commentators say that to a
     Jew this would mean the day before the Passover, i.e. Nisan 14, and
     not 'Friday in Passover' (NEB mg.); but there is still the question
     whether John meant what a Jew would mean. For the disagreement
     with the Synoptists, see note on 13¹. *it was about the sixth hour*: i.e. noon;
     contrast Mark 15²⁵ ('it was the third hour, when they crucified him'—
     i.e. 9 a.m.). John's point may be that the Passover lambs were
     slaughtered during that afternoon, and that Jesus was crucified at the
     time when this was happening. *Here is your King!* contrast v. 5 above,
     'the man'. Pilate again speaks as one who is inspired; see note on 18³⁴.
15 f. The demand for crucifixion is repeated (cp. v. 6 above). The taunt
     of Pilate, *Shall I crucify your King?* leads the chief priests to say that only
     Caesar is their king, and thus deny the sovereignty of God over
     Israel. Pilate waits till this has been said before he hands Jesus over
     to them to be crucified, which cannot mean that he literally committed
     Jesus to the Jews, but must mean surrendered him to their wishes.

19: 17–30 *The crucifixion*

   John's account of the crucifixion is set out in four short
   paragraphs, which deal with the title on the cross, the disposal
   of Jesus' clothes, his mother and the disciple whom he loved,
   and the drink of vinegar. In most of these incidents John's
   purpose is clear: they explain to the reader the meaning of
   the crucifixion. Pilate insists on his wording of the title, 'Jesus of
   Nazareth, the King of the Jews', and refuses the emendation
   which the Jews ask for: he is bearing witness to the kingship of
   Christ. The soldiers, in dividing the clothes, fulfil scripture,
   and in this way show that what is happening is God's will; and
   the drink of vinegar likewise happens in fulfilment of a Psalm.
   The meaning of the entrusting of his mother to the beloved

18 Hebrew Golgotha. There they crucified him, and with him
two others, one on either side, and Jesus between them.

17. The Isenheim Altarpiece: *Grünewald*, sixteenth century

disciple is more obscure, but though we may not know for
certain what John's meaning was, it seems likely, in view both
of his method of writing elsewhere in the Gospel, and of the
doubtful historicity of the incident, that he saw some symbolic
significance here also.

Although some scholars have claimed that John is dependent
on a non-Marcan tradition (e.g. Dodd, *HTFG*, pp. 121–36),
there seems less need for such a hypothesis, the more John's
methods and intentions are borne in mind.

17   *bearing his own cross*: contrast Mark 15²¹ and parallels, in which
Simon of Cyrene is compelled to carry the cross. Various explanations

19 Pilate also wrote a title and put it on the cross; it read, 'Jesus
20 of Nazareth, the King of the Jews.' Many of the Jews read
   this title, for the place where Jesus was crucified was near the
   city; and it was written in Hebrew, in Latin, and in Greek.
21 The chief priests of the Jews then said to Pilate, 'Do not
   write, "The King of the Jews," but, "This man said, I am
22 King of the Jews." ' Pilate answered, 'What I have written
   I have written.'

23   When the soldiers had crucified Jesus they took his garments and made four parts, one for each soldier; also his

---

of this apparent contradiction have been offered, e.g. that John is
alluding to Gen. 22⁶ (Isaac carrying the wood for his sacrifice); that
he is denying the Docetic belief that Simon was crucified in place of
Jesus; that he is emphasizing the all-sufficiency of Jesus; that he has
the saying of Jesus in Luke 14²⁷ ('whoever does not bear his own cross
and come after me, cannot be my disciple') in mind; or that Simon
was brought in to help after Jesus had fallen. *the place of a skull* and
Golgotha are both mentioned in Mark 15²², Matt. 27³³.

18   The *two others* (cp. Mark 15²⁷ and parallels) will be referred to again
in vv. 31 ff.

19   It was the normal Roman practice to put up a notice indicating the
offence for which a criminal was being executed. On *Nazareth* (which
formed part of the title only according to John), see note on 18⁵.

20   John explains how it happened that *many of the Jews read this title*:
Golgotha *was near* Jerusalem, and the title was written in the three
most common languages. It is possible, however, that John means
more than this by the second half of his explanation; namely, that
Jesus is the Saviour of men of all nations and languages (cp. 4⁴², 11⁵²).

21 f.   The Jews object to the apparent statement of fact, and ask Pilate to
change it to a statement of what *This man said*. Pilate refuses, and thus
again acts as an unconscious witness to the truth (see note on 18³⁴).

23 f.   Mark said that they cast lots for the clothes (Mark 15²⁴) but left his
readers to see the fulfilment of Ps. 22¹⁸ for themselves: John quotes *the
scripture* (cp. John 12¹² f. with Mark 11²ff. for a similar procedure). The
tunic was the under-garment, and John says that it was *without seam*;
this was why the soldiers *cast lots* for it, thus fulfilling the two lines
of the Psalm exactly (but misunderstanding the poetic parallelism,
as Matthew also did in his account of the entry into Jerusalem,

tunic. But the tunic was without seam, woven from top to
24 bottom; so they said to one another, 'Let us not tear it, but
cast lots for it to see whose it shall be.' This was to fulfil the
scripture,

> 'They parted my garments among them,
> and for my clothing they cast lots.'

25   So the soldiers did this. But standing by the cross of Jesus
were his mother, and his mother's sister, Mary the wife of
26 Clopas, and Mary Magdalene. When Jesus saw his mother,
and the disciple whom he loved standing near, he said to his
27 mother, 'Woman, behold, your son!' Then he said to the
disciple, 'Behold, your mother!' And from that hour the
disciple took her to his own home.

28   After this Jesus, knowing that all was now finished, said (to
29 fulfil the scripture), 'I thirst.' A bowl full of vinegar stood

---

Matt. 21[2-5]). It is not certain whether John saw some significance in
the seamless robe; or, if he did, what that significance was (see 21[11]).
25   Mark also records the presence of women (Mark 15[40f.]), but he
says they were 'looking on from afar': John says that they were *by the
cross of Jesus*. He probably intends his readers to contrast the four
soldiers (implied in v. 23) with four women, but this also is not certain.
For the *mother* of Jesus, cp. 2[1, 12], and 6[42]. *Mary Magdalene* will be
mentioned again in 20[1-18].
26 f.   *the disciple whom he loved*: see note on 13[23]. *Woman*: see note on 2[4],
where Jesus addresses her in the same way. It is difficult to think that
John did not mean this also as an allegory; and in view of the symbolism in Rev. 12 (notice particularly Rev. 12[17]) it is possible that his
mother is to be understood as the Church, and the beloved disciple
as the typical believer (cp. Introduction pp. 12 f.).
28   *Jesus, knowing that all was now finished*: John says that Jesus knew
what was to happen, and that it had now taken place, in order to
show that he was in command of the situation throughout (cp. e.g.
13[1, 3], 18[4]). *to fulfil the scripture*: probably Ps. 69[21] ('for my thirst they
gave me vinegar to drink'). John says that Jesus' motive was not the
satisfaction of his thirst, but the fulfilment of scripture.
29   Those commentators who maintain that John's primary interest is
in the symbolic significance of what he says think that *hyssop* is an

there; so they put a sponge full of the vinegar on hyssop and
30 held it to his mouth. When Jesus had received the vinegar, he
said, 'It is finished'; and he bowed his head and gave up his
spirit.

31   Since it was the day of Preparation, in order to prevent the
bodies from remaining on the cross on the sabbath (for that

---

allusion to the Passover ceremonies (see Exod. 12²²; and cp. 10⁷, *I am
the door*): those who think that John is using a non-Marcan tradition
and is concerned to describe the facts suggest that *hyssop* (Gk. ὑσσώπῳ)
is a primitive error for a similar word meaning 'a javelin' (Gk. ὑσσῷ;
e.g. Dodd, *HTFG*, pp. 123 f., n. 2), which is the reading of one MS.
and has been accepted by the translators of NEB.

30   *It is finished*: i.e. the work which the Father gave him to do has been
completed; Jesus has done everything necessary for the salvation of
the world (cp. 17⁴).   *he bowed his head and gave up his spirit*: Jesus 'remains the subject' until the end (Barrett, p. 460): some commentators
think the second half of the sentence should be translated 'and handed
over the Spirit' (i.e. to those who were standing near by, v. 25).

31–42 *The burial*

In order to keep the Law, the Jews ask for permission to
hasten the death of those who have been crucified, and to
remove the bodies. Jesus, however, is found to be dead already,
so instead of breaking his legs a soldier pierces his side, and
blood and water come out. John sees great significance in this,
part of which he explains in terms of the fulfilment of scripture.
After this, Joseph of Arimathea and Nicodemus see to the
burial in accordance with Jewish custom.

John's account of these things is fuller than the Synoptists':
they do not record the breaking of the legs, the piercing of the
side, or the scriptural fulfilments; Nicodemus is not mentioned
by them, nor the garden close to the place of the crucifixion.
John claims the evidence of an eye-witness for the effusion of
the blood and water, and this raises the question of the historical element in the Fourth Gospel in its most acute form (see
Introduction, pp. 16 ff.).

31   *the day of Preparation* here means Friday, the day on which the Jews
prepared for the sabbath (contrast v. 14); it is also used in this sense
below, v. 42.   *in order to prevent the bodies from remaining on the cross on the*

sabbath was a high day), the Jews asked Pilate that their legs
32 might be broken, and that they might be taken away. So the
soldiers came and broke the legs of the first, and of the other
33 who had been crucified with him; but when they came to
Jesus and saw that he was already dead, they did not break his
34 legs. But one of the soldiers pierced his side with a spear, and
35 at once there came out blood and water. He who saw it has
borne witness—his testimony is true, and he knows that he
36 tells the truth—that you also may believe. For these things

---

sabbath: cp. Deut. 21[22 f.] ('. . . his body shall not remain all night upon
the tree, but you shall bury him the same day'). *for that sabbath was a
high day*: according to John's chronology the sabbath was the Passover;
see note on v. 14 above. *that their legs might be broken*: thus hastening
death by increasing the difficulty of breathing.

32   The *two others* were mentioned briefly in v. 18.

33   John seems to imply that Jesus had died unusually quickly (cp.
Mark 15[44], and note that the crucifixion began later according to
John; see note on v. 14.) *they did not break his legs*: see v. 36.

34   *pierced his side*: presumably to make certain that he was dead. The
resulting wound in the Lord's side will be referred to again in 20[20,
25, 27]. *at once there came out blood and water*: it has been argued that this
can happen in cases of death from traumatic shock (e.g. Dodd, *HTFG*,
p. 136, where he quotes from R. Schmittlein); but in view of what
John has said earlier about the *blood* of the Son of man (6[52 ff.]) and
water (4[10 ff.], 7[37 ff.], 13[1–11]), it is possible that John intends to record
something more than a physical event. 1 John 5[6 ff.] supports this theory
though the meaning of these verses also is not clear.

35   *He who saw it has borne witness*: probably John means the beloved
disciple (v. 26), though he does not say so unequivocally. *his testimony
is true, and he knows that he tells the truth*: possibly *he knows* refers to the
witness (= *he who saw it*), but it is a question whether the Evangelist is
referring to himself, or to somebody else. The meaning may be: I am
the beloved disciple; I saw the blood and water; I have borne witness;
my testimony is true; I know that I am telling the truth; all this is in
order that you too may believe. Alternatively, the Evangelist would
be saying that there was one who saw this and bore witness, etc. See
Introduction, p. 10.

36   *these things took place that the scripture might be fulfilled*: cp. vv. 24, 28.
Not a bone of him shall be broken: this is one of John's composite

took place that the scripture might be fulfilled, 'Not a bone of
37 him shall be broken.' And again another scripture says,
'They shall look on him whom they have pierced.'

38   After this Joseph of Arimathea, who was a disciple of Jesus,
but secretly, for fear of the Jews, asked Pilate that he might
take away the body of Jesus, and Pilate gave him leave. So he
39 came and took away his body. Nicodemus also, who had at
first come to him by night, came bringing a mixture of
40 myrrh and aloes, about a hundred pounds' weight. They
took the body of Jesus, and bound it in linen cloths with the
41 spices, as is the burial custom of the Jews. Now in the place

---

quotations; see Exod. 12⁴⁶, Num. 9¹², Ps. 34²⁰ (the first and second
refer to the Passover lamb).

37   The *scripture* referred to here is Zech. 12¹⁰, in the Hebrew, not the
LXX. *They shall look* (Gk. ὄψονται) refers back to 'he who saw it' (Gk.
ὁ ἑωρακὼς) in v.35; and since 'he who saw it has borne witness', and as a
result of his witness there are believers, the plural (*they shall look*) has
been fulfilled: the Christians look at Christ, i.e. they are saved by
faith in him; cp. 3¹⁴ ᶠ· and Num. 21⁸ ᶠ· ('. . . when he sees it, shall
live . . . he would look at the bronze serpent and live'). Zech. 12¹⁰ is
also quoted in Rev. 1⁷.

38   *Joseph of Arimathea*: Mark said that he was 'also himself looking for the
kingdom of God' (Mark 15⁴³): perhaps John has changed this to *was
a disciple of Jesus*: he has not used the expression *the kingdom of God*,
except in 3³, ⁵. *for fear of the Jews*: cp. 7¹³, 9²², 12⁴², 20¹⁹. All four
Gospels give detailed accounts of the burial, partly perhaps because
belief in the resurrection and the empty tomb needed buttressing with
the evidence that the Christians were well informed concerning the
burial; but perhaps also because Jews laid great emphasis on the
duty of burying the dead (see D. Daube, *The New Testament and
Rabbinic Judaism* (London, 1956), pp. 310 ff.).

39   For *Nicodemus* see also 3¹ ᶠᶠ·, 7⁵⁰ ᶠ·. *about a hundred pounds' weight*: some
commentators compare 'the prodigious supply of wine implied in
2⁶⁻⁸' (Lightfoot, p. 327), but possibly John's point is that this quantity
of material for embalming (*myrrh*) and perfuming (*aloes*) was unnecessary in the case of Jesus (contrast 11³⁹ ᶠ·, and see note on 20¹).

40   Compare the description of Lazarus coming from the tomb (11⁴⁴)
and see further references to the *linen cloths* in 20⁵ ᶠᶠ·.

41   For *garden*, cp. 18¹. *a new tomb where no one had ever been laid*: cp.
Luke 23⁵³ for an almost identical description of the tomb.

where he was crucified there was a garden, and in the garden
42 a new tomb where no one had ever been laid. So because of
the Jewish day of Preparation, as the tomb was close at hand,
they laid Jesus there.

20 NOW on the first day of the week Mary Magdalene came to
the tomb early, while it was still dark, and saw that the stone

---

42   *the Jewish day of Preparation*: i.e. Friday, as in v. 31.

20: 1–23 *The first day of the week*

In the three paragraphs which deal with the events of Easter
Day John describes, first, the finding of the empty tomb;
second, the revelation of the Lord to Mary Magdalene; and
third, his revelation to the (ten) disciples in the evening, and
their commissioning.

Part of the purpose of the Evangelist in writing these paragraphs is to show that the Lord fulfilled the promises which he
had made before the crucifixion, particularly in the discourses
in Chapters 13–16. He had said there, 'I will come to you'
(14^{18}), and it may be significant that John says 'came' rather
than 'appeared' in 20^{19}. He had said 'a little while, and you
will see me' ($16^{16 \text{ ff.}}$); and now Mary Magdalene can say 'I have
seen the Lord' (20^{18}). He had said 'I go to the Father' (e.g.
14^{12}); and now he tells Mary to say to the disciples, 'I am
ascending to my Father . . .' (20^{17}). He had promised them the
gift of the Holy Spirit (14^{26}, 15^{26}, $16^{7 \text{ ff.}}$) and peace (14^{27}, 16^{33}),
and had assured them that they would do the works that he
had done (14^{12}); and now he says to them 'Peace be with you
. . . Receive the Holy Spirit', and he sends them just as he
himself had been sent ($20^{21 \text{ f.}}$).

But this is not the whole of John's purpose here. Like the
Synoptists, he too shows that the disciples were unready for
what happened, and slow to believe. Like them again, he
believes that the tomb was empty and that the risen Lord was
identical with the body which was crucified.

In places John seems to show knowledge of the Synoptic
accounts of the appearances, but if this is so, he has rewritten

2 had been taken away from the tomb. So she ran, and went to
   Simon Peter and the other disciple, the one whom Jesus
   loved, and said to them, 'They have taken the Lord out of
   the tomb, and we do not know where they have laid him.'
3 Peter then came out with the other disciple, and they went
4 toward the tomb. They both ran, but the other disciple out-
5 ran Peter and reached the tomb first; and stooping to look in,
6 he saw the linen cloths lying there, but he did not go in. Then

---

them in his own idiom, and for his own purposes. It is impossible to say how much of this material is traditional, how much
Johannine elaboration; and whether the traditional material
is simply the Synoptic material, or whether John had access
to other sources.

1   *Mary Magdalene*: mentioned only once before in this Gospel (19^{25});
contrast Mark 16^1, where she is accompanied by 'Mary the mother of
James, and Salome', and see note on next verse. *while it was still dark*:
contrast Mark 16^2 ('when the sun had risen'). *the stone* had not been
mentioned in the account of the burial (contrast Mark 15^{46}): perhaps
John's story of the embalming fulfilled much the same function in his
narrative, as the stone did in Mark's, i.e. it drew attention to the power
of the risen Lord (see note on 19^{39}).

2   *Simon Peter* and the beloved disciple are again mentioned together;
see $13^{23\,f\cdot}$, and the note there. *They have taken the Lord out of the tomb*:
there is irony here, in that she refers to Jesus as *the Lord*, and yet thinks
him to be still dead. No character in this Gospel has, up to this point,
spoken of Jesus as *the Lord*. The Evangelist has used this title (e.g. 6^{23},
11^2), and the vocative (Gk. Κύριε) has been used in address, but that
may mean simply 'Sir' (cp. e.g. v. 15, where Mary uses it of one whom
she supposes to be a gardener). For *the Lord* in its full sense, see vv. 13,
18, 20, 28 and $21^{7,\ 12}$. *we do not know*: the plural is possibly an echo of
the Synoptic accounts, in which a number of women visit the tomb
(see note on v. 1).

f.   John seems concerned to show that the beloved disciple was the
first at the tomb, and the first to see the evidence of the resurrection.
For the previous mention of *the linen cloths*, see 19^{40}, and contrast the
raising of Lazarus (11^{44}). Lazarus returned to life in a resuscitated
body, still 'bound with bandages', whereas the Lord's body has been
transformed into a body which is not subject to physical limitations
(cp. vv. 19, 26; and 1 Cor. $15^{42\,ff\cdot}$).

Simon Peter came, following him, and went into the tomb;
7 he saw the linen cloths lying, and the napkin, which had been
on his head, not lying with the linen cloths but rolled up in
8 a place by itself. Then the other disciple, who reached the
9 tomb first, also went in, and he saw and believed; for as yet
they did not know the scripture, that he must rise from the
10 dead. Then the disciples went back to their homes.

11   But Mary stood weeping outside the tomb, and as she
12 wept she stooped to look into the tomb; and she saw two
angels in white, sitting where the body of Jesus had lain, one
13 at the head and one at the feet. They said to her, 'Woman,
why are you weeping?' She said to them, 'Because they have
taken away my Lord, and I do not know where they have

---

7   *the napkin* (Gk. τὸ σουδάριον): the same word is translated 'a cloth', in
the story of Lazarus (11⁴⁴).

8   The point John wishes to make is that the beloved disciple was the
first to believe in the resurrection—not Mary Magdalene, not Peter
(contrast the Synoptists, and 1 Cor. 15⁵).

9   This verse explains that the faith of the beloved disciple (mentioned
in the previous verse) was something new to him, and to all the disciples; none of them understood from the Old Testament (as they
were to do later) that the Lord must rise from the dead. John is probably not referring to any particular Old Testament passage, but to a
large number of texts which Christians interpreted as prophecies of
the resurrection (cp. 1 Cor. 15⁴).

10   *went back to their homes*: this translation is not certain; John may
mean simply that they went away from the tomb.

11 f. Mark says that the women saw 'a young man sitting on the right
side, dressed in a white robe' (Mark 16⁵), Matthew says 'an angel'
(Matt. 28² ᶠᶠ·), and Luke 'two men in dazzling apparel' (Luke 24⁴; but
cp. Luke 24²³, 'a vision of angels'); John agrees with Luke here.

13   The angels' question provides the cue for Mary Magdalene to
repeat what she had said to the two disciples (v. 2), with these slight
alterations: *my Lord* instead of 'the Lord'; and *I do not know* instead of
'we do not know'; see note on v. 2. She, unlike the beloved disciple
(v. 8), does not yet believe. *Woman*: cp. 2⁴, 19²⁶, and v. 15 below [also
8¹⁰].

14 laid him.' Saying this, she turned round and saw Jesus
15 standing, but she did not know that it was Jesus. Jesus said
to her, 'Woman, why are you weeping? Whom do you seek?'
Supposing him to be the gardener, she said to him, 'Sir, if
you have carried him away, tell me where you have laid him,
16 and I will take him away.' Jesus said to her, 'Mary.' She
turned and said to him in Hebrew, 'Rabboni' (which means
17 Teacher). Jesus said to her, 'Do not hold me, for I have not
yet ascended to the Father; but go to my brethren and say to
them, I am ascending to my Father and your Father, to my
18 God and your God.' Mary Magdalene went and said to the

---

14   Cp. Matt. 28¹⁷ and Luke 24¹⁶ ᶠᶠ· for disciples not recognizing Jesus
after the resurrection.

15   *Woman*: see note on v. 13. *Whom do you seek?* cp. 13³³, 'You will
seek me.' *the gardener* (Gk. κηπουρός, from the word translated
'garden' in 18¹, ²⁶, 19⁴¹): it is unlikely that John intended any allusion
to the garden in Gen. 3, or to Adam, though the idea has been put
forward; entirely different words are used in John from those in the
LXX. Mary's words are an example of John's use of misunderstanding
and irony (see Introduction, pp. 19 ff.).

16   Cp. 10³ ('he calls his own sheep by name'). *Rabboni* apparently
means the same as 'rabbi' (see note on 1³⁸); John translates both by the
word *Teacher*.

17   The interpretation of the first part of this verse is uncertain, but the
meaning may be 'Do not hold on to me (cp. Matt. 28⁹), I have not
yet ascended to the Father; when I have done so, then the Spirit will
be given (see 7³⁹, etc.) and a new relationship will be inaugurated, in
which there will be a new kind of fellowship between me and you'.
my brethren: i.e. the disciples (cp. Matt. 28¹⁰ and Mark 3³⁴). The
disciples have not been called *brethren* by Jesus before in this Gospel
(cp. 1¹² '. . . he gave power to become children of God'). *I am ascending
to my Father and your Father, to my God and your God*: John puts the ascension of Jesus on the same day as the resurrection; the only New
Testament writer who distinguishes ascension from resurrection in time
is Luke (Acts 1⁹). The repeated *my . . . your*, maintains the difference
between Jesus and the disciples (he is the eternal Son of God, they are
sons by adoption); but the use of the same titles, *Father* and *God*, indicates
the fellowship between Jesus and the disciples which is now a reality.

18   *the Lord*: see note on v. 2.

disciples, 'I have seen the Lord'; and she told them that he
had said these things to her.

19   On the evening of that day, the first day of the week, the
doors being shut where the disciples were, for fear of the
Jews, Jesus came and stood among them and said to them,
20   'Peace be with you.' When he had said this, he showed them
his hands and his side. Then the disciples were glad when
21 they saw the Lord. Jesus said to them again, 'Peace be with
22 you. As the Father has sent me, even so I send you.' And
when he had said this, he breathed on them, and said to

---

19   *that day, the first day of the week*: cp. v. 1. *the disciples*: Thomas was
not present (see v. 24) nor presumably (though John does not say so)
was Judas; but it is not clear whether John means the other ten, or a
larger group of disciples. *for fear of the Jews*: cp. 19³⁸, and references
there. *Jesus came*: cp. 14¹⁸. *Peace be with you*: the conventional greet-
ing is used by John, but with a richer sense; see 14²⁷, 16³³, and cp.
vv. 21, 26, below.

20   *he showed them his hands and his side*: i.e. the marks left by the nails
(v. 25) in his hands, and by the spear in his side (19³⁴). No mention
is made of the marks of nails in his feet, and the Synoptic accounts do
not mention either nails or wounds (but cp. Luke 24³⁹). It has been
suggested that Jesus was tied to the cross with ropes, and that the
wounds are not historical: they might have entered the tradition from
Ps. 22¹⁶ ('they have pierced my hands and my feet'), but, if that were
so, one would have expected a reference here to feet. *were glad* (Gk.
ἐχάρησαν): the verb from the noun 'joy' (cp. 16²⁰ ᶠᶠ·); but *were glad* is a
weak translation; contrast NEB 'they were filled with joy'.

21   *Peace be with you*: see note above on v. 19. *As the Father has sent me,
even so I send you*: cp. 17¹⁸, 'as thou didst send me into the world, so I
have sent them into the world'. The Father sent the Son to bring life
to the world; the Son sends the disciples into the world for the same
purpose, and under the same conditions, i.e. dependence on the
Father and obedience to him.

22   This is John's version of Luke's narrative in Acts 2¹ ᶠᶠ·; see note on
v. 17, and note that John puts resurrection, ascension, and the gift of
the Spirit on the same day. *he breathed on them*: the same word is used
in Gen. 2⁷ (LXX) ('the Lord God . . . breathed into his nostrils the
breath of life'). *Receive the Holy Spirit*: thus fulfilling the promises in
14²⁶, etc.

23 them, 'Receive the Holy Spirit. If you forgive the sins of any, they are forgiven; if you retain the sins of any, they are retained.'

24 Now Thomas, one of the twelve, called the Twin, was not
25 with them when Jesus came. So the other disciples told him, 'We have seen the Lord.' But he said to them, 'Unless I see in his hands the print of the nails, and place my finger in the mark of the nails, and place my hand in his side, I will not believe.'

23　The Church will continue the judgement of the world which Jesus has inaugurated, dividing men by its existence and its witness into those who believe (and are forgiven), and those who do not believe (and are not forgiven); the nearest parallel of this in the Gospel is the conclusion of Chapter 9: notice particularly the last words there, 'your sin remains' (9^{40}).

20: 24–31 *Jesus and Thomas*

The previous account of the coming of Jesus to the disciples had mentioned only one reaction on their part, joy (v. 20); Matthew and Luke on the other hand recorded their doubt and disbelief (Matt. 28^{17} and Luke $24^{11, 25, 37, 41}$). John now tells the story of Thomas and his faithlessness, and uses it to lead up to what many commentators think was the original conclusion of the Gospel (see notes at the beginning of Chapter 21).

There is no parallel passage in the Synoptic Gospels and it is probable that this is an entirely Johannine creation.

24　*Thomas* is also mentioned in this Gospel at 11^{16}, 14^{5}, 21^{2}: notice particularly the first of these, which prepared the reader for the description of his doubts here. *called the Twin*: see note on 11^{16}. *was not with them when Jesus came*: cp. v. 19, and note again the use of the verb 'to come' (see p. 200).

25　*We have seen the Lord*: cp. v. 18. *Unless I see . . . I will not believe*: Thomas lays down the conditions on which he will 'believe', so providing the cue for the words of the Lord in v. 29. It is perhaps significant that, though he will be invited to touch the Lord, John does not record that he did so. It is also possible that John intends Thomas' words to sound absurd, since this kind of evidence, if it were made available, would do away with faith.

26   Eight days later, his disciples were again in the house, and Thomas was with them. The doors were shut, but Jesus came and stood among them, and said, 'Peace be with you.'

27 Then he said to Thomas, 'Put your finger here, and see my hands; and put out your hand, and place it in my side; do not

28 be faithless, but believing.' Thomas answered him, 'My

29 Lord and my God!' Jesus said to him, 'Have you believed because you have seen me? Blessed are those who have not seen and yet believe.'

30   Now Jesus did many other signs in the presence of the

---

26   *Eight days later*: i.e. the following Sunday (by inclusive reckoning); see v. 1. *The doors were shut*: cp. v. 19: John does not repeat the reason given there ('for fear of the Jews'), perhaps because he means that faith has banished fear (cp. 1 John 4[18]); the coming of Jesus to the enclosed house is a sign of the transformation of his body effected by the resurrection. *Jesus came*: cp. vv. 19, 24. *Peace be with you*: cp. vv. 19, 21.

27   Jesus repeats the words of Thomas (with slight variations), and commands him to believe.

28   *My Lord and my God!* This is the climax of the Gospel, bringing the reader back to what was said in the prologue, particularly 1[1] ('the Word was God'). It is one of the few places in the N.T. where Jesus is unequivocally called God. It may also be no accident that the Emperor Domitian (perhaps at the time when the Gospel was written) made use of the same title, for himself: *Dominus et deus noster* (Suetonius, *Domitian*, 13).

29   *Have you believed because you have seen me?* These words can be taken as a statement, rather than a question (so NEB, 'Because you have seen me you have found faith') and this may be what John intended. The faith of Thomas, like the faith of those who will not believe unless they see signs and wonders (4[48]), is not the only kind of faith; there will be others who have not experienced these events, yet will believe. The readers of the Gospel, and all later generations of believers, are included in this beatitude (cp. v. 31).

30 f.   *many other signs*: those who think that John had among his sources a book of signs, suggest that this verse originally stood as the conclusion to that book (see e.g. D. M. Smith, *The Composition and Order of the Fourth Gospel* (New Haven, 1965), pp. 34 ff.); this would explain the use of *signs* here. Otherwise, we must say that John regarded the words

31 disciples, which are not written in this book; but these are
written that you may believe that Jesus is the Christ, the Son
of God, and that believing you may have life in his name.

21 AFTER this Jesus revealed himself again to the disciples by
the Sea of Tiberias; and he revealed himself in this way.

---

and deeds of Jesus, taken together, as *signs*, that is, as revelatory
events. *these are written that you may believe*: cp. Rom. 10^{17} ('Faith comes
from what is heard, and what is heard comes by the preaching of
Christ'); the written Gospel is a form of preaching, and the Evangelist's purpose is the same as that of the preacher. *and that believing
you may have life in his name*: *life* here, as throughout this Gospel, means
eternal life, that is, salvation, which Jesus is himself (14^6), and gives
to the believer (cp. 3^{15} ,'that whoever believes in him may have eternal
life').

21 *An appendix*

The confession of Thomas, and the words of Jesus, together
with the note of the Evangelist on the purpose of his book
(20$^{28\,ff.}$), formed a climax and a conclusion to the Gospel.
Chapter 21 therefore presents us with a problem, because it
seems unnecessary in its present position. Moreover, there are
certain differences in the contents and in the style of writing
of Chapter 21, from those of Chapters 1–20 (see Barrett,
pp. 479 f.) Position in the Gospel, subject matter, and style, thus
combine to support the view that Chapter 21 is not part of the
original Gospel. The only argument against this view (and it
is a powerful argument) is that there are no manuscripts or
versions which do not contain this chapter: therefore if it was
added to an original Gospel which ended at 20^{31}, it was added
very early; but when all the evidence is considered, this seems
to be the most likely conclusion.

The chapter describes what it calls 'the third time that Jesus
was revealed to the disciples after he was raised from the dead'
(v. 14). The scene is the Sea of Tiberias. There is a miraculous catch of fish, through which Jesus, whose identity was
previously unknown, is recognized as the Lord. This is followed
by a meal at which Jesus is the host, and by a conversation

2 Simon Peter, Thomas called the Twin, Nathanael of Cana in
   Galilee, the sons of Zebedee, and two others of his disciples
3 were together. Simon Peter said to them, 'I am going fishing.'
   They said to him, 'We will go with you.' They went out and
   got into the boat; but that night they caught nothing.
4   Just as day was breaking, Jesus stood on the beach; yet the

---

between Jesus and Peter, dealing with the future ministry of
Peter, and with a question concerning the beloved disciple.
We are then told that the beloved disciple 'has written these
things' and his truthfulness is vouched for. Finally, there is
another conclusion similar to, and perhaps modelled on, the
conclusion in 20³⁰ᶠ·.

Similar material is found in Luke's Gospel; namely, a story
of a miraculous catch of fish (Luke 5¹⁻¹¹ at the beginning of the
ministry, not after the crucifixion), and an account of Jesus
eating with his disciples after the resurrection (Luke 24⁴¹ ᶠᶠ·).
We cannot tell whether the author of Chapter 21 used these
narratives or other sources.

1   *revealed himself again*: contrast 20¹⁹, ²⁴, ²⁶, where John said that Jesus
'came' to the disciples. *the Sea of Tiberias*: see note on 6¹.

2   *Thomas, called the Twin*: see 11¹⁶, 14⁵, 20²⁴ ᶠᶠ·. *Nathanael*: see 1⁴⁵ ᶠᶠ· *of
Cana in Galilee*: Cana is not mentioned in the Synoptic Gospels; see
2¹, ¹¹, and 4⁴⁻⁶ for references to Cana in John. *the sons of Zebedee* were
not mentioned in this Gospel (cp. e.g. Mark 1¹⁹). As the beloved
disciple is one of the group listed here (see v. 7), it has been suggested
that the author of Chapter 21 assumed that he was John, the son of
Zebedee. But he might have been one of the *two others of his disciples*
who are mentioned but not named in this verse (see Introduction,
pp. 11–13).

3   It was not said anywhere in John 1–20 that Peter had been a
fisherman. Notice Mark 1¹⁷ ('Follow me, and I will make you become
fishers of men'): it is not altogether clear whether this symbolic sense
is intended here. *that night they caught nothing*: cp. Luke 5⁵, and the
use of *night* in the Gospel (3², 9⁴, 11¹⁰, 13²⁰, 19³⁹). Their lack of success
is contrasted with the great catch (vv. 6, 11), and the *night* with the
day in which Jesus is present (v. 4).

4   The references to dawn and to the unrecognized presence of Jesus
recall the account of Mary Magdalene at the tomb (20¹⁻¹⁸).

5 disciples did not know that it was Jesus. Jesus said to them,
6 'Children, have you any fish?' They answered him, 'No.' He
said to them, 'Cast the net on the right side of the boat, and
you will find some.' So they cast it, and now they were not
7 able to haul it in, for the quantity of fish. That disciple whom
Jesus loved said to Peter, 'It is the Lord!' When Simon Peter
heard that it was the Lord, he put on his clothes, for he was
8 stripped for work, and sprang into the sea. But the other disciples came in the boat, dragging the net full of fish, for they
were not far from the land, but about a hundred yards*m* off.
9   When they got out on land, they saw a charcoal fire there,
10 with fish lying on it, and bread. Jesus said to them, 'Bring
11 some of the fish that you have just caught.' So Simon Peter

m Greek *two hundred cubits*

---

5   *Children* (Gk. παιδία): Jesus does not address his disciples in this way
in the Gospel, but cp. 1 John 2[14, 18]: a different word, 'little children'
(Gk. τεκνία), is used in 13[33].

6   *to haul it in* (Gk. ἑλκύσαι): the word was used of disciples being drawn
to Christ at 6[44] and 12[32].

7 f. The beloved disciple and Peter are mentioned together, as in 13[23 f.],
(18[15 ff.]?), 20[2 ff.], and below, vv. 20 ff.   *It is the Lord*: see note on 20[2].
Notice that the beloved disciple recognizes the Lord before Peter, and
cp. 20[8]; whereas Peter comes to the Lord first (cp. 20[4]).

9   With the *fish* and *bread* here cp. 6[9] (the feeding miracle). If the catch
of fish is a symbol of the evangelistic mission of the disciples, the meal
seems to be in some sense a symbol of the Eucharist.

10   The command to bring the fish (presumably to eat) fits awkwardly
into the symbolism; it may simply provide the link for the next verse,
in which the fish are counted.

11   The number of fish is almost certainly significant, and various
explanations of it have been suggested;[1] so also is the statement that

[1] e.g. that it was thought that there were a hundred and fifty-three
different species of fish; in this case, the number is a symbol of the Gentile
converts. Or that $17 + 16 + 15 + \ldots + 1 = 153$; then the problem is to account
for the number 17. Or that 17 and 153 are the numerical equivalents of two
places mentioned in Ezek. 47[10], En-gedi and En-eglaim (cp. J. A. Emerton,
'The Hundred and Fifty-three fishes in John XXI. 11', *JTS*, NS, ix (April
1958), pp. 86–9).

went aboard and hauled the net ashore, full of large fish, a
hundred and fifty-three of them; and although there were so
12 many, the net was not torn. Jesus said to them, 'Come and
have breakfast.' Now none of the disciples dared ask him,
13 'Who are you?' They knew it was the Lord. Jesus came and
14 took the bread and gave it to them, and so with the fish. This
was now the third time that Jesus was revealed to the disciples
after he was raised from the dead.

15   When they had finished breakfast, Jesus said to Simon
Peter, 'Simon, son of John, do you love me more than these?'
He said to him, 'Yes, Lord; you know that I love you.' He
16 said to him, 'Feed my lambs.' A second time he said to him,
'Simon, son of John, do you love me?' He said to him, 'Yes,
Lord; you know that I love you.' He said to him, 'Tend my
17 sheep.' He said to him the third time, 'Simon, son of John,
do you love me?' Peter was grieved because he said to him the
third time, 'Do you love me?' And he said to him, 'Lord, you
know everything; you know that I love you.' Jesus said to
18 him, 'Feed my sheep. Truly, truly, I say to you, when you

---

the net was not torn: perhaps this means that the unity of the Church
will not be impaired by the great number of converts (cp. 19²³ ᶠ·).

12   See note on 20².

13   Cp. 6¹¹, and Luke 24³⁰ ᶠ·, ³⁵: eucharistic allusions are strong here.

14   The reference is to the two 'revelations' of the Lord in 20¹⁹⁻²⁹; see
note on v. 1.

15 ff.   *Simon, son of John*: see note on 1⁴². *more than these*: i.e. (probably)
more than the other disciples do: contrast Peter's three denials (18¹⁵ ᶠᶠ·,
ᶠᶠ·). The words translated *love* are different in Greek: in Jesus'
question in vv. 15, 16, he uses ἀγαπᾶν, and Peter answers with φιλεῖν,
and in the question in v. 17 Jesus uses φιλεῖν; but there is probably
no significance in this change of word, nor in the variation between
lamb and *sheep*, *tend* and *feed*. *Feed my lambs*: in these words, Jesus
commissions Peter to be the shepherd, that is, the one who is to care
for the Church as an apostle.

18 f. Jesus foretells the death of Peter, which, like his own death, will reveal
the glory of God, i.e. cause people to praise him (cp. 13³¹, 17¹).

were young, you girded yourself and walked where you
would; but when you are old, you will stretch out your hands,
and another will gird you and carry you where you do not
19 wish to go.' (This he said to show by what death he was to
glorify God.) And after this he said to him, 'Follow me.'

20   Peter turned and saw following them the disciple whom
Jesus loved, who had lain close to his breast at the supper and
21 had said, 'Lord, who is it that is going to betray you?' When
Peter saw him, he said to Jesus, 'Lord, what about this man?'
22 Jesus said to him, 'If it is my will that he remain until I come,
23 what is that to you? Follow me!' The saying spread abroad
among the brethren that this disciple was not to die; yet
Jesus did not say to him that he was not to die, but, 'If it is
my will that he remain until I come, what is that to you?'

24   This is the disciple who is bearing witness to these things,

---

Moreover, Jesus foretells *by what death* (= by what kind of death;
cp. 12³³) Peter will die. The author means that Peter will be crucified:
this is referred to in the words *you will stretch out your hands* (i.e. on
a cross), *and another will gird you* (i.e. tie you to a cross with a rope).
Follow me: cp. 13³⁶ ('you shall follow afterward').
20   For Peter in the company of the beloved disciple, see note on vv.
7 f. above. Notice the parallels in 1³⁸, where Jesus turns and sees two
of John the Baptist's disciples following. See 13²⁵ for the beloved disciple's question at the supper.
21   Peter's question will be answered by Jesus, and this will then be
explained in such a way as to clear up a misunderstanding which had
arisen over what Jesus had meant.
22   Jesus says that Peter is to follow him (cp. v. 19) and not to be concerned about the future of the beloved disciple, even if his future were
to be that he should remain alive until the second coming, in fulfilment of sayings such as that in Mark 9¹ ('Truly, I say to you, there
are some standing here who will not taste death before they see the
kingdom of God come with power').
23   The misunderstanding of Jesus' reply is corrected: presumably the
beloved disciple has died, and this has caused perplexity among
believers (= *the brethren*; cp. 20¹⁷).
24   Compare 19³⁵, but note that the present verse goes further in what
it claims; it states that the beloved disciple wrote *these things*, which

and who has written these things; and we know that his testimony is true.

25   But there are also many other things which Jesus did; were every one of them to be written, I suppose that the world itself could not contain the books that would be written.

---

probably means the whole Gospel. And that this cannot be taken literally is shown by the final clause in this verse, *we know that his testimony is true*. The pseudonymous character of the Gospel is thus suggested by the author of Chapter 21.

25   Cp. 20³⁰: similar hyperboles can be found both in Greek and Jewish writers; there is a rather less exaggerated example in 1 Macc. 9²²; see also I. and P. Opie, *The Oxford Dictionary of Nursery Rhymes* (Oxford, 1951), pp. 436 ff.

ADDITIONAL NOTE

The Story of the Woman taken in Adultery, 7⁵³–8¹¹

THIS paragraph presents modern translators of the Bible with a problem. It is printed in the margin of the RSV (1946) with a note at 7⁵²: 'Other ancient authorities add 7.53–8.11 either here or at the end of this gospel or after Luke 21.38, with variations of the text.' On the other hand, the editors of the RSVCE (1966) print it as part of John's Gospel, with a note at 8¹¹: 'Some ancient authorities insert 7.53–8.11 either at the end of this gospel or after Luke 21.38, with variations of the text. Others omit it altogether'; and in the Explanatory Notes at the end of the volume they say: 'This passage, though absent from some of the most ancient manuscripts, is regarded as inspired and canonical by the church. The style suggests that it is not by St. John, and that it belongs to the Synoptic Tradition' (p. 243). In *The New English Bible* (1961), the paragraph is printed after John 21, with a note explaining that it 'has no fixed place in our ancient witnesses'; but in *The Jerusalem Bible* (1966) is it printed as part of the text of the Fourth Gospel, with a note in the margin: 'The author of this passage . . . is not John . . .'

It is certainly not part of John's Gospel, for the following reasons:

(*a*) A large number of the earliest manuscripts and versions does not include it, nor do many of the patristic writers refer to it.

(*b*) It fits awkwardly into the Gospel, between 7⁵² and 8¹², nor is there any other place in this Gospel from which it could have become detached. The suggestion has often been made that it was inserted at this point to illustrate the Lord's saying in 8¹⁵, 'I judge no one.'

(*c*) It makes use of a number of words and expressions not used elsewhere by this evangelist, some of which are noted below.

As we have seen, 'some ancient authorities' (namely, the Ferrar group, that is, family 13 of minuscule manuscripts[1])

[1] See B. M. Metzger, *The Text of the New Testament* (Oxford, 1964), pp. 61 f.

have this passage after Luke 21³⁸, and it may be that it was at one time part of the text of Luke: it uses many Lucan expressions (see below), and the teaching of the passage is similar to that in the Third Gospel.

The point of the story is to teach that no one should take it upon himself to execute God's judgement upon sinners, because no one is 'without sin', except Jesus; and he will not, because he came 'not to destroy men's lives but to save them' (Luke 9⁵⁵ mg.; cp. Luke 19¹⁰).

7⁵³–8¹¹   Cp. Luke 21³⁷ f.; if, as has been suggested, this story originally stood at that point in Luke's Gospel, and was later omitted (perhaps because it was thought that it taught too lenient an attitude to sin), Luke 21³⁷ f. may have been composed in order to fill up the gap created by its omission.

the Mount of Olives is not mentioned elsewhere in John's Gospel.

2   *Early in the morning* (Gk. ὄρθρου): this word is only used by Luke elsewhere in the N.T. (Luke 24¹, Acts 5²¹). *all the people* (Gk. πᾶς ὁ λαός): this way of referring to the crowd is not Johannine, but is typically Lucan. *he sat down and taught them*: in John, Jesus stands to teach (e.g. 7³⁷, but note 6³); contrast Luke 4²⁰, 5³.

3   *The scribes* are not mentioned elsewhere in John.

4   *Teacher*: this form of address is used in John only when the speaker is a disciple (1³⁸, 20¹⁶; but cp. 3²).

5   *in the law Moses commanded us to stone such*: see Lev. 20¹⁰, Deut. 22²²ff..

6   *This they said to test him, that they might have some charge to bring against him*: cp. Luke 6⁷. Their intention is to see whether Jesus will endorse the Law, or teach something that is contrary to it. *Jesus bent down and wrote with his finger on the ground*: various explanations of this have been offered; some think there is a reference here to Jer. 17¹³ ('those who turn away from thee shall be written in the earth'); another suggestion is that Jesus was imitating Roman judicial procedure, in which the judge first wrote his sentence, and then read it out (see J. Jeremias, *The Parables of Jesus* (2nd ed. London, 1963), p. 228); others see it as 'simply a studied refusal to pronounce judgement' (Barrett, p. 492); cp. Luke 12¹³ f..

7   *Let him who is without sin among you be the first to throw a stone at her*: according to Deut. 17⁷, the witnesses of a transgression are to be the first to carry out the execution of the sentence ('The hand of the witnesses shall be first against him to put him to death, and afterward the hand of all the people'). Jesus' answer means that 'God's action in punishment or mercy can be exercised only through an entirely sinless agent' (Hoskyns, p. 681).

8   See note on v. 6 above.

9 f.   Jesus is *left alone with the woman*, and the reader believes that he alone is 'without sin' (e.g. 2 Cor. 5^{21}, Heb. 4^{15}).

11   Cp. Rom. 8$^{33\,f.}$ ('It is God who justifies; who is to condemn? Is it Christ Jesus, who died, yes, who was raised from the dead, who is at the right hand of God, who indeed intercedes for us?') Notice however that the gospel which proclaims the forgiveness of sins does not thereby provide a licence to sin; Jesus says to the woman, *Go, and do not sin again.*

INDEX

PRINTED IN GREAT BRITAIN
AT THE UNIVERSITY PRESS, OXFORD
BY VIVIAN RIDLER
PRINTER TO THE UNIVERSITY